VIGNETTES OF COLONIAL VIRGINIA

Vignettes of Colonial Virginia

❧ • ❧

REMARKABLE STORIES FROM
THE FOUNDING OF AMERICA

Brent Tarter

RIVANNA BOOKS
UNIVERSITY OF VIRGINIA PRESS
Charlottesville and London

The University of Virginia Press is situated on the traditional lands of the Monacan Nation, and the Commonwealth of Virginia was and is home to many other Indigenous people. We pay our respect to all of them, past and present. We also honor the enslaved African and African American people who built the University of Virginia, and we recognize their descendants. We commit to fostering voices from these communities through our publications and to deepening our collective understanding of their histories and contributions.

RIVANNA BOOKS
An imprint of the University of Virginia Press

© 2025 by the Rector and Visitors of the University of Virginia
All rights reserved
Printed in the United States of America on acid-free paper

First published 2025

1 3 5 7 9 8 6 4 2

LIBRARY OF CONGRESS CATALOGING-IN-PUBLICATION DATA

Names: Tarter, Brent, author
Title: Vignettes of colonial Virginia / Brent Tarter.
Description: Charlottesville : Rivanna Books, University of Virginia Press, 2025. | Includes bibliographical references and index.
Identifiers: LCCN 2024060720 (print) | LCCN 2024060721 (ebook) | ISBN 9780813953908 hardback acid-free paper | ISBN 9780813953915 trade paperback | ISBN 9780813953922 ebook
Subjects: LCSH: Virginia—History—Colonial period, ca. 1600–1775 | Virginia—Social life and customs—To 1775
Classification: LCC F229 .T177 2025 (print) | LCC F229 (ebook) | DDC 975.5/02—dc23/eng/20250401
LC record available at https://lccn.loc.gov/2024060720
LC ebook record available at https://lccn.loc.gov/2024060721

Cover art: Detail from drawing of St. Stephen's Episcopal Church in New Kent County, Virginia. (Library of Virginia)
Cover design: Cecilia Sorochin

CONTENTS

PREFACE vii

ACKNOWLEDGMENTS xi

1. Alien Invasion   1
2. The Werowansqua of Appamattuck Meets the Alien Invaders   5
3. Hughe Pryse and the Loss of Faith   16
4. Lawes Divine, Morall and Martiall   22
5. Richard Bucke, the Book of Common Prayer, and the Bible   25
6. Thefts from Edward Grindon's Warehouse   29
7. Anthony Johnson's Enslaved Man   39
8. Elizabeth Key and the Law of Slavery   47
9. Cockacoeske and the Fate of the Powhatan Confederacy   56
10. Jamestown in 1676   62
11. The Grievances of the People   66
12. A Dead Bastard Child   71
13. No Obey   79
14. Grace Sherwood Charged with Witchcraft   82
15. Exemplary Punishment for Salvadore and Scipio   92
16. Drinking More Than Necessary   98
17. Releese Us out of This Cruell Bondegg   103
18. William Byrd and His Vine and Fig Tree   111
19. The Air of a City   116
20. The Head of Hampton   123

21. Susannah Sanders Cooper and Her Tavern   126
22. One Pistole   131
23. Lowe Jackson Hanged   135
24. Long and Painful Service During the War with France   139
25. All Was Not Tobacco   144
26. John Wayles's Neighbors and His Families   149
27. The Candidates   153
28. George's Marked Face and Broken English   158
29. The Great Fresh of 1771 and Its Consequences   162
30. Patrick Lunan Exposed   167
31. Subversive Religious Doctrines   172
32. *Robin v. Hardaway*   176
33. New Virginias in the West   186

SUGGESTED READING   191

INDEX   207

PREFACE

I chuckled when I encountered a short entry dated March 21, 1714, in the records of York County. It is on pages 397–98 in the fourteenth volume of the series of hand-written record books entitled York County Orders, Wills, Etc. The justices of the peace, who presided as judges in the county court, received a complaint "agnst Edward Rippon Ordinary keeper in Williamsburgh"—that is, the keeper of an inn or tavern—that he permitted a servant named John Creightong (Creighton?) "to drink more than was necessary in time of divine Service." I immediately asked myself, How much alcohol *was* it necessary to drink "in time of divine Service"? Then, was this not also about keeping the peace? County court records from colonial Virginia abound in descriptions of people who drank more than was good for them and disrupted public meetings, court proceedings, or even church services.

These brief vignettes of episodes in the lives of several Virginians, including the innkeeper and servant, whose names are not familiar to most people illuminate how people lived during the colonial portion of Virginia's long and complex history. None of the people were representative Virginians or typical of most of their contemporaries. Instead, their personal experiences left behind documentary evidence from which we can learn about some events that were both important and commonplace and also about the changes that took place in what we now call Virginia.

The first vignette features two people whose names we do not know. It is a lightly revised portion of the opening of chapter 2 from my 2020 book, *Virginians and Their Histories*. The fifth is a lightly revised portion of chapter 1 from my 2013 book, *The Grandees of Government: The Origins and Persistence of Undemocratic Politics in Virginia.* I have also adapted small portions of some other of my previous publications for the purpose, and I include a few eighteenth-century examples from a biography of Robert Carter Nicholas on which I have been working.

I could easily have selected other episodes from the lives of other colonial Virginians for the same purpose or chosen to write about more of them or about fewer of them, but the events in the lives of these men and women are intrinsically interesting and revealing, and we know enough about the episodes and about the people and their lives and times to place them into historical perspective and therefore understand them better. Taken together, these vignettes illuminate some very important subjects, such as relations between people of different cultural, genetic, and class backgrounds; slavery; religion; economic change; and how the institutions of government and society functioned. All of those subjects affected how the different populations of Virginia in the different portions of the colony lived during different epochs of the colonial period. Life for everyone in Virginia then was radically different from life for anyone in Virginia now.

When I began to read about and research Virginia history fifty-several years ago, the subjects in the historical literature were almost all white, almost all male, overwhelmingly political, somewhat repetitious, and therefore often rather dull. The scholarship and popular histories exhibited a feeble attempt, by concentrating on a few admirable white men, to make inspiring a long narrative that exhibited a lack of change and that generally slighted or left out Black people, members of First Nations tribes, women of all races and classes, and most poor or otherwise ordinary white people. Important subjects like religion, economic change, social change, demographic change, material culture, women and gender relations, and other topics that directly affected the lives of the residents of Virginia got short shrift. Most appallingly, the subjects of slavery and racism got glossed over with apologetic language that almost literally whitewashed them and left behind a harmful residue of falsehood and misunderstanding. As I hope that these vignettes will demonstrate, the field of Virginia history and our understanding of Virginia history have changed dramatically.

I have had the almost unique opportunity to work in the original primary source documents of every decade of Virginia's history since the

English invasion of 1607. I have also learned a great deal from a very large body of scholarship that excellent researchers published during my time as a Virginia historian. As a consequence of this published scholarship, historians no longer view Virginia history as we once did. My work in the original records has, I hope, enabled me to exploit what I found there to explain what nobody taught us when my generation was in school and what has been entirely too slow to get into the textbooks and popular literature that still shape how people understand their past.

We need to know about our shared past. The undoubtedly admirable portions of Virginia history cannot be understood properly without understanding the neglected portions or, most importantly, the unfortunate or even terrible portions of that past. Even as I have been writing, we still see people who are ignorant about that past or who have a narrow political agenda attempting to reshape the narrative of American history back into a celebration of elite white men and to deny or even prohibit students and curious readers from learning and fully appreciating that all history is shared and that we all live in the aftermath of events that preceded us.

With *Vignettes of Colonial Virginia*, I hope to contribute to and continue to spread a more complete and accurate view of Virginia history outside the guild of professional historians. I said in April 2006 at the conclusion of my remarks at the opening session of the first Virginia Forum, the annual Virginia history conference, that "we have now an opportunity for the very first time to try to rewrite the history of all of Virginia and include the histories of all Virginians, including the Very First Families and African Americans, and not as add-ons or afterthoughts but as essential and integral dramatis personae. We need to try to make a history of Virginia that is a history that not only happened to everybody but a history that everybody made." I published a revised and expanded version of that talk as "Making History in Virginia," *Virginia Magazine of History and Biography* 115 (2007): 2–55. My earlier needs-and-opportunities article that makes a similar point is "The New Virginia Bookshelf," *Virginia Magazine of History and Biography* 104 (1996): 7–102. I incorporated many of the new insights into my narrative history of Virginia, *Virginians and Their Histories* (Charlottesville, 2020).

ACKNOWLEDGMENTS

Most of these vignettes, or very short stories, come directly from my own research into the original records of colonial Virginia, but I gladly thank all of my former colleagues at the Library of Virginia during the half-century that I researched and wrote about Virginia history there, especially the editors of the library's *Dictionary of Virginia Biography* project, without which the lives of many Virginia men and women would remain almost entirely unknown, and the roles that they played, sometimes unwittingly, in shaping the state in which we live would remain hidden from view. That work and other projects that I took part in at the Library of Virginia led me directly or indirectly to the stories of these people and to the documents that form the heart of these vignettes of life in colonial Virginia.

Serendipity, every historian's favorite research assistant, led me to some excellent episodes that help explain Virginia's history. Very often, when looking for one thing, we find another that is itself of great use. That was the case with the innkeeper and servant. I also thank the many historians, librarians, archivists, genealogists, local history researchers, and other people who published their discoveries about Virginia's history in the *Dictionary of Virginia Biography*, in the Virginia Humanities online *Encyclopedia Virginia*, in scholarly books, in articles in the professional literature, or in the form of oral presentations at the annual state history conference, the Virginia Forum. Their work provided details and context and suggested how these episodes could inform us about aspects of Virginia's history in ways that the lives of the famous men and women whose stories populate our historical narratives often do not. That guild of scholars, like the Americans of whom Walt Whitman sang, contains multitudes, too many to list individually.

The particular scholarship that some of those many researchers engaged in that illuminates the episodes in these chapters is listed in the suggestions for further reading at the end of the volume. The readings may enable readers whose curiosity these vignettes arouse to explore more deeply into the excellent scholarly literature that has made it possible for us to learn about aspects of the lives of colonial Virginians that old textbooks and much of the popular literature have omitted or slighted.

I also thank Mark Mones, acquisitions editor at the University of Virginia Press, who was enthusiastic about this project from the beginning; Lynne Bonenberger, who copyedited the manuscript with a keen eye, admirable patience, and insightful questions and comments; Kate Gruber, formerly of the Colonial Williamsburg Foundation and of the Jamestown-Yorktown Foundation and more recently of the Virginia Commission for the Two-Hundred-Fiftieth Anniversary of the American Revolution, and Warren M. Billings, emeritus distinguished professor of history at the University of New Orleans, both of whom read the manuscript for the press, made useful suggestions, and endorsed publication; Nat Case for the map; and Dale Neighbors and his colleagues in the Special Collections at the Library of Virginia for advice and assistance in selecting the illustrations.

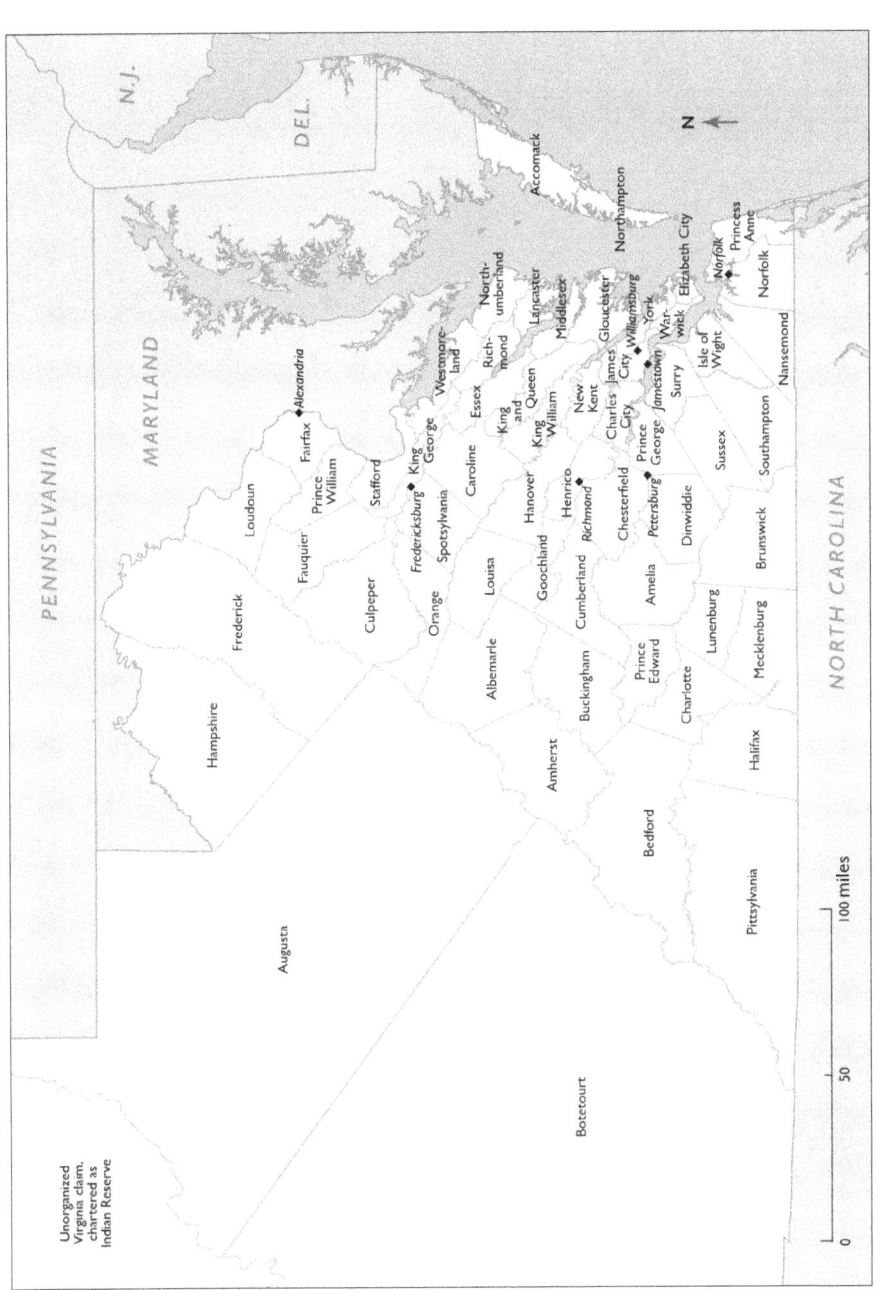

Virginia in 1770, near the end of the colonial period. (Map by Nate Case, INCaseLLc)

VIGNETTES OF COLONIAL VIRGINIA

1

Alien Invasion

IT BEGAN IN THE TIME OF PLANTING, as residents of the Chesapeake Bay area reckoned the changing of seasons and the passing of time. It began on April 26, 1607, as English people reckoned the changing of seasons and the passing of time.

Two people saw the beginnings of the invasion that permanently altered the landscape and history of the Chesapeake Bay region. One of them was probably a member of the Chesapeake tribe that dwelled near the coast and could have been male or female, child or adult. The other was a man or boy and probably English. We do not know the name of either, nor do we know precisely what they thought about what they saw. We know something about what they saw and what they and other people with them did, which allows us to understand in a general way what they may have thought.

The first person who saw the beginning of the invasion from the land probably saw a ship's sail far out to sea as the sun rose behind it. That woman or girl, man or boy, probably stood at the edge of the woods or on the beach near where the coastline bends from north-south to east-west at the south end of the great bay, at what the invaders called and modern maps identify as Cape Henry, which the invaders named for the young first son of their king.

The person on the coast probably watched as the ship and two others slowly approached. He or she probably knew that for several generations, ships like the ones approaching had suddenly and without any warning appeared and then disappeared. Some remained for a short time and entered the bay. Some actually set ashore strangely attired hairy men who carried large, loud weapons that could wound or kill at a distance with tiny metal balls that invisibly flew through the air much faster than the arrows of even the most powerful bowman.

He or she may possibly have known a little something about the missionary settlement that Spanish explorers had established two or three generations earlier on the banks of one of the rivers that emptied into the bay. He or she probably knew something about the settlement that English men and women made in the time of his or her parents or grandparents on a thin strip of sandy land that we now call the Outer Banks of North Carolina. It would be safe to assume that the person who first caught sight of the sails that spring day would have been surprised at the sight because it was unexpected, but because of what the people there knew about the past, he or she would most likely have assumed that just another short-term visit from those strange people was about to begin. He or she probably quickly informed family members, friends, and the tribe's leaders, who later in the day approached the coast to see for themselves. Perhaps that day or soon thereafter a tribal leader sent messengers farther inland to alert other tribes nearby or farther away in Tsenacomoco, the area of what is now southeastern Virginia where about twenty tribes affiliated as the Powhatan confederacy resided.

The other person who was the first witness to the invasion was a man or boy aboard one of the three ships, *Susan Constant*, *Godspeed*, and *Discovery*, that the Virginia Company of London had sent to establish a trading and exploring outpost on the east coast of North America. The man or boy who was the first to catch sight of the land as the sun rose behind him might have been a common sailor standing watch before dawn, or he might have been a ship's officer or even a passenger on deck peering keenly to the west as they approached the coast. There were no women or girls aboard the three ships, only the 104 men and boys who were passengers plus the crewmen and officers who worked the lines, set the sails, and calculated latitude and estimated longitude as the three ships followed the wind southwest from England to the Azores, west to the islands of the Caribbean, then north and west to the place they called Virginia. The ship's crew very likely included men from several parts of the British Isles and also from elsewhere in Europe, the Mediterranean, or even Africa, as was common at the time, so it is not certain that the first witness on the ship was English. Whoever he was and wherever he was from, he loudly called out the landfall, and the other men and boys aboard the ships crowded to the rails to get their first sight of the New World.

What those men and boys knew in greater or lesser detail was that they were approaching a large landmass that differed in many ways from the island they had left. They knew that it had its own populations of people who spoke different languages than they did and lived in what Englishmen and Europeans early in the seventeenth century regarded as a very primitive manner. They were what anthropologists later called Stone Age or Neolithic people, who although they had copper implements and adornments did not have bronze or iron tools or weapons.

The educated men certainly knew that for more than a century, sailing ships from different nations had coursed along that coast and sometimes landed briefly to explore the fringe of the mainland. The Spanish had been there several times, as had other Englishmen, some Frenchmen, and probably Dutchmen, too. The men aboard the ships may not have known about the Spanish settlement, but they did know at least something about the earlier English expedition that had established the small, short-lived colony on the Carolina coast. From oral and published accounts that the people on that expedition took back to England, from drawings they had made of the landscape and its inhabitants, and from printed reports about the people who traveled with them to England and then back home, some of the men on those ships in 1607 could have learned enough about the New World to have a reasonably good mental image of what they would see when they landed.

They also probably knew that the men, women, and children who did not return to England from that sandy settlement had mysteriously disappeared, never to be seen again by any European eye. The men aboard the ships were probably as apprehensive about what would happen when they landed as they were excited about getting off their cramped ships and setting foot on firm, dry land. Would they meet hostile inhabitants on the beach? Would they meet a friendly welcome? They did not know.

One person saw ships approaching land from the sea; another aboard one of the ships first spied the land. In both cases, many more people quickly saw what they had seen, and before the day was done some of the people who dwelled on the land and some of the Englishmen on the ships had their first encounter. Englishman George Percy left a written account of what happened that day. "The six and twentieth of Aprill, about foure a clocke in the morning," he wrote, "wee descried the land of *Virginia;* the same day wee entered into the Bay of *Chesupioc* directly, without any let or hinderance; there wee landed and discovered a little way, but wee could find nothing worth the speaking of, but faire meddowes and goodly tall Trees, with such Fresh-waters running through the woods, as I was almost ravished at the first sight thereof. At night, when wee were going aboard, there came the Savages creeping upon all foure, from the Hills like Beares, with their Bowes in their mouthes, charged us very desperately in the faces, hurt Captain *Gabrill Archer* in both his hands, and a sayler in two places of the body very dangerous. After they had spent their Arrows, and felt the sharpnesses of our shot, they retired into the Woods with a great noise, and so left us."

Percy's account of the encounter that first day was published with the title "Observations gathered out of a Discourse of the Plantation of the Southerne Colonie in Virginia by the English, 1606, Written by that Honorable Gentleman Master George Percy," in Samuel Purchas, ed., *Purchas His Pilgrimes, In Five Bookes . . .* (London, 1625), 4:1686. The publisher printed the date as 1606, the year that the ships departed England, not 1607, the year of their first landing in Virginia.

No member of a First Nations tribe left a record of the events that survives, but from what they did we know that they reacted with anxious uncertainty. Like the first Englishmen who went ashore armed for self-defense, or perhaps to take some game for fresh meat, the men who attacked them also appeared on the shore armed, probably also for self-defense. We do not know why they attacked the landing party; perhaps some of the Englishmen had done something that angered or frightened them. A smart little skirmish marked the end of the first day of the invasion, but it is entirely likely that both parties had wished to avoid violence.

2

The Werowansqua of Appamattuck Meets the Alien Invaders

WE DO NOT KNOW the name of the woman whom Gabriel Archer called the "Queen of Appomattac" following a meeting with her on May 26, 1607. A ruler of a village or tribe or clan (the English words could all have been used almost interchangeably) in that part of what is now southeastern Virginia was called a werowance if male, a werowansqua if female. Early English observers like Gabriel Archer usually referred to them as kings, queens, chiefs, or with other terms of English or European derivation, which implied a greater degree of coercive authority than many of them actually exercised. Even if we do not know her name, we should identify her not as the queen, but as the werowansqua of Appamattuck.

We also do not know the names of her parents, or of her husband or husbands or children, if any; nor do we know just when or where she was born or precisely when or where she died. We do know roughly where she lived in 1607. Her residence is marked on the map that Captain John Smith prepared from data collected when he and some of the men aboard the three ships that the Virginia Company of London sent out to Virginia in the winter of 1606–7 explored the Powhatan River, which they renamed the James River, for their king. The men explored as far inland as the impassable rapids where the city of Richmond now stands. Smith's map indicated that the seat of the werowansqua of Appamattuck was north of the confluence of the Appomattox and James Rivers, not far from the modern city of Petersburg, possibly at what has long been called Matoaca.

Her town/tribe/clan was one of about twenty that Wahunsonacock, also known as Powhatan, had formed into a league or confederacy twenty or thirty years earlier. They shared an Algonquian language, common social and religious customs, and use of the land and waters in what they called Tsenacomoco, which meant densely inhabited land. It encompassed the portion of what is now Virginia from roughly south of the Rappahannock River to North Carolina and east of the fall line, where eastward flowing rivers passed over hard bedrock and created rapids and turbulent areas that were difficult or impossible for large watercraft to navigate. The line runs south and a little west from the Falls of the Potomac a few miles above Alexandria through Fredericksburg, Richmond, and Petersburg. We often refer to that league as a paramount chiefdom because Wahunsonacock was the principal chief, and it is also known as the Powhatan confederation, but each village had its own leader.

Most of what we know about the werowansqua is from a short section of a manuscript narrative that English invader Gabriel Archer prepared. The relation narrates events of the exploration of the James River from May 21 through June 21, 1607. He gave it the title "A relayton of the discovery of our River, from James Forte into the Maine." It is preserved with the records of the Colonial Office, in series 1, volume 1, with the account of the meeting with the werowansqua on folio 49^v, in the National Archives of the United Kingdom, formerly known as the Public Record Office (PRO).

What little that we know about the werowansqua's encounter with the alien invaders from Archer's brief narrative gives us insights into the manner in which she and her people lived at the time of the invasion as well as into the perspectives of one of the invaders who recorded the event and described the werowansqua herself. Unfortunately, we have no written record of precisely what any of the native inhabitants of Tsenacomoco said or thought when they encountered the invaders. Surviving English-language accounts describe many of their actions, though, from which we can perceive some of their attitudes toward the arrival of Englishmen.

We have several accounts that invaders recorded. Those records, including Gabriel Archer's narrative, can make for difficult reading. They abound in antique or unfamiliar spellings and abbreviations, and their syntax does not always resemble twenty-first-century English writing or speech. It is best to read the passages out loud and let the rhythms and sense of the text emerge through the human voice.

As Archer recorded the encounter between the English invaders and the werowansqua on May 26, an exploring party under the command of Captain

Christopher Newport and including Captain John Smith and a native guide and interpreter named Nauirans arrived at what Archer called "Queene Apumatecs bower." Nauirans guided the party from the riverbank "through a plaine Lowe grownd prepared for seede, part whereof had ben lately Cropt," or planted. There, "we sawe the Queene of this Country cominge in self same fashion of state as Pawatah or Arahatec," two powerful male werowances they had already encountered farther up the James River. She conducted herself "wth more majesty" than either of the two men. The werowansqua "had an usher before her who brought her to the matt prepared under a faire mulbery tree, where she satt her Downe by her selfe." Archer noted that "she would permitt none to stand or sitt neere her."

The werowansqua thus set herself apart from the people over whom she ruled precisely as members of the nobility and royal families in England and in Europe did. Archer and the other invaders had all grown up during the final years of the long reign of Queen Elizabeth I and understood that some elite women could rule and that all rulers exhibited their superiority by standing or sitting apart from common men and women. The werowansqua had what Archer called "a stayed Countenance," meaning that her face and the movements of her body displayed the dignity and solemnity appropriate for a monarch. He also wrote, "she is a fatt lustie manly woman," by which he meant that the werowansqua looked and acted the part of a ruler in every way. The word *lustie* implied vigor or strength, not carnal appetites. She wore a copper crown and had what Archer described as "long black haire, wch hanged loose downe her back to her myddle." She wore a deer skin about her waist but otherwise was "all naked." Archer also recorded that "she had her woemen attending on her adorend much like her selfe (save they Wanted the Copper)."

The werowansqua clearly impressed Archer, and she probably impressed the other members of the exploring party. That was undoubtedly her intention. That she was prepared to receive them—she sat on a mat that somebody had already placed underneath a mulberry tree—indicates that she had advance notice from some tribal messenger that they were coming.

"Here," Archer continued his narrative, after the werowansqua had seated herself, "we had our accustomed Cates, Tobacco and Wellcome." The old and now obsolete English word *cates* referred to food or refreshment. The werowansqua furnished her guests the refreshment as well as tobacco, which they passed around for all of the visitors and residents to smoke. That was the custom among the people of the region, a custom of welcoming visitors that Archer's description of the ceremony as "accustomed" means that the invaders had already encountered several times, and they were well aware of its significance in local culture. As was also the custom, Archer reported, "Our Captayne presented her wth guyftes"—gifts—"liberally, whereupon shee cheered somwhat her Countenance." That is to say, the presents that Captain Newport presented to her appeared to please her.

The werowansqua then requested that one of the men "shoote of a peece," or fire one of their guns, "wherat (wee noted) she shewed not neer the like fear as Arahatec though he be a goodly man." Firearms were sometimes called pieces then, as cannon sometimes were even into the twentieth century, as artillery pieces.

Archer concluded his brief account of the visit to the bower by noting that the werowansqua "had much Corne in the grownd" and that "she is subject to Pawatah as the rest are; yet wthn herselfe of as great authority as any of her neighbour Wyoances. Capt Newport stayed here some 2 houres & Depted"—departed.

We can, as students of cultural customs sometimes phrase it, "unpack" what this brief narrative reveals to us about the werowansqua and other Eastern Woodland tribes of Tsenacomoco and about the English invaders. To do that, we have the help of other narratives of encounters of the time that also contain descriptions and explanations of the customs.

From contemporary English-language accounts, we know that the site of the werowansqua's "bower" probably contained several lodges, perhaps a few dozen in number, where the men, women, and children lived. We do not know how many people resided there or how many in nearby settlements regarded themselves as living within her realm. Elsewhere in Archer's account of the spring explorations, he recorded that the people "live comonly by the water side in litle cottages made of canes and reedes, covered wth the barke of trees; they dwell as I gues by families of kindred & allyance some 40^{tie} or 50^{ti} in a Hatto or small village; wch townes are not past a myle or half a myle asunder in most places." The men, he observed, were "proper lusty streight men" and "very strong," that they "runn exceeding swiftly," and that when they fought, it was "alway in the wood wth bow & arrowes, & a short wodden sword."

The town, or hatto, of the werowansqua of Appamattuck in 1607 may have resembled this stylized representation of the town of Secotan, on the Outer Banks of North Carolina, that Theodore de Bry published in 1695 in *Admiranda narratio*. (Library of Virginia)

The cornfields that Archer mentioned produced but one of the sources of food for the people there. In seventeenth-century English, the word *corn* signified any or all small grains, not what twenty-first-century Americans call corn. Those Englishmen usually identified what we call corn as Indian corn. The people at the bower and in other towns also grew beans and gourds, and because they lived in the vicinity of marshes and swamps, they had access to wild rice and other water plants, including the starchy tuckahoe, as well as to grapes and a wide variety of other edible land plants, plus fish and game, such as turkeys, deer, and bears.

Archer also included in his narrative of events late in the spring of 1607 what he called "A Briefe discription of the People." It began, "There is a king in this land called great Pawatah"—Wahunsonacock, or Powhatan—"under whose dominions are at least 20^{ty} severall kingdomes, yet each king potent as a prince in his owne territory." The werowansqua of Appamattuck was one of them, a female prince. This is one of the examples of an English observer projecting European perceptions of hierarchy and governance onto Eastern Woodland people. In reality, none of the First Nations tribes or leagues of tribes was part of a hierarchical arrangement held together by coercion or force. Instead, leaders and members of communities reinforced alliances and relations among them through cultural rituals, exchanges, and marriages.

Powhatan society was what is known as a modified matriarchal one. Legitimate authority to rule descended through the female line. Most tribes had male rulers who inherited their authority from their mothers or grandmothers, but as in England, in the absence of male heirs the authority descended to the next female descendants.

The werowances and werowansquas, such as in the case of the "Queen of Appomattac," had "their Subjects at so quick Comaund," Archer believed, that a simple beckoning "bringes obedience, even to the resticucion"—restitution—"of stolen goods which by their naturall inclinacon they are loth to leave." Other narratives contain numerous references to what the Englishmen regarded as thefts of the implements of warfare and agriculture that the English brought with them aboard their ships. Those episodes could have been simple demonstrations of curiosity about the unfamiliar items, many of which were made of iron. Nevertheless, Englishmen often punished what they regarded as thefts, sometimes even going so far as to cut off the hand of the person who so much as picked up an item.

"They goe all naked," Archer continued, "save their privityes"—private parts—"yet in coole weather they weare deare skinns, wth the hayre on loose: some have leather stockings up to their waistes, & sandalls on their feet, their hayre is black generally; wch they weare long on the left side, tyed up on a knott, about wch knott the kinges and best among them have a kind of Coronett of deares harye colored redd." It may be that, like the legendary Amazon women, the men cut off some of their hair so that it would not interfere when they raised their bows to shoot an arrow.

The near nakedness initially shocked the Englishmen, who concealed themselves in clothing that completely covered their bodies and limbs, all but their faces, and they wore hats, too, or suits of armor. Such modesty and clothing were in part an expression of cultural values and in part consequent on the Englishmen having lived in a cooler climate than the Eastern Woodland people they encountered; but, as with other matters of cultural and practical consideration, including religious ideas and social norms, the beliefs and practices of the two peoples diverged in ways that certainly must have made comfortable interactions between them difficult or, as in the case of the relative nakedness of the werowansqua and her people, even shocking to the English invaders.

Archer noted that some of the people adorned themselves in different ways than Englishmen did, but not for different reasons. Some of the men wore copper or pearl necklaces or knotted their hair, and "the comon sort stick long fethers in this knott." He "found not a grey eye among them all" and believed that they were not born with dark or tawny "skynn" but darkened their bodies by "dying and paynting them selves, in which they delight gratly." By that last five-word phrase Archer inadvertently revealed that he might have thought of them in some respects as childlike in beautifying themselves in what he may have regarded as a primitive manner. "The women are like the men" in apparel, Archer observed, "onley this difference; their hayre groweth long al over their heades save clipt somewhat short afore."

In describing gender roles, the same as in suggesting European notions of hierarchical society, Archer and other English observers found themselves perplexed, and they consequently misrepresented the roles of men and women in the society because the roles differed from what the invaders understood as correct or normal, that is to say, English. The women, Archer wrote, "do all the labor and the men hunt and goe at their plesure." What he described was, in fact, a productive distribution of labor, not a degradation of women, who in England did not usually do the work of planting and harvesting except perhaps in modest kitchen gardens. English women took care of the household and the children, and English men did the farming and hard outdoor labor. In England, hunting was a recreation of high-status gentlemen or an illegal means of gaining subsistence among poor men who poached on other people's land. In Tsenacomoco, a hunting and gathering society that also practiced agriculture, men were the hunters and women planted and gathered.

George Percy, who was also present in 1607, made the same mistake when he wrote, "I saw Bread made by their women which doe all their drugerie. The men takes their pleasure in hunting and their warres, which they are in continually one Kingdome against another." Percy probably exaggerated the frequency of intertribal conflicts. Actual warfare between towns or tribes was not continual and probably not even common, certainly not within populations in league with one another, as in Tsenacomoco. Such conflicts had probably occurred with some frequency several generations earlier after small hunting and gathering parties settled down to practice agriculture and therefore had the greater incentive to protect their crops, fisheries, and hunting grounds from neighbors who appeared threatening. And they probably occasionally continued to occur between residents of villages that were close to villages of other clans or tribes.

Archer found them to be "a most kind and loving people," that "They sacrifice Tobacco to the Sunn" and washed their bodies with water every morning. Some of the men had multiple wives. "The women are very cleanly in making their bread and prepareing meat." He concluded that they were "a very witty and ingenious people, apt both to understand and speake our language, so that I hope in god . . . he will make us authors of his holy will in converting them to our true Christian faith by his owne inspireing grace and knowledge of his deity."

A mere month after the invaders landed at what they called Cape Henry, some of them and some of the people of Tsenacomoco had learned enough of each other's languages that they could converse with one another. Nauirans acted as both guide and interpreter, but we do not know for certain how he came to have an understanding of English. Perhaps when Manteo, originally an inhabitant of what we now call the Outer Banks of North Carolina, returned to North America from England a generation before the invasion of Tsenacomoco, he brought back some knowledge of the English language; or perhaps the Englishmen who temporarily resided on the Outer Banks at that time recorded some of the Algonquian words that they learned, which rudimentary knowledge of the language some of the men on the three ships of 1607 could have brought with them. From either source or from a concerted effort to understand each other from the beginning, the people who encountered each other at the time of the invasion of 1607 soon conversed. Not long thereafter, a few English boys went to live with Powhatan people to learn the language, and some Powhatan children, including Matoaka, also known as Pocahontas, lived with the Englishmen to learn their language. The children were some of the first interpreters and therefore important people to leaders of both the indigenous people and the invaders.

Captain John Smith compiled a short vocabulary that he published along with the map that he made after the first explorations. He listed Powhatan words and their English counterparts—words for man, woman, boy, house, fire, arrows, copper, fish, friend, enemy, and the words they used to number things. Strangely, right in the middle of the list is the Powhatan word *wepenter*, which Smith indicated meant cuckold. At first sight, that word in such a list is surprising; but if the two populations were attempting to learn about each other and their customs and beliefs, perhaps it should not be surprising. The English would certainly have been curious about the legitimacy of power relations in the Powhatan towns, and being accustomed to royalty and nobility inheriting their authority from their parents (fathers, mostly) in England, they would likely have wished to understand whether sexual relations outside marriage affected the inheritance of the right to rule in Powhatan society. Hence the word *wepenter* in the vocabulary, which Smith reprinted in his 1624 *Generall History of Virginia*.

Gabriel Archer described the people he encountered as "a most kind and loving people." He might have been disposed to think the opposite after he was hurt "in both his hands" when he went ashore with the first landing party near Cape Henry a month earlier. Both parties were armed, the Englishmen with guns, the members of one of the First Nations tribes with their bows and arrows. Almost certainly, both groups were armed for self-defense and not for attacking the other party because neither acted in a hostile manner toward the other until the end of the first day. Most of the first encounters in the spring of 1607 were peaceful. The Powhatan sometimes welcomed the invaders with hospitality, as was the case with the werowansqua of Appamattuck, and not with hostility. The longer the English stayed, however, the more opportunities for conflicts arose, and the more unwelcoming some werowances and werowansquas became.

Another interesting episode at the meeting between the Englishmen and the werowansqua of Appamattuck was her request that one of the Englishmen "shoote of a peece." That indicates that she already knew at least a little about English guns, though how she learned is far from clear. Ships from England, Spain, and perhaps France and the Netherlands had visited Chesapeake Bay from time to time during the previous decades, and it is possible that information about the loud and deadly weapons spread throughout Tsenacomoco or that she had learned from one of the neighboring towns where the invaders had already visited and fired a gun. Moreover, when the man fired the gun, "she shewed not neer the like fear as Arahatec though he be a goodly man." The werowansqua probably knew exactly what to expect and asked the man to fire his gun so that she could demonstrate her courage by not being startled at the loud report.

Although some of the native residents may have already known about guns, they certainly did not know about everything that the Englishmen brought with them. About a week before Captain Newport met the werowansqua of Appamattuck, the werowance of Paspehay, a village near Jamestown, sent some of his people to deliver a deer to the invaders, who were then preparing to make that site their principal settlement. One of the Englishmen set up a board or heavy target and asked one of the Paspehay to shoot it. He did, and the arrow pierced the stiff target and stuck out the back more than a foot. The Englishman was impressed at the strength of the bowman. He then set up a "steele Target" for the man to shoot at. George Percy watched as "he shot again, and burst his arrow all to pieces, he presently pulled out another Arrow, and bit it in his teeth, and seemed to bee in a great rage, so hee went away in great anger." He had not before seen steel and did not know that even the strongest bowman would not penetrate it with an arrow.

We do not know much about the werowansqua of Appamattuck after the brief encounter she had with Captain Christopher Newport's party of explorers. Four years later, in May 1611, a new invader, Sir Thomas Dale, a career military man, took charge of the English settlements. He almost immediately attacked a Nottoway village on the south side of the James River from Jamestown. He ruthlessly killed its inhabitants and burned the town. In December of that year, Dale attacked the Appamattuck towns and then established a new outpost near there that he named Henricus, after Prince Henry, the eldest son of King James I. It is entirely possible that Dale destroyed the werowansqua's town and killed her and some of the other residents at that time, as he had done at the Nottoway town.

It is also possible that if she lived through that event, the werowansqua of Appamattuck ordered her own warriors to take part in the coordinated attacks that Opechancanough, a younger brother of Wahunsonacock, launched against several outlying English settlements on March 22, 1622, fifteen years after Captain Newport and his exploring party visited her. If so, she might have had a role in killing some of the people Dale had sent to the settlement of Henricus, which is now a county historical park in Chesterfield County; or she might have had a role in the killing of the Englishmen who were then at work at a recently discovered vein of iron near Arahatec's town to establish the first ironworks in North America. The site was only a few miles from her "bower," near where Falling Creek empties into the James River. The site is also now a very small county historical park in Chesterfield County, in the median between the lanes of US 1 south of Richmond.

3

Hughe Pryse and the Loss of Faith

"HUGHE PRYSE"—PERHAPS HUGH, perhaps Price—suffered through part of the most deadly tragedy that the English invaders experienced following their arrival in the spring of 1607. His role is unique and appears in the only detailed account that we have of the events at Jamestown. Hughe Pryse, according to that account, "In a furious distracted moode did come openly into the markett place Blaspheaminge exclameinge and Cryeing outt thatt there was noe god." Hughe Pryse lost his faith in Jamestown during the winter of 1609–10 in what has been known ever since as the Starving Time.

The exclamation, the causes for his crying out, and the consequences for him and the other residents of Jamestown are recorded on pages 17–18 of a manuscript that George Percy composed entitled "Trewe Relacyon of the proceedings and ocurrents of momente wch have hapned in Virginia from the tyme Sr. Thomas Gates was shippwrackte upon the Bermudes Ano: 1609 untill my departure outt of the country wch was in Ano: Dmi 1612." The manuscript is in the Elkins Collection, Free Library of Philadelphia, and a photocopy of it is in the collections of the Virginia Historical Society. Mark Nicholls edited and published all of it as "George Percy's 'Trewe Relacyon': A Primary Source for the Jamestown Settlement," *Virginia Magazine of History and Biography* 114 (2005): 212–75.

Hughe Pryse was not one of the original party of invaders in 1607. He arrived later aboard a ship in one of the several fleets that transported people, foodstuffs, farm animals, farming implements, and other supplies to the new Virginia outpost. The supply fleet that sailed for Virginia in 1609 ran into a fierce tropical storm early in the season, and the flagship of the fleet, which carried the bulk of the supplies, was wrecked on the uninhabited island of Bermuda. Almost all of the supplies sank with the ship and were lost. The survivors worked for months, through the winter, to salvage enough useable timber from their ship to construct a smaller craft that eventually took them to their intended destination in May 1610. The episode of the shipwreck inspired William Shakespeare to write *The Tempest*.

Without the supplies, the little garrison at Jamestown faced famine. George Percy was in command during the winter of 1609–10 and a few years later wrote his account of the Starving Time. He may also have been to some extent responsible for it. A much smaller party of men spent that winter a few miles downstream at Fort Algernon on the north bank of the mouth of the James River, where the city of Hampton now is. Percy knew that the men there fared well during the winter. They harvested and ate fish and oysters and gathered ample supplies of other provisions thereabouts. Percy and the men in the fort at Jamestown, though, did little to help themselves. Perhaps Percy provided no leadership, or perhaps he foolishly expected the supply ship to arrive any day even months after the other ships of the fleet had come and gone. He evidently took no action to provide for the residents of the fort in the meantime. Supplies ran low even before the winter set in and the Starving Time began.

For many decades, historians speculated that many of the invaders died during the early years because too many of them were haughty gentlemen who refused to demean themselves by working and consequently starved. Captain John Smith's 1624 history of the founding of Virginia included his account of issuing an order that "he that will not worke shall not eate," which may have been the origin of the myth. Smith had been injured in a gunpowder explosion before the Starving Time, though, and returned to England. The Starving Time may have been more the result of inactive or incompetent leadership than of an unwillingness of men to provide for themselves.

Percy's account, as with the narratives that recorded the events of 1607, is best read aloud to let the voice carry past the unconventional spellings and syntax. Percy wrote later, "Now all of us att James Towne beginneinge to feele the sharpe pricke of hunger wch noe man trewly descrybe butt he wch hathe Tasted the bitternesse thereof." It is a gruesome narrative of shocking events, one of the most grim passages in all of early American literature. Percy wrote, "A worlde of miseries ensewed," which in the beginning forced him to execute some men who robbed the common storehouse and thereby reduced the supply of food that remained for the others.

"Then haveing fedd upoun horses and other beastes as longe as they Lasted, we weare gladd to make shifte wth vermin as doggs Catts Ratts and myce." From that comment, we know that not later than 1609, Englishmen had brought horses, cats, and dogs to Jamestown, and rats and mice probably crossed the ocean on the ships, too, and joined native rodent species in plaguing the invaders. Percy quoted an old maxim that "all was fishe thatt Came to Nett to satisfye Crewell hunger." They ate their boots, shoes, and other items of leather; "and those beinge Spente and devoured some weare inforced to search the woodes and to feede upon Serpentts and snakes and to digge the earthe for wylde and unknowne Rootes."

It got worse. Some of the men who went out in search of something to eat encountered members of First Nations tribes who in some instances attacked and killed them. The other men apparently cowered fearfully in the fort at Jamestown. "And now famin beginneinge to Looke gastely and pale in every face," Percy continued, "thatt notheinge was Spared to mainteyne Lyfe and to doe those things wch seame incredible, as to digge upp deade corpes outt of graves and to eate them. And some have Licked upp the Bloode wch hathe fallen from their weake fellowes." One man killed his pregnant wife, "Ripped the Childe outt of her woambe and threwe itt into the River," then chopped up and salted down his wife's corpse and fed on it until somebody discovered what he had done. Percy tortured the man and hung him up "by the Thumbes wth weightes att his feete a quarter of an howere" to make him confess and then executed him.

About Hughe Pryse, Percy vividly recalled, "one thinge hapned wch was very Remarkable wherein god sheowd his juste Judgmt For one Hughe Pryse beinge pinched wth extreme famin, In a furious distracted moode did come openly into the markett place Blaspheaminge exclameinge and Cryeing outt thatt there was noe god, alledgeing thatt if there were a god he wode nott suffer his creatures whome he had made and framed to indure those miseries and to perish for wante of foode and Sustenance."

"Butt itt appeared the same day," Percy continued with the lesson, "thatt the Almighty was displease wch him" because Pryse "goinge thatt afternoene wth a Butcher a corpulennt fatt man, into the Woode to seke for some reliefe, bothe of them weare slaine by the salvages, and after beinge fownde gods Indignacyon was sheowed upon Pryses corpes wch was Rente in pieces wth wolves or other wylde Beastes and his Bowles Torne outt of his boddy, being a leane spare man. And the fatt Butchers nott lyeing above six yards from him was found altogether untouched onely by the salvages Arrowes whereby he recieved his deathe."

Hughe Pryse denied the existence of God and, according to Percy, suffered God's just punishment. Pryse and the butcher died at the hands of "salvages" for unwisely venturing out into the woods without protecting themselves properly. Percy deduced from the fact that the wild animals did not touch the body of the dead fat man but attacked the lean body of Hughe Pryse that the damage that the animals did to Pryse's corpse was God's own method of punishing the man. It is difficult to ascertain from Percy's narrative of the Starving Time which terrible sinner was worse, the murderer and cannibal who killed and ate his wife, or the blasphemer who denied the existence of God. Nor can we know for certain whether people who later read Percy's account regarded Hughe Pryse or the murderer and cannibal as the worse sinner of the two.

The English men and women who colonized—invaded—Tsenacomoco in and after 1607 were all, or almost all, Protestant members of the Church of England. The events of the English Reformation were recent enough, a mere few decades, to be part of their family histories and memories. Under the terms of the royal charters that King James I issued to the Virginia Company that sponsored the invasion until 1624, the men, women, and children in Virginia were supposed to observe all of the daily and weekly religious ceremonies of the Church of England. The first Jamestown settlers hung an awning between some trees and placed a board between two trees to serve as a pulpit and altar when they first arrived and shortly thereafter erected a rude place of worship.

The invaders relied on their religion and had learned to fear Catholics or other people who threatened their religious institutions and the preservation of their faith. It is true that early in the time of settlement they allowed a few Italian glassmakers to reside near Jamestown and attempt, without much success, to establish a glassmaking industry in Virginia. But those few men, although undoubtedly Catholic, were foreigners and subject to strict control over their lives and behavior; and the company did not permit them to enjoy the ministry of a Catholic priest.

Denying the existence of God, as Pryse did, was a direct threat to the stability and success, even to the very survival, of the settlement. English men and women of the time believed that without God, there could be no morality, no civilization, no safety. It is not too much to say that for those English invaders, their religious beliefs were the most important things that they brought with them to North America.

We used to believe that people in colonial Virginia were not much interested in religion or did not take church attendance or religious beliefs and services very seriously; that they were only interested in getting rich off the resources that they found and exploited in Virginia; that because Virginians of the seventeenth century left behind few commentaries on religion, their faith was therefore not very important to them in the same way that it was somewhat later to the Puritans and other immigrants to New England who created and preserved a very large written and printed record of their religious beliefs, practices, and disagreements.

English residents of colonial Virginia did care about God and the manner in which their religious faith enabled them to try to live wholesome, civilized lives and hope to attain eternal salvation. They probably could not imagine living otherwise. Hence, when somebody like Hughe Pryse, even in the utmost desperation of the terror of starvation, cried out "thatt there was noe god," it is not too much to suspect that had he not gone out into the woods and been killed by the Indians and mutilated by wild animals later that day, George Percy might very well have executed him, too, as he did the men who robbed the common storehouse and the man who killed and ate his wife.

George Percy's gruesome account of the Starving Time does not indicate that he was squeamish about death. What disturbed him about what he had witnessed was the manner of the suffering and death of the residents of Jamestown that winter, especially Hughe Pryse's death and the dismembering of his corpse as a result of his blasphemy. Percy witnessed more deaths than any person should have to see in a short period of time. In an earlier account, he had recorded a list of the men who died in Jamestown in August and September of 1607. Every two or three days one or more men had died, some from violent encounters with members of nearby First Nations tribes, others from one of several diseases. The men may have weakened their systems by drinking slightly brackish, or salty, water from the first well that they dug, which was too close to the shore of the James

River. By the autumn, more than half of the men who landed at Jamestown in the spring had died.

Percy, like most other Englishmen who acted in responsible roles during the colonization period, did not mind killing people if he believed that they were dangerous or deserved to be killed. He recorded in another passage in his "Trewe Relacyon" that in August 1610, at the direction of the new governor, he raided the nearby Paspehay town. Percy and his raiding party burned all the houses there and cut down the corn, then they killed fifteen or sixteen men, one of them by cutting off his head. Next, they seized "the Quene and her Children" to transport them back to Jamestown. Along the way and with Percy's permission, "itt was agreed upon to putt the children to deathe the wch was effected by Throweing them overboard and shoteinge owtt their Braynes in the water." When the raiding party arrived back in Jamestown, Percy's soldiers prepared to burn the werowansqua alive. Percy recalled that he had already seen enough cruelty that day, so he stabbed her to death with his sword to spare her the torture of being burned.

4

Lawes Divine, Morall and Martiall

IN 1612, WILLIAM STRACHEY, an official of the Virginia Company of London, compiled and published a pamphlet in London. He entitled it *For the Colony in Virginea Britannia, Lawes Divine, Morall and Martiall, &c.* It has three parts, plus an introduction by the governor whom the Virginia Company had appointed and sent to Virginia in 1611, Thomas West, Baron De La Warr. The first part contains laws relating to religion; the second, laws relating to morality and civil behavior; and the third, a section of the law martial. The collection is sometimes and wrongly referred to as Dale's Laws, perhaps because Sir Thomas Dale contributed the law martial a year after Sir Thomas Gates and Lord De La Warr promulgated the laws divine and moral, and also because Sir Thomas Dale was not only commander of the military forces in Virginia from 1611 to 1616, but because he enforced all the laws, including the law martial, with notorious rigor, even against civilians.

The provisions of the first code were not laws in the same sense that acts of Parliament were laws in England because the House of Commons, the House of Lords, and the king had together enacted them, and a system of royal courts enforced them. In fact, the laws divine and moral were not even prepared in Virginia. Gates or De La Warr brought them to Jamestown in 1610, just at the time that the survivors of the Starving Time had abandoned the settlement and were sailing down the James River to try to get to Newfoundland and hitch a ride back to England aboard the fishing fleet that worked the waters thereabouts every summer. The ships of the supply fleet brought regulations that Virginia Company officials had written for the better organization and control of the settlers. Gates and De La Warr put them into effect in the summer of 1610, a year before Dale arrived and added the law martial to them. Dale may possibly have also added a few other provisions to the law moral.

The "Lawes" prohibited any person from leaving the safety of the settlement without permission; required everybody to attend religious services both morning and evening; forbade speaking impiously about God, the Trinity, the Holy Ghost, or the articles of faith of the Church of England, all on pain of death; prohibited people from uttering blasphemous statements, to be punished severely for a first offense, to have a bodkin, a long sharp needle, thrust through the tongue for a second offense, and to be executed for a third offense; prohibited traitorous words on pain of death; punished criticism of any member of the clergy with death; required men and women to repair the church when it needed work; prohibited sabbath breaking by gambling or neglecting private prayers at home; and required ministers to conduct religious services twice a day.

The "Lawes" imposed a punishment of death for murder, sodomy, and rape, and for fornication a whipping for first or second offenses and a whipping three times a week for a month for a third. The code imposed a penalty of death for stealing anything of value from the common storehouse or from another resident, including clothing, hats, stockings, shoes, or tools made of iron or steel. One long paragraph punished criticism of company officials, including the men in authority in Virginia, with corporal punishment or for a third offense with death. The laws prohibited settlers from engaging in unauthorized trade with members of local First Nations tribes or stealing anything from them on pain of death.

The code also regulated residents' dealings with sailors on ships that visited Virginia, and imposed whipping or other corporal punishment for actions that reduced the number of cattle in the colony. It prohibited people from throwing soapy water or foul water into the streets or from doing "the necessities of nature" within a quarter of a mile of the palisades of the fort. The laws required everybody to labor at his or her own trade daily and prohibited anybody from running away to live with "Powhathan, or any savage Weoance else whatsoever" on pain of death.

The physical punishments for the many offenses seem exceptionally severe by twenty-first-century standards, but in most instances, particularly in matters of religion and physical security, they were not notably more strict and did not impose notably more harsh penalties than English courts imposed on people who violated similar provisions of the common law. The origins of American law, as seen in the *Lawes Divine, Morall and Martiall*, were in essence right out of English common law practices that, in most instances, residents of Jamestown would have already understood.

One thing that has given the code a bad reputation in later centuries, after brutal physical punishments began to disappear from criminal codes, was that Sir Thomas Dale imposed punishments on people through the rigor of the law martial that he carried with him to Virginia for the government of the soldiers under his command. The law martial was a fairly common military code for disciplining soldiers, and he probably did not intend, at least in the beginning, to impose it on civilians. Surviving records do not disclose that he formally imposed martial law on the whole population, but he sometimes acted as if he had. In one famous instance, when a man was found taking food from the common stock, Dale ordered him tied to a tree and left him there to starve to death, both as a punishment and as a deterrent, to terrify other people into not doing likewise.

Insofar as we know, and there is much that we do not know because of the loss of many original records, the *Lawes Divine, Morall and Martiall* probably governed the actions of the people of Jamestown and the other small, new settlements that people established elsewhere until the creation of a more formal government structure, beginning with the first meeting of the General Assembly in the summer of 1619 and the royal proclamations of 1624 and 1625 that converted the company settlement into a royal colony.

5

Richard Bucke, the Book of Common Prayer, and the Bible

ON THE MORNING OF Friday, July 30, 1619, the governor, members of the Council of State, the secretary of the colony, and twenty-two elected burgesses met in the church at Jamestown as members of the very first session of the General Assembly of Virginia. Richard Bucke opened the session with a prayer "that it would please God to guide & sanctifie all our proceedings, to his owne glory, and the good of this plantation."

The assembly was a creation of the Virginia Company, and the rules and regulations that it adopted, like the *Lawes Divine, Morall and Martiall,* were company orders for the good management of the English people who lived in the young settlement. Nevertheless, in several important respects, the assembly conducted its business in much the same manner that Parliament did at that time, except that the governor, council members, secretary, and burgesses all met together in one room in unicameral session, not with burgesses meeting separately from council members in bicameral session as became the practice in 1643.

Before the members of the assembly met, most of them had probably attended the morning service of the Church of England that Bucke led in the same church. Bucke conducted the morning service prescribed for the day in the Book of Common Prayer, the established form of worship for the Church of England that Parliament had enacted in the sixteenth century. During the service, Bucke read from his copies of the Bible and the Book of Common Prayer. Precisely which words he read and the men and women assembled in the church heard is unclear. The Latin, Greek, and Hebrew texts had been translated by then into several English-language editions of the Bible, each with subtle or sometimes significant differences in tone and meaning.

Bucke probably had a copy of what was called the Geneva Bible, which was the English-language version that was the most widely used at the beginning of the seventeenth century and the edition that the church's reformers, known as Puritans, preferred. The Virginia Company's shareholders and officers included many Puritans, and several of the colony's early clergymen, including Bucke, were sympathetic to the Puritans. Bucke might possibly have had a copy of the new translation of the Bible, the one that King James had commissioned not long before he issued the first charter to the Virginia Company in 1606 and that was published in 1611, not long after Bucke first stepped ashore in Virginia in 1610 and walked among the starving men in Jamestown.

Directions printed in Bucke's copy of the Book of Common Prayer required that he read the service and the words of Scripture distinctly and with a loud voice that the people might hear, that none by virtue of being unlettered remain ignorant of the word of God. The words that he read would have been familiar to the people in the church. The services of the church were so arranged that the same significant texts were read aloud once each year and select psalms once every month, "that the people (by daily hearing of holy scripture read in the Churche)," according to the explanatory preface in the 1559 edition of the Book of Common Prayer, "shoulde continually profite more and more in the knowledge of God, & be the more enflamed with the love of his true religion."

If Bucke conducted the full morning service for the thirtieth of July, the first of the three psalms for the day was Psalm 144, which began, in the words of the Geneva Bible, "Blessed *be* the Lord my strength, w^c teacheth mine hands to fight, & my fingers to battel. *He is* my goodness & my fortres, my tower & my deliverer, my shield, and in him I trust, which subdueth my people under me." Those words may have carried a special significance that morning to the men and women who gathered in the little church in that little town on the bank of a great river on the edge of a vast continent that contained no more than a few hundred Protestant Christians. They needed all the earthly help and divine aid that they could get. The psalm concluded with the prayer "That our corners"—places for storing things— "may be ful, and abunding with divers sorts, *and* that our shepe may bring forthe thousands, and tens thousands in our streetes: That our oxen may be strong to labour: that their be none invasion, nor going out, nor no crying in our streetes, Blessed *are* the people, that be so, *yes,* blessed *are* the people, whose god is the Lord."

Those words of the psalmist must have resonated in the souls of the men and women in the church that day. They needed moral and spiritual support to make a reality of their dreams of peace, full storehouses, and plentiful flocks. One wonders what Richard Bucke thought about those words. He had been shipwrecked on the way to Virginia in 1609 and had been in the first ship to reach Jamestown in May 1610 at the end of the Starving Time. His wife had died. It is possible that he married a second time and that his second wife died, also. He named his children Mara (meaning bitter), Gershon (expulsion), Peleg (division), and Benoni (sorrow), and Benoni was feebleminded. Bucke's life in Virginia was hard, but that was one of his bonds with every other man and woman who entered the church on that day or on any other day.

Bucke then read the two passages from Scripture prescribed for that day. From chapter 8 of the book of Jeremiah, he read about how the kings and people of Judea had sinned and ignored God's warnings and how as a consequence their bones were taken out of their tombs and spread "as dung upon the earth." In the third verse were the words of warning that would have made anyone shudder who recalled or knew about the Starving Time in Virginia: "And death shalbe desired rather then life of all the residue that remaineth of this wicked familie, which remaine in all the places where I have scatred them, saith the Lord of hostes." Bucke then read from chapter 18 of the book of John about the arrest of Jesus in the garden, how Peter thrice denied him, how Jesus denied that he was a mere earthly king, and how Pilate prepared to hand Jesus over to the Jews for trial and execution.

The lessons that day, for both the lettered and the unlettered, reminded men and women of their duty to obey God and to avoid sin, to recognize Jesus as a greater king than an earthly king, and that even earthly kings were subject to the word of God through the words of Jesus. To the people in the church in Jamestown that day, the words in the psalm about subduing "my people under me" meant not only the unchristianized and possibly dangerous members of First Nations tribes in their midst, they also meant all of the men and women, all of the people who were free as well as those who were bonded by indenture to labor for other people or for the company. Except the king, every soul was under some other person's temporal and spiritual authority.

Among the laws that the General Assembly enacted during the ensuing four days, several concerned religion. One required all ministers "to read divine service, and exercise their Ministerial function, according to the Ecclesiasticall lawes and orders of the churche of england, and every Sunday in the afternoon shall Catechize suche as are not yet ripe" to take Communion. Another required the ministers and churchwardens to present to the court evidence of "all ungodly disorders" and "skandalous offenses, as suspicions of whordomes, dishonest Company-keeping with woemen, and suche like." Yet another specified punishments, including excommunication from the church, if "any person, after two warnings doe not amende his or her life, in point of evident suspicion of Incontinency"—sexual misbehavior—"or of the commission of any other enormous sinnes."

The assembly, in effect, established the Church of England as the official church in Virginia. By the time that the king revoked the charter of the Virginia Company in 1624 and made Virginia a royal colony in 1625, the Church of England was firmly established in Virginia.

6

Thefts from Edward Grindon's Warehouse

VOLUME 15 IN SERIES 8 of the Thomas Jefferson Papers in the Library of Congress preserves original records, some of them in fragmentary form, of actions of the governor and his council of advisors, officially the Council of State, from early in 1623 to early in 1633. The documents have been published in H. R. McIlwaine, ed., *Minutes of the Council and General Court of Colonial Virginia* (Richmond, 1924). Those records contain several depositions taken almost two decades after the Starving Time, about a series of robberies during the winter of 1627–28. The documents indicate that residents of Virginia by then had access to a considerable variety of things to eat and to other items of commerce. The documents also include other revealing, tangential information about life in the colony in the early days.

The documents concerning the thefts consist of several depositions, which were probably affidavits or sworn statements that the governor and his advisory council considered before they issued their final judgment on or about February 7, 1628. The testimony appears here in the sequence in which the paragraphs are recorded in the record book; but because the first of them is the confession of the principal accused person, that is probably not the sequence in which the judges heard the evidence.

The testimony of William Mills, the accused, is the first. He was Edward Grindon's servant, identified as "aged 21 yeares or thereabouts borne at Purton in Wiltshire," England. Grindon owned and operated a small store near Jamestown at a place the depositions called Grindon's Hill. Mills confessed "that at divers times before Christmas last past" he had stolen from Grindon's warehouse as much tobacco as he "could carry away under his arme." Mills also admitted that not long thereafter, one morning "a little before Sun rising," he "pulled downe three boards" from one side of the warehouse at Grindon's Hill, "went in & stole a way his capp full of currants, & carried them" to the house of John Tios "& gave them unto him" and his wife, Jane Tios.

Mills also testified that "on Newe Yeeres day in the morning" he "went into the store againe & stole from thence more currants & brought them away" and delivered them to John and Jane Tios "& Thomas Hall, (who all were privy to the stealing of the currents)." Mills also confessed that he "stole 6 paire of shoes & one shirte," and on another occasion, "on Sunday in the Morning," he "went into the store againe and took from th[ence] some Currants in a bagg wch Thomas Hall gave him," as well as some sugar. Mills asserted that John Tios told him to "take heed that he was not seene & specially take heed that one Rich: Littlefere should not see him for he was a very Knave."

"Richard Littlefere aged 30 years & borne in the Bishoppricke of Durrham" testified that "about 2 of the clocke in the night on the 14th of January last past" he was asleep in his bed and heard somebody "walk about the hous in the Fort at Grindalls Hill." About half an hour later, perhaps after he heard another sound, and thinking "that it was noe time of the night for any one to be abroad," he got out of bed and looked out the window. He saw "one Willm Mills coming out at an hole in the wall of the store some boards being down at one end." Littlefere wakened "his Mate John Dunfy who lay wth him, & sayd there is one comeing out of the store, shall wee take him, & the sayd John Danfy answered noe." Danfy having declined to act with him, Littlefere was perhaps afraid to act alone and merely continued to watch. He "saw the sayd Willm Mills after he was come out to set downe his cappe uppon the ground & after-wards putt upp the boards wth his hands into their places againe." Littlefere concluded his testimony by swearing that he did not see Mills bring anything else out of the store.

"John Danfy, aged 25 years bourne in the Citty of Worcester" was then "sworne & examined sayth that about two of the clocke in the night time on the 14th of January last past," he was "a sleepe in his bed at Grindons Hill one Rich: Littlefere being in bed wth him." Littlefere awakened him "& calling uppon him said looke yonder looke yonder," and so Danfy asked what was happening. Littlefere "answered there is Mills comeing out of the store," but Danfy merely "layd himselfe downe againe to sleepe." Three days later, Danfy testified further, he "went unto the ho[us]e of John Tios & Thomas Hall wth Mr Grindon to serch for stolne goods." When the two men "asked the said Thomas Hall for the shoes & other things that his man had brought unto him," Hall "presently went unto his Chest & delivered the said Mr Grindon seaven paire of shoes & one shirt & said these was all that he had."

"Edward Grindon gent" swore that his wife had informed him that Littlefere had told her that he had seen William Mills "Comeing out of the store" in the night. The next day, Grindon questioned Mills, "who confessed that he had stollen out of the store, twice some currants & once some suger & six paire of shoes & one shirte." Grindon then "went downe unto the house of John Tios & Thomas Hall, & asked the sayd Thomas Hall where were the shoes & other things that his man Willm Mills had brought thither, & the sayd Tho: Hall answered there was halfe a dozen paire of shoes" and then "brought out a course shirte."

Grindon obtained a search warrant, "& goeing againe to the house of the said John Tios & Thomas Hall to serch," he "went upp in to the loft & found a bagg of fowle"—dirty or ragged—"cloathes, & in the said Bagg there was two other small Baggs, the one haveing about six pounds of currants, & the other about 3 pounds of suger." Jane Tios told Grindon, as Grindon testified, that she and her husband had purchased the sugar from a Frenchman who was aboard a ship in the James River and had bought the currants from another man. About that time, John Tios returned home, and Grindon "asked him, what currants & suger those were that he had in the house, & the sayd Tios answered, if there were any there, they were not his for he knew of none." Grindon "went upp againe & brought downe the said currants & suger & gave them unto Edward Temple to keep." After Grindon "made serc[h] in the chests of the sayd John Tios," but found "none of his owne goods therein," he concluded his investigation into the theft of his merchandise.

The governor and council also heard testimony from "Peter Climgeon aged 26 yeares borne in the parish of St Olives in Southwarke neare London," who swore that he had heard William Mills confess to Grindon that he had "carryed a certain quantity of sugar & Currants unto the house of John Tios, & likewise six paire of shoes & one shirt." Climgeon also swore that he heard Mills curse "them that had enticed him to it," evidently referring to John and Jane Tios and Thomas Hall.

"John Tyos aged 26 yeares borne at Lowe Layden in Essex" testified that "in the Christmas holydayes last," William Mills brought to his house two hens. Tios asked where he got them, and Mills "answered, that he bredd upp three henns & a capon of his owne, whereof his Mistris"—the wife of Edward Grindon—"had killed one wch caused him to kill the other two." Mills took them to Tios's house. Tios related that Mills explained "that there was noe keeping of henns at his Masters house, for my Mistris will kill them all" to feed the members of her own family. Tios related that he and the residents of his house had eaten the fowls and that about four days later Mills brought him "one blacke capon, wch was likewise dressed & eaten at his house."

Tios also testified that William Mills played cards at his house and lost the hens in gambling; and that Mills also offered to sell Tios "six pairs of shoes wch he refused," because he had no tobacco on hand to pay for them. "Whereuppon," Tios continued, "Thomas Hall did buy the sayd shoes." Tios concluded his testimony by stating that he had no knowledge of how Hall came into possession of tobacco, which could have suggested that he believed that Hall was complicit in the theft of the tobacco.

"Jane the wife of John Tyos aged about 22 yeares borne at Wombarne in Staffordshire, examined confesseth that the aforesaid Willm Mills did at severall times bring poultry into her house but knoweth not how many, wch were there dressed & eaten; & futher shee confesseth that the said Willm Mills did bring a certaine quantity of sugar & Currants in a bagg unto her house, when Edward Allen, John Edwards, & Tho: Hall & others of Mr Grindons servants were there present." Jane and John Tios did not go to church while the goods were in their house, perhaps for fear that the other servants whom she named would steal the bag or steal some of the currants in it. She also testified "that the said Mills did bring once or twice certaine Currants in his pockett wch he did eate & give away." Jane Tios concluded by stating "that there was one shirte & shoes in her house, but how & by what meanes they came she knoweth not."

"Tho: Hall aged about 26 yeares borne at Wisbige in Cambridgshire" testified that "Willm Mills did at severall times bring certaine poultry unto the house of John Tios wch were there eaten," but he did not recall how many. Jane and John Tios, he related, had given him a piece of cloth that

Mills had provided them and asked him "to sowe it & make a bagg of it to carry currants." Hall believed that Jane Tios understood that Mills had purchased seven pair of shoes from Grindon for two and a half pounds of tobacco per pair.

The governor and council having heard all the testimony concerning the charge that Mills had stolen the items from Grindon, the governor "demaunded if there were any inditemt."—indictment—"preferred agst. him by any one, And the Provoust Marshall openly made Proclamation of the same, And none being found the Court thought fitt to adjuge him for his fault to be whipped at the cartes taile from the Towne unto the Gallowes & back again." Moreover, "the Court hath adjudged that the said John Tios shall receave 40 stripes at the whipping post, & the said Thomas Hall to receave in like sort 40 strippes more: And the Court doth discharge & free the said Jane Tios it being most probable that shee was drawne thereunto by the will & power of her husband, & in expectation of her amendmt of her life hereafter."

Without our being able to know for certain whether this was the record of an actual trial with the accused present or a compilation of written evidence from which the governor and council drew their conclusions, we are not able to ascertain to what extent the judges in the case obeyed the commands in the charters that King James I issued to the Virginia Company of London and the proclamation that King Charles I made in 1625 that stipulated that the English residents of Virginia enjoy all the rights and liberties of residents of England and required that Virginia laws and courts must conform as closely as unique local circumstances permitted to the laws and practices of England. That Edward Grindon obtained a warrant from somebody to search the Tios house and that the governor asked about indictments, or formal charges, against the people whose testimony the court considered suggests a certain close similarity to court proceedings in England at the time.

The supply of currants, shoes, and other merchandise that Edward Grindon had in his warehouse or store indicates that by the end of the second decade of the settlement, English residents of Virginia had access to much more in the way of supplies and foodstuffs than the residents of Jamestown had during the misery of the Starving Time three years into the first decade of the settlement. Two reports from 1634, toward the end of the third decade, state that Virginians produced more than enough food to feed themselves and that in 1633 they had shipped 5,000 or 10,000 bushels of grain (the reports vary about how much) to New England.

The testimony of Mills implicated Tios and Hall in his theft, but the evidence of Tios, Hall, and the others placed the entire blame on Mills. That raises the question, how did the governor and members of the council know who to believe? Their judgment indicates that by and large they agreed with "Edward Grindon gent," as the copy of his evidence identified him. They almost certainly gave a gentleman (the only person so identified) more credit for veracity than any of the other people, who were all merely servants, and all of whom at least one of the depositions implicated in the thefts or as a receiver of stolen goods.

And how many shoes were there, six or seven pair? The testimony contains several discrepancies. Moreover, John Tios declined to buy any of the shoes because he had no tobacco with which to pay for them, but Thomas Hall did have enough tobacco. That tells us that a servant could have his own supply of tobacco, more than he needed for smoking. It also tells us that within a very short time after tobacco became the essential cash crop for Virginia residents in the 1610s, they began using tobacco as a currency. Very early records contain other evidence that people generally agreed that the prices for some items be expressed in terms of a certain number of pounds of tobacco. By the middle of the century, the General Assembly even levied taxes on people to be paid in specified weights of tobacco.

Another question: how, in a time and place where clocks or other instruments of telling time were undoubtedly very scarce, did Littlefere know that it was 2 o'clock in the morning when the noises that Mills made at the warehouse awakened him? References to the hours of the day and night occur with some frequency in the early colonial records. How did they know? At that time and both long before and long after, during the daytime when the sun was shining people could hold up an open hand, fingers touching and perpendicular to the ground, and look at the hand with the sun immediately above it and the ground below. One hand held that way at arm's length measured about an hour, so that if a person knew roughly at what hour the sun rose or set that day, estimating the hour would not be difficult. But did people merely guess about what the hour was in the dark? Did they still have a night watch that patrolled the perimeter of the settlement as armed men had done during the first years, a guard who would call out the hours during the night and reassure the people that all was then well? If they did, why did the guard not detect Mills entering and leaving the store in the dark?

Also, Littlefere and Danfy shared a bed, and Thomas Hall resided in the house with John and Jane Tios. It is almost certain that the dwelling places of servants would have been small cabins, probably rude one-room structures made of logs without panes of glass or, as at the Tios place, maybe a small loft or garret between the ceiling and the roof. Working people lived cramped together in small spaces when they were not at work and probably lacked all of the conveniences of privacy that later generations of people enjoyed and prized.

About a year before the thefts of currants, sugar, and shoes, five men testified that they were all trying to sleep in the same room with a sixth man when a seventh, Captain William Epes, and Alice Boise drank a large quantity of wine and then "three or fowre times" in the night awakened the men with a "great busseling and joggling of the bed" during sexual intercourse. One of the men deposed that "there was soe great a motion in the bed that this deponent rose and sayd for shame doe not doe such thinges before soe many people then the said Capt Epes answered fye brother thats too plaine." Two other men testified that Epes replied in almost exactly the same words, but in one instance the scribe spelled the final word as plaint, which suggests that the captain dismissed the rebuke as an unnecessary or insignificant complaint.

People in the first decades of the English settlement of Virginia had little or no privacy, and it would have been very difficult for anybody to keep secrets.

The short, final two paragraphs of the surviving record of the proceedings against William Mills record that "the Court thought fitt to adjuge" that Mills "for his fault to be whipped at the cartes taile from the Towne unto the Gallowes & back again." It also ordered that "John Tios shall receave 40 stripes at the whipping post, & the said Thomas Hall to receave in like sort 40 strippes more." The punishments were very much of the kind that local courts in England would have ordered at that time and that remained common in Virginia well into the eighteenth century.

Whipping a culprit was a common form of punishment long before it became associated in later generations as a form of punishment for enslaved people. Whipping left on people's backs long, painful, and bloody marks—called "stripes"—that could have remained visible for a lifetime. The sentence that Mills be "whipped at the cartes taile from the Towne unto the Gallowes & back again" meant that he would be tied to the end of a cart and continually whipped as a horse drew the cart from Jamestown all the way out to the gallows and then back for everybody to witness. Public whipping was a painful punishment, but it was also a form of terrorism intended to frighten people into not committing similar or other offenses.

Physical punishment and public humiliation were the common forms of punishment for breaches of the peace in England and in the North American colonies. Hanging was reserved for the most serious offenses, but corporal punishment was probably common. It is probable that Jamestown in the 1620s had the same implements of law enforcement and punishment that Virginia law later required every county to have. Those included a gallows to hang convicted felons; a jail for confining people who awaited trial (convicted people seldom spent time in jail, as they did later, when sentenced to imprisonment); a whipping post, where people could be tied up to receive their stripes; a pillory to which the sheriff or jailer could nail a culprit's ears, which he would cut off to free the person when the hour or hours of punishment expired; a ducking stool to confine people in a chair so that they could be lowered into a pond or a creek, which was a common punishment for rumormongers or common scolds; and stocks for restraining people by locking their heads, hands, and perhaps feet securely while other people probably mocked them and where officials hoped that by being thus humiliated they would see the errors of their ways and promise themselves to live better lives in future.

Finally, the court discharged and freed "Jane Tios it being most probable that shee was drawne thereunto by the will & power of her husband, & in expectation of her amendmt of her life hereafter." In that, the court exactly followed proper legal practice in England. The English law of marriage made the husband and wife as one. The wife had no separate legal existence from the husband and could not act in any lawful capacity without his permission. If a wife should be found complicit in an unlawful act, the presumption of the criminal law was that she acted under instructions from or under the control or her husband and was therefore not guilty by virtue of her own volition. It was that presumption of the common law that led exasperated

A ducking stool similar to this one and other implements of public punishment and humiliation were common sights near the courthouses of colonial Virginia. (Library of Virginia)

Mr. Bumble in Charles Dickens's nineteenth-century novel *Oliver Twist* to exclaim, "If the law supposes that, the law is a ass—a idiot."

One final thing. The people who gave depositions or testimony in this case ranged in age from about twenty-one to thirty and came from various places in England. Only "Edward Grindon gent" is not identified by the place of his birth. The others came from Wiltshire, Durham, Worcester, the outskirts of London, and the counties of Essex, Stafford, and Cambridge. Even so early as the 1620s, the white population of Virginia was extremely varied. Counting the presence after 1619 of natives of different parts of Africa and from the beginning of members of a large number of First Nations tribes, the population of Virginia could scarcely ever be characterized, even in the very early years, in broad generalities without taking account of local, regional, cultural, religious, linguistic, and other important differences.

7

Anthony Johnson's Enslaved Man

Folio 10 in the record book entitled Northampton County Deeds, Wills, Etc., 7 (1655–68), contains a report of the proceedings of the county court that fairly leaps off the page because it contains surprising information. It indicates that Anthony Johnson, a "Negro," lived on the Eastern Shore of Virginia, the peninsula between Chesapeake Bay and the Atlantic Ocean, that he was a free, married man who owned property, and that he claimed lifetime ownership of John Casor (or Casar), also a "Negro," and held him in slavery.

The date on the court record is March 8, 1655, but that is what is called an old-style date. The British Calendar Reform Act of 1752 discontinued use of the old Julian calendar that had been the legal calendar in England for centuries in favor of the Gregorian calendar of 1582 that was then in use throughout most of western Europe. Before that, English and colonial officials almost always used old-style dates. Under the old calendar, the new year began on March 25. That is, December 31, 1655, was the day immediately before January 1, 1655, and March 24, 1655, was the day immediately before March 25, 1656. The old-style date March 8, 1655, was March 8, 1656, by the new-style calendar, which some people made clear in their record-keeping by writing it as March 8, 1655/6. They rendered only dates between January 1 and March 24 in this manner. People were accustomed to two New Year's Days, the legal Julian calendar one and the modern Gregorian one. Recall that William Mills admitted to a theft from Edward Grindon's store "on Newe Yeeres day" between Christmas and the public revelation of his criminal acts in January and February.

The names of Anthony Johnson and his wife, Mary Johnson, are familiar to students of the origins of slavery and of the history of seventeenth-century Virginia, but even though some speculative or derivative statements about them can easily be found on the internet and in ill-informed books and magazine articles, most twenty-first-century people have not heard of them and probably find it difficult to believe that a "Negro" could enslave another person.

We do not know much for certain about Anthony Johnson, and almost nothing about his early life. He and his wife were native Africans, and at some time, probably in the 1620s, they had been kidnapped, given Spanish, Portuguese, or English names, and sold to a ship captain who transported them to North America. It is possible—indeed, probable—that the ship landed in the West Indies, where the human cargo could have been broken up into smaller groups of people and distributed to European settlements in the islands, in the Caribbean, or, as in their case, to the relatively new colony of Virginia.

Whether they had been captured separately or together and transported aboard the same ship is not known for certain. They both survived the long, brutal ordeal aboard the slave trading ship. Many men, women, and children died during those long voyages, and the ship captains tossed their bodies into the sea to feed the sharks. The ships always stank, especially in the summer heat, from the combined odors of sweat, vomit, and—to be blunt—farts, piss, shit, menstrual blood, and rotting flesh worn raw by the iron shackles that confined them all packed closely together below deck all night every night and nearly all day nearly every day. If the wind was wrong, people could smell the putrid stench of a slave trading ship from far away.

Exactly when and where they reached Virginia is not positively recorded, nor when or why Anthony took the surname Johnson. Their given names, Anthony and Mary, could have easily been anglicized from Antonio or Maria if they had received Spanish or Portuguese names when enslaved or shipped out of Africa. Those names that appear in some surviving early Virginia records have led to unverifiable conjectures that the documents actually dated their arrivals in Virginia; those conjectures are based more on coincidence of names than on ascertainable fact.

The legal status of Africans in Virginia was very unclear during the first decades after the earliest well-documented arrival in August 1619 of "20.

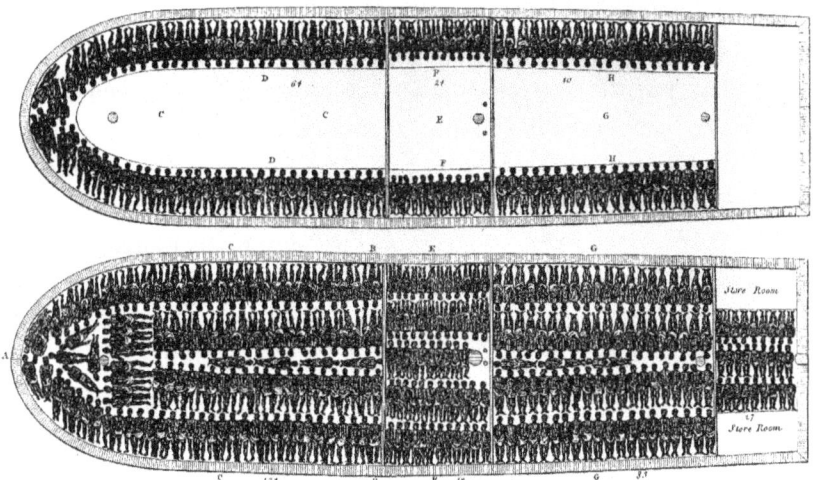

This early nineteenth-century schematic diagram of the cargo decks of a slave trading ship illustrated the inhumane conditions under which men, women, and children were tightly packed together for the long and dangerous trip to the Americas. (Library of Virginia)

and odd Negroes," as John Rolfe reported the following January. He also wrote that Governor Sir George Yeardley and Abraham Peirsey, the cape merchant, who managed the communal storehouse, bought them. It is unclear from what we know, however, whether Yeardley and Peirsey paid the ship captain a sum of money in order to claim legal ownership of the people as slaves or if the two men intended to treat them as laborers, either paid workers or unpaid servants.

The words *slave* and *slavery* appear in surviving public and private documents during the first half of the seventeenth century but not in the colony's laws. Those words did not always have very precise meanings then; some people used them interchangeably with *servant* then as well as later without regard to the legal status of people. English common and statute law did not either authorize or prohibit slavery. By the middle of the eighteenth century, though, many able lawyers concluded that English law did not recognize property in human beings.

In practice, however, beginning even before the first English invasion of North America early in the seventeenth century, a few Englishmen had purchased Turks, Arabs, and Africans who had been captured and enslaved as prisoners of war. International law sanctioned that form of enslavement on the grounds that it was more humane to enslave captured people than to kill them, which was the usual alternative. That form of slavery was not linked to race, as it later was in the English colonies, nor was it always regarded as slavery for life. (Captain John Smith had been captured and briefly enslaved in Turkey before he traveled to Virginia in 1607.)

English common law treated as property anything that anybody legally purchased or acquired by inheritance or other lawful means and protected the rights of all owners to all of their property. That even included the people whom Englishmen purchased outside of England and then brought into the kingdom. All this arose without the government taking any action at all, such as passing or amending any laws. In a sense, slavery in England's North American colonies was the product of an unregulated international free market economy in which white Virginians began to participate very soon after they first arrived in North America. Virginia planters later created new laws to protect their ownership and control of their human property.

Most of the laborers who toiled in Virginia during the seventeenth century were not enslaved Africans; they were white indentured servants, the large majority of them from England. They labored in agricultural fields, as servants in households, and sometimes even as farm managers or clerks. Each of them had a labor contract that he or she made a mark on or signed. The person who owned their labor for a stated, limited number of years also signed the contract. It was called an indenture because to create that form of labor contract required two identically worded documents that both parties signed, one for the master, one for the servant. The person who wrote out the two documents placed one on top of the other and cut one side along a wavy or jagged (indented) line so that both documents precisely matched in shape as well as in wording. The contract specified the rights and responsibilities of both parties and how long one owed loyal service to the other. The English law of master and servant provided legal recourse for either party in the event of the failure of the other to meet the terms of the indenture. A servant could take a master to court.

Captured Africans, however, arrived in Virginia without any indentures and lived there without the protections that English and Virginia law provided to indentured servants or to hired workers. Whenever and wherever Anthony Johnson and Mary Johnson arrived in Virginia, and whether separately or together, they did not come with indentures, but somehow they did not become entrapped in lifetime slavery. They may have worked as paid laborers or as unpaid laborers, or they might possibly have negotiated terms of employment that made them, either separately or individually, hired servants for a stated period of time and with the legal protections of the English law of master and servant.

By the 1640s they lived together in Northampton County, Virginia, and identified themselves, and their neighbors described them, as husband and wife. They had begun to accumulate property, first a cow, then other farm animals, and eventually a small farm. They also learned to understand and speak the English language well, although neither apparently ever learned to read or write it. As an owner of land—real property—Anthony Johnson had his name recorded in the official public records of the county. Those references to him are actually the earliest known records that provide documented facts about him and his family, which by the 1650s included several children.

According to the entry that the county clerk made in the county court's record book on March 8, 1655/6, "Anthony Johnson Negro made his complaint to the Court agt mr. Robert Parker & declared that hee deteyneth his servant Jno. Casor negro (under pretence that the sd Negro is a free man.)." To ascertain the facts, the members of the county court that day heard what Johnson had to say and considered a deposition from a white man, Captain Samuel Goldsmith.

Goldsmith swore that he had been "att the howse of Anth: Johnson Negro (about the beginninge of November last to receive a hogsh of tobac.)." A hogshead was a large wooden keg, or barrel, in which Virginia tobacco planters packed their tobacco for shipment to England to be sold. Goldsmith stated that at that time "a Negro called Jno. Casar . . . told him that hee came into Virginia for seaven or Eight yeares (per Indenture.) And that hee had demanded his freedome of his master Anth: Johnson; And further sd that Johnson had kept him his servt seaven yeares longer than hee ought." Casor asked Goldsmith for help. Goldsmith informed the court that Anthony Johnson denied that he had ever seen any indenture but said that "hee had him for his life"; that is, Anthony Johnson stated that John Casor was his slave for life.

Goldsmith also swore that the brothers Robert Parker and George Parker, also white men, evidently, because the court record did not identify them otherwise, "knew that the sd Negro had an Indenture." According to Goldsmith, they "sd that if the sd Anthony Johnson did not tell the negro goe free The said Jno. Casor would recovr. most of his Cowes of him," which indicated that they or Casor believed that Casor should sue Johnson for damages and claim Johnson's "Cowes" as compensation for his labor during the time after he should have been freed at the expiration of the indenture. In Goldsmith's opinion, Johnson "was in a feare" then and allowed "his Sonne in lawe, his wife & his 2 sonnes" to persuade him "to sett the sd Jno. Casor free."

"The Court seriously consideringe & maturely weighinge the premisses," the clerk recorded in the court record book, "doe fynde that the sd Mr. Robert Parker most unjustly keepeth the sd Negro from Anth: Johnson his master as appeareth by the deposition of Capt Samuel Goldsmith & many probable circumstances. It is therefore the Judgmt. of the Court & ordered That the sd Jno. Casor Negro forthwth returne unto the service of his sd master Anthony Johnson; And that mr. Robert Parker make paymt. of all charge in the suit."

The county court ordered Casor back into Johnson's lifetime service. The court record does not indicate whether the members of the court heard any other evidence or indicate what the "many probable circumstances" were that contributed to their determination. We can nevertheless conjecture with some confidence that the failure of Casor or anybody else to produce the indenture as evidence of his status weighed against him heavily and in Johnson's favor. The assertions that Casor had once had such a legal document were not proof; and without the written terms of the document, had there been one, Casor's rights and the limit of his term of service could not be known beyond what Casor had told Goldsmith and that Goldsmith in turn had told the court, which was in fact only hearsay evidence and not proof. Casor was a mere servant who produced no document or other evidence that he was legally entitled to be free. That leaves one more unanswered question: why did the court not hear from Casor himself?

Among the "many probable circumstances" that could have inclined members of the court to rule in favor of Johnson was the fact that Johnson owned his own farm, had a family, planted tobacco, and was a man of good behavior and a productive member of the community. The occasional references to Johnson in the county records provide enough evidence to believe that his neighbors regarded him as a respectable man. The references that contain information about him as an owner of land sometimes omitted identification of him as a "Negro." That is suggestive. It does not prove anything, but it suggests that Johnson's being of African birth was not in every instance relevant or as significant as was his ownership of his farm. It would be important to identify him as an African to differentiate him from some other Anthony Johnson who was white, but the county records apparently do not have references to anybody else by that name who was not a member of that particular family. Anthony Johnson the farmer who owned his own land was respectable in a way that ordinarily a "Negro" might not be.

That conjecture about how the county clerk recorded information about Johnson also suggests that identification of a man, woman, or child as a "Negro" might not yet have become, as it did later in the seventeenth century, a default method of identification, as if being a "Negro" was itself an important distinction to make even if the place of birth or the ancestry of the person did not matter, or even if the status of the person as free, indentured, or enslaved was not relevant to the matter at hand.

During the decades that Anthony and Mary Johnson lived in Virginia and later to the northward in Maryland, they prospered in their freedom. During those same decades, though, being a "Negro" became a greater stigma than it had formerly been as the system of slavery became more important and as the blight of racism grew in importance along with it. John Casor, lacking the paper indenture that he claimed that he had once possessed, was by default at a disadvantage in his claim to freedom from Anthony Johnson. And being a "Negro" perhaps put him at a greater disadvantage in contesting the word of a tobacco planter who owned his own land, even though the tobacco planter was also a "Negro."

For the record, Anthony Johnson, Mary Johnson, and their family later moved to Maryland and farmed there until he died, probably sometime before 1672, when Mary Johnson bequeathed a cow to each of her grandsons. John Casor, on the other hand, being reduced to the status of lifetime servant or slave, disappears from our view. Whether he lived the remainder of his life in slavery to Johnson or to some other person is not possible to know. We can say for certain, though, that references scattered through the incomplete surviving records of seventeenth-century Virginia indicate that his claim to being detained in servitude longer than was legally required was far from unique. In some of those instances, people who had been held in slavery gained their freedom.

Slavery as it evolved in Virginia during that century came to appear in hindsight to be inevitable, but it was not. The deliberate individual decisions that white men and women (or even an occasional "Negro") made in particular instances and the later legislative enactment of a body of law to protect the institution of slavery and the rights of enslavers to that property demonstrate that slavery was not inevitable. In the beginning when Yeardley and Peirsey purchased some human beings in 1619, it might have seemed a small deviation from the contemporary legal practices of acquiring white indentured servants, but it was far from inevitable that their decisions would lead to the chattel racial slavery that residents of the English colonies shackled onto millions of people during the ensuing two and a half centuries. That was a tragedy with far-reaching and brutal consequences. It did not have to happen as it did. It could have been very different, and therefore the entire history of North America would have been different. "For of all sad words of tongue or pen," John Greenleaf Whittier wrote in 1856 when slavery flourished in fifteen of the United States of America, "The saddest are these: 'It might have been.'"

8

Elizabeth Key and the Law of Slavery

ELIZABETH KEY FILED the earliest known, reasonably well-documented, successful lawsuit in Virginia to free an enslaved person, herself. She began the lawsuit in 1655, a few months before Anthony Johnson's case came up in Northampton County, and she received her freedom in 1656, a month after his case concluded. She was then about twenty-four or twenty-five years old. The incomplete records pertaining to her life and lawsuit were recorded in the Northumberland County Court order book and have been published in Warren M. Billings, ed., *The Old Dominion in the Seventeenth Century: A Documentary History of Virginia, 1606–1700*, rev. ed. (Chapel Hill, 2007).

As with most other residents of Virginia at that time, free or enslaved, we know very little about Elizabeth Key. Almost the only references to her that we have are from the documents in her lawsuit, some of which spell her name Kay or Kaye, not Key, which may suggest how people pronounced it. Depositions taken in connection with the suit indicate that she was born sometime between 1630 and 1632, probably at the site of her father's settlement, which was in what became Warwick County and is now part of the city of Newport News, where the James River empties into Chesapeake Bay. Her father, Thomas Key, was a prominent local white man and was a burgess member of the General Assembly of Virginia in 1630. He was married to a white woman and had at least one white son.

The name of Elizabeth Key's mother does not appear in the surviving records of the court case. Depositions that Elizabeth Key filed as part of the lawsuit indicate that her mother was of African birth or descent and labored on Thomas Key's property. By the time of the lawsuit in the 1650s, people referred to Elizabeth Key's mother as a slave of Thomas Key, but the lack of surviving local records from the time of Elizabeth Key's birth do not indicate whether people referred to her or regarded her in that way at the time.

Elizabeth Key's freedom suit was one of many events that in the 1660s prompted Virginia lawmakers to create a new law of slavery alongside the traditional laws of master and servant and of indentured servitude that had ancient lineages in English law. Most of the laborers who toiled in Virginia during the seventeenth century were white indentured servants. Most of them were from England. By the middle of the seventeenth century, when Elizabeth Key filed her suit, it appears that the assumption among most white people was that Africans and descendants of Africans were enslaved for life, not indentured under a contract to work for a stated period of years. The timing of Elizabeth Key's lawsuit was coincidentally important in the history of the evolution of the law of slavery in North America, not just immediately important to her personally.

One of the documents in the case indicates that Thomas Key had paid a fine for impregnating Elizabeth Key's mother. English common and statute law, which were good Virginia law, provided for punishment of men and women who committed adultery or fornication and also required that the father of an illegitimate baby be required to pay the costs of bringing up and caring for the child; otherwise, the parish would raise the child and tax the parishioners to pay for it. That may be what the reference to a fine indicated: Thomas Key had confessed to or been convicted of adultery and of fathering a bastard. It was not until much later that Virginia law punished interracial sexual intercourse consistently—that is, between Black men and white women, not between white men and Black women—or prevented people of African birth or descent or members of First Nations tribes from marrying white people.

In the autumn of 1636, Thomas Key and his white family prepared to return to England. He transferred his young daughter, who might also have been known then as Black Bess, to a neighbor, Humphrey Higginson, for a period of nine years. That certainly suggests that Key did not regard his daughter as enslaved for life and implies that he probably did not regard Elizabeth Key's mother as enslaved for life, either. Key specified that Higginson treat her humanely and also that if Higginson returned to England before the end of the nine years, he must either take the girl with him or free her from her responsibility to labor for him. Key also insisted that if Higginson remained in Virginia and died before the end of the nine years, Elizabeth would become free at the time of his death. No surviving record indicates what became of her mother.

Thomas Key died first, not long after he and Higginson made their agreement, even before Key and his white family left Virginia. Later, in one or more transactions for which complete documentation does not survive, Elizabeth Key passed out of Higginson's service and into that of John Mottrom, a prominent tobacco planter in Northumberland County, between the Rappahannock River and Chesapeake Bay, about seventy-five miles north of where she had been born and lived with Thomas Key and then with Humphrey Higginson. Whether that transfer happened before or after the nine years that Thomas Key specified is not certain.

John Mottrom died in 1655. By then, ten years after the agreement between Thomas Key and Higginson should have made Elizabeth Key free, she and William Grimstead—or Grimsted, as the local records sometimes spelled his name—one of Mottrom's white indentured servants, had a son. They had also had another child who died in infancy. The inventory of Mottrom's estate, dated July 4, 1655, indicates that the administrators of his estate regarded Elizabeth Key as enslaved for life. That assumption about people of African birth or ancestry was becoming common among white Virginians at that time. As was the case in several other contemporary instances, the inventory of the Mottrom estate listed six servants by their first and last names (which indicates that they were English indentured servants) and six "Negroes" by their first names only. Throughout the almost two and a half centuries of slavery in Virginia, white men and women who kept records almost never recorded surnames of Africans or enslaved descendants of Africans. (The instance of Anthony Johnson's man John Casor was unusual even then.) Elizabeth Key had a surname, the surname of her father, and she and other people knew it. In the estate inventory, though, she is listed simply as "Elizabeth the Negro & her sonne." Some estate inventories assigned monetary values to the servants and enslaved people, with servants always worth less because they had fewer years left to serve than enslaved people who served for life.

Elizabeth Key knew enough about her early life and about the agreement that her father and Humphrey Higginson had made that after the filing of the estate inventory, she sued Mottrom's estate for her freedom. She had to enlist and rely on one or more white men to collect copies of the relevant documents, including the agreement between her father and Higginson, and take depositions to document that Thomas Key was her father. She needed white, male help to instigate a lawsuit.

William Grimstead, the father of her child, is identified in one of the court records as her attorney. He was not a lawyer, though, and acted as what was often described in court records of the time as her *prochein ami*, or "next friend." Grimstead, if other documents that refer to him about that time are correct, was not even literate then and was certainly not a lawyer. He acted on her behalf as what we would call an attorney in fact, not as an attorney at law, as if he had a power of attorney to represent her. White women, minors, and other people who were not responsible adult white men often participated in lawsuits through the agency of a "next friend." That would be the only way that a person being held in slavery could commence a legal action in a court at that time.

Elizabeth Key sued on the grounds that the common law defined the child of an Englishman as a free person. Whether she initially knew of the English legal doctrine of *partus sequitur partem*, that a father's status determined the status of his children (whether royal, noble, gentleman, or commoner), is not clear—it is, in fact, rather unlikely—but somebody knew and informed her. On January 20, 1655/6, a jury in the county court of Northumberland, after hearing the evidence, including the affidavits and other documents that she or her white male assistant(s) assembled, decided that she should be free.

The administrators of Mottrom's estate appealed the verdict to the General Court, more commonly known then as the Quarter Court. The court held four sessions each year in Jamestown and heard all appeals from county courts and also had an extensive docket of civil and criminal cases that it heard on original jurisdiction. The members of the royal Council of State, who were also executive advisors to the governor and constituted the upper House of the General Assembly, sat together as the judges of the court. Humphrey Higginson had been a member of the Council of State for several years by then, but it is not clear, because of the loss of most of the court's midseventeenth-century records, whether he was present when the judges heard the case on March 12, 1655/6. In fact, he died about that time, possibly even before the court heard the appeal. The General Court overruled the Northumberland County Court, but the loss of the court's records leaves the reasons for the judges' decision unknown. (Many of the seventeenth-century records of the General Court and almost all of its eighteenth-century records were destroyed at the end of the American Civil War in a fire that burned the State Court House in Richmond. Records of many eastern counties, which had been sent there for safekeeping, also burned.)

Elizabeth Key then appealed the court decision to the General Assembly. Some white man or men gave her additional and important legal advice. At that time and until the 1680s, people had a right to appeal a General Court verdict to the General Assembly. Many of the records of the spring 1656 session of the assembly do not survive, but a copy of one document, probably the recommendation of the Committee for Private Causes of the House of Burgesses, contains this language respecting its consideration of the appeal of Elizabeth Key: "by the Common Law the Child of a Woman slave begott by a free-man ought to bee free." The sentence indicates that the burgesses believed that Elizabeth Key's mother had been enslaved and that Mottrom and his estate had improperly held Elizabeth Key in slavery.

The committee report also indicates that she was a baptized Christian and "by report shee is able to give a very good account of her fayth." That could have been good grounds for freeing her, too, because English and Virginia law then prohibited holding Christians of any race in slavery. Nevertheless, because nobody appeared at the General Assembly to represent the Mottrom estate and contest Elizabeth Key's appeal, the burgesses recommended that the case be sent back to the county court.

Early in the summer of that year, one of the administrators of Mottrom's estate asked the governor to order that the county court not act until the General Court could hear the case again, but the county court acted on its own, anyway. On July 21, 1756, it freed Elizabeth Key and ordered the estate to pay her the customary allowance of corn and clothing that indentured servants received at the end of their terms of service. The judges of the county court did not, however, require that the estate pay her anything for her service during the nearly eleven years that had elapsed since the agreement between Thomas Key and Humphrey Higginson should have made her free.

On the same day that the county court freed Elizabeth Key, she and William Grimstead posted their banns and publicly declared their intention to marry. A short time later, an administrator of Mottrom's estate signed over to Grimstead the estate's claim to ownership of Elizabeth Key or to her labor. Although she was free, she was still only a married woman and therefore not able to be party to a legal agreement, which the instrument that relinquished the estate's claim to her or her labor was. The estate delivered the document to her next friend, her husband. But Elizabeth Key was free of enslavement at last.

There is no doubt that white men played essential roles in bringing about Elizabeth Key's freedom. Without her courage and determination to go ahead, without her ability to persuade them to assist her, and without their willingness to help, she would not have been able to succeed. Undoubtedly, many other people in similar circumstances were unable to sue for or obtain their freedom. Scattered surviving documents from the middle decades of the seventeenth century indicate that she was not the only person who believed that she or he had been detained in service longer than legally allowed.

After Elizabeth Key received her freedom and married William Grimstead, her name disappears from surviving public records. Ordinary people who did not own property or get into trouble with the law typically did not engage in actions that generated entries in court records or produced deeds, wills, or other kinds of documents that enable us to learn about their lives. A few entries about other people in the record books of Northumberland County nevertheless hint at some events in the remainder of her life.

By the summer of 1660, an entry in the county records indicates that she had a second son and a daughter named Elizabeth. Her husband died sometime after the county clerk made that entry in the county records, and she evidently married a second time. The will of John Parse (or Pearce) that was recorded in the county court on May 20, 1667, contains circumstantial evidence that he had married the widow Elizabeth Key Grimstead, but because the will did not provide for her at all, we must conclude that she died before her second husband died. In the will, Parse bequeathed 300 acres of land, a substantial amount at that time, plus domestic household items and livestock to John Grimstead and William Grimstead, whom he identified as his sons-in-law. They were actually his wife's sons, not his daughters' husbands. The phrase son-in-law did not always mean a daughter's husband. It indicated that a boy or man stood in the same relationship to an adult as a son and was a son in the eyes of the law, even if not a son of the body. That is good evidence that Parse had married Elizabeth Key Grimstead.

In time, the fact that Elizabeth Key Grimstead Parse had an African mother and had been illegally held in slavery receded from the memories of the people of Northumberland County. In 1685, the county court ordered that two of her grandsons be bound out as apprentices to learn a trade, which was common for white orphans or for the children of white people who were poor or paupers but uncommon for Black children. Her grandsons had one-eighth African ancestry and may have appeared white.

The following year, the father of those boys, Elizabeth Key Grimstead Parse's son (one-quarter African), served on a jury that the county court impaneled. The members of the county court regarded him as a loyal, native-born (and possibly even white) subject of the king of England and no longer as a man with enough African ancestry to affect his economic, social, or legal status. They had apparently forgotten about his illegally enslaved mother and her ancestry.

During the 1660s, beginning a few years after Elizabeth Key successfully sued for her freedom, the General Assembly of Virginia passed several laws to protect the institution of slavery and the interests of enslavers. Students of history generally agree that legislators do not often pass laws without some experiences that demonstrated the need for new laws or for amending existing laws, experiences that in Virginia included the freedom suit of Elizabeth Key. The loss of many record books from the archives of seventeenth-century Virginia makes it impossible to know whether or how many other such lawsuits worked their way through the county courts or even reached the General Court. It is almost certain that some did, just as it is almost certain that other events occurred that prompted legislators in the 1660s to create a new body of law, the Virginia law of master and slave, alongside the old English law of master and servant.

In 1662, the preamble of the first of the new laws declared that because "some doubts have arisen whether children got by an Englishman upon a negro woman should be slave or ffree"—the exact circumstance of Elizabeth Key—legislators reversed the common law legal doctrine of *partus sequitur partem* and declared that thereafter "all children borne in this country shalbe held bound or free only according to the condition of the mother." By Virginia law from then until the abolition of slavery in the 1860s, the children of enslaved women belonged to the owner of the mother, exactly as newborn calves or kittens belonged to the owner of the cow or cat.

Notice, too, the language of the law: "children got by an Englishman upon a negro woman." Being a "negro," a person with known or observable African ancestry, indicated probable enslavement. No person with exclusively English ancestry could be enslaved, but in the case of Elizabeth Key, she had English ancestry. She was 50 percent English and 50 percent African.

A 1667 law reversed another rule of English law and declared that the conversion of an enslaved person to Christianity did not terminate the owner's legal right to continue to hold that person in slavery. Virginians easily stretched that law to validate the purchase of already enslaved Christians.

A law passed in 1668 required owners of women with African ancestry or who employed them as hired laborers to pay taxes on them, just as they paid taxes on horses, white males older than sixteen years, hired or enslaved male laborers, and some other forms of valuable property. The legislators did not levy taxes on adult white women, which indicates that they did not believe that adult white women were economically productive in the same way that all other free and forced laborers were, and white women were not in any way a form of property and therefore not commercially valuable.

Another law of 1668 entitled An Act About the Casuall Killing of Slaves—"Casuall" in the title meant unintentional or accidental—declared that it was not murder if a "negro" died during moderate correction or after being punished. In this context, too, "negro" meant enslaved. The common law definition of murder was the willful infliction of an injury to a person that resulted in the death of the person within one year and one day. The General Assembly did not define the killing of a "negro" during correction as murder because, as the law explained, nothing "should induce any man to destroy his owne estate" on purpose. Death as a consequence of punishment was therefore by legal definition an accident. An enslaved person was property within the meaning of Virginia law, as well as a person. That the law specified the race of the human property to which it referred is one of many signals that slavery and race had come, or were coming, to be inseparable categories.

A law of 1670 also included race among the factors that limited its application. It forbade free people with African ancestry and members of First Nations tribes, but not white Virginia men and women, from purchasing "christian servants." The laws and practices of slavery evolved in tandem with the laws and practices of race, of racism, and of racial discrimination.

County courts also made new laws to protect slavery and the interests of enslavers. By the 1660s, the courts began reversing the common law doctrine of *caveat emptor,* let the buyer beware. *Caveat emptor* placed the burden on buyers to ascertain whether goods or services were of good quality and did not require sellers to disclose defects in merchandise or even in an animal or servant. The great demand for sound laborers in Virginia led the county courts to reverse that doctrine in transactions relating to indentured servants and enslaved people and to place on sellers a responsibility to disclose if a person was of unsound health or pregnant. Either condition could reduce the labor the buyer could hope to extract from the servant or enslaved person and thereby depress the worker's market value.

The new doctrine became good law throughout Virginia without any legislative enactment, which might have resulted in the Crown disallowing a legal practice that clearly violated an important principle of the common law. When the General Court of Virginia heard arguments on the legality of the doctrine in 1735, the judges affirmed it in *Waddill v. Chamberlayne* even after hearing a long, scholarly argument from the colony's very able and learned attorney general, Edward Barradall, that the common law required the judges to reinstate *caveat emptor.* Manuscript and printed forms for bills of sale and lease for servants and enslaved people often included a warranty of sound body or an explicit disclosure of an infirmity straight through to the final end of slavery in the spring of 1865.

9

Cockacoeske and the Fate of the Powhatan Confederacy

COCKACOESKE, THE IMPRESSIVE WEROWANSQUA of the Pamunkey, appeared before a committee of the House of Burgesses in Jamestown in June 1676. Virginia was then on the verge of civil war between competing white factions and at the same time in danger of attacks from First Nations tribes that lived or roamed near the most exposed white settlements on the frontier. The members of the legislature debated how to respond to the proposal of a young member of the Council of State, Nathaniel Bacon, to appoint him a general to wage war on the tribes that had already attacked some outlying settlements and killed a considerable number of white people. The committee had apparently asked or required Cockacoeske to go down to Jamestown from her residence somewhere between the Mattaponi and Pamunkey Rivers so that the committee members could ascertain how many men the Pamunkey could furnish to defend the white settlers.

We know about Cockacoeske's meeting with the committee of the House of Burgesses from an incomplete manuscript account of Bacon's Rebellion that one of the committee members later wrote. Thomas Mathew, from the northernmost frontier county of Stafford, included the event on pages 28–33 of his narrative "The Beginning Progress and Conclusion of Bacons Rebellion in Virginia in the Years 1675 & 1676," which survives in series 8, volume 1, Thomas Jefferson Papers, in the Library of Congress.

Many years after the event, Mathew vividly recalled the impression that Cockacoeske made when she entered the committee room with her retinue in attendance on her. "Our committee being sat," Mathew reported, "the Queen of Pamunky (Descended from Opechankenough a former Emperor of Virginia) was Introduced, who entred the Chamber with a Comportment

Gracefull to Admiration, bringing on her right hand an Englishman Interpreter, and on the left her Son a Stripling Twenty Years of Age." Mathew recalled that Cockacoeske wore "round her head a plat of Black & White Wampum peague"—that is, a band of beads—"Three Inches broad in imitation of a Crown, and was Cloathed in a Mantle of dress't Deerskins with the hair outwards & the Edge cut round 6 Inches deep which made Strings resembling twisted frenge from the Shoulders to the feet."

Mathews described the scene. "Thus with grave Courtlike Gestures and a Majestick Air in her face," he wrote, "she Walk'd up our Long Room to the Lower end of the Table, Where after a few Intreaties She Sat down; th' Interpreter & her Son Standing by her on either side as they walked up."

It is not clear how old Cockacoeske was at the time. She had been werowansqua of the Pamunkey for many years by then, after her husband, Totopotomoy, died fighting alongside white Virginians in the last large-scale warfare with neighboring tribes. How many children she had is also not clear. The son who accompanied her that day in Jamestown was born after the death of Totopotomoy. The boy's father was a member of the West family from England that had furnished Virginia a governor who arrived in 1610, shortly after the Starving Time, and an acting governor in the mid-1630s. Her son, "to whom the English tongue was familiar," as Mathew noted, was "the Son of an English colonel" and went by the name Captain John West.

The chair of the committee asked Cockacoeske how many Pamunkey men could serve as "Guides in the Wilderness & to assist us against our Enemy Indians." She asked her interpreter to inform her what the committee chair had said, "tho' we believed She understood him," Mathew interjected in his narrative. The interpreter informed the chair that he should address his questions to her son. Captain John West, though, declined to speak for his mother. The werowansqua initially insisted on following the etiquette of diplomacy as it was practiced in Virginia and in Europe at the time and intended to conduct her business through interpreters and her subordinates, not in her own person. She was not in the least inclined to assist white Virginians or allow them to treat her in an undignified manner.

The chair of the committee repeated his question: how many Pamunkey men could assist the forces of Virginia? After "a little Musing" during which Cockacoeske considered her grievances and options, she "with an earnest passionate Countenance as if Tears were ready to Gush out and a fervent sort of Expression made a Harangue about a quarter of an hour" long during which she several times "with a high shrill voice & vehement passion" cried out, "Tatapatamoi Chepiack," which translated as Totopotomoy is dead. She remembered her old grievances as clearly as her recent ones.

When Cockacoeske concluded her statement, a member of the committee who sat next to Thomas Mathew "Shook his head." Mathew "ask'd him what was the matter, he told me all she said was too true to our Shame, and that his father was Generall in that Battle, where diverse years before Tatapatamoi her Husband had Led a Hundred of his Indians in help to th' English against our former Enemy Indians, and was there Slaine with most of his men; for which no Compensation (at all) had been to that day Rendered to her." For that ill treatment, the burgess explained to Mathew, "she now upbraided us."

The chair of the committee undoubtedly knew all of that but said nothing "towards asswaging the Anger & Grief her Speech and Demeanour Manifested under her oppression, nor taking any notice of all She had said." The committee chair, "Neither Considering that we (then) were in our great Exigency" and were in the desperate role of "Supplicants to her for a favour of the same kind as the former, for which we did not Deny the having been so Ingrate, He rudely push'd againe the same Question What Indians will you now Contribute, &c.?"

Mathew recalled that Cockacoeske "signified her Resentment by a disdainfull aspect, and turning her head half a side," sat mute until the chair asked the same question yet again. She still did not turn her face toward the committee members "but answered with a low slighting Voice in her own Language," six. Asked again, "She sitting a little while Sullen, without uttering a Word," eventually said twelve, "tho' she then had a hundred & fifty Indian men, in her Town," Mathew understood. Cockacoeske, with the painful memories fresh in her mind and her dignity affronted, "rose up and gravely Walked away, as not pleased with her Treatment."

It was a remarkable scene. The committee of burgesses needed assurance that for the protection of the white people of the colony, the Pamunkey and other tribes at peace with the government of Virginia would assist the frontier settlers. Cockacoeske, much like the werowansqua of Appamattuck who greeted Captain Christopher Newport in 1607, used her best theatrical skills to avoid being abused or exploited and to impress, or perhaps overawe, the arrogant white men with her steadfastness.

Cockacoeske was and had been for many years, perhaps as long as two decades, the most important and influential of the tribal rulers in the old Powhatan confederacy. Following the end in 1646 of the last of what have come to be called the Anglo-Powhatan Wars, a peace treaty between the governor of the colony and Necotowance, then the paramount chief, stipulated that the tribes would reside peacefully between the York and James Rivers. (The York River commences at what has come to be known as West Point, where the Mattaponi and Pamunkey Rivers converge. The northern of the two rivers, the Mattaponi, became the northern boundary of their home territory.) As a pledge to keep the peace and to enforce the terms of the treaty, Necotowance, on behalf of the tribes, promised to pay "unto the King's Govern'r. the number of twenty beaver skins att the goeing away of Geese yearely."

The tribes at peace with the government have since come to be known as tributary tribes because they paid an annual tribute to the government of Virginia. Under the treaty of 1646, which still remains in force, the Pamunkey and the Mattaponi nations maintain tribal reservations within the prescribed area and are exempt from taxation. During the twentieth century, though, somebody moved the annual payment of tribute from "the goeing away of Geese" in the spring to the autumn to coincide with the modern celebration of Thanksgiving in November. The tribute is usually paid in deer or turkeys, and no longer in beaver skins.

After Cockacoeske left Jamestown, Nathaniel Bacon returned to the capital city and at gunpoint demanded and received a commission to lead his men into the field against the government of Governor Sir William Berkeley, during which Bacon burned Jamestown to the ground. Bacon died in October 1676, and the rebellion collapsed during the winter.

We do not know what Cockacoeske thought about one provision in the law that the General Assembly passed in June 1676 to declare war on the hostile tribes and appoint Nathaniel Bacon general "and commander in chiefe." Perhaps to stimulate white men to enlist, the provision declared "that all Indians taken in warr be held and accounted slaves dureing life." (The practice in Virginia before that time had sometimes been to limit the terms of enslavement of members of First Nations tribes, comparable in some ways to the limitation of obligation under an indenture.) Under authority of the June 1676 law, poor farmers might, if they enlisted and survived the fighting, acquire an enslaved person to assist in the labor on their farms and probably raise their economic and social standing.

The unfortunate werowansqua suffered terribly when she was caught up in the bizarre events of Bacon's Rebellion. In the summer of 1676, after months of fighting, including raids on First Nations towns, plunged the colony into civil war and after she appeared before the committee of the House of Burgesses, Nathaniel Bacon and a party of men attacked several First Nations villages, including her main town. They killed several Pamunkey people, took others captive, and plundered the village. To save her life, Cockacoeske abandoned all of her possessions and fled into the inhospitable Dragon Swamp, where she nearly starved before she could safely return to her people.

Royal commissioners of investigation arrived in Virginia from England early in 1677, and on May 29, 1677, Cockacoeske, together with the werowansqua of the Weyanoke, the werowances of the Nottoway and the Nansemond, and Captain John West (son of Cockacoeske), made their marks on the Treaty of Middle Plantation, which the royal commissioners also signed, to keep the peace between the First Nations tribes and white Virginians. The werowances and werowansquas acknowledged that they owed allegiance to the king of England; that they retained their lands under the authority of the king and the government of the colony; and that in lieu of taxes, they would pay to the king "onely Three *Indian* Arrows" in tribute yearly.

The treaty also included several protections that the tribal leaders apparently insisted on for the benefit of their people, including that no colonists establish farms or households closer than three miles from "any *Indian* Town"; that by application to the governor, the tribal leaders could obtain redress for any injuries done to their people; that their people continue to have the right to hunt, fish, and gather natural foods on their lands; that to prove that they were on peaceful business and not a threat to white people they have passes to enter white settlements; and that their people be supplied with firearms and gunpowder sufficient to defend themselves and harvest game.

Article XII of the treaty stipulated that the werowances and werowansquas each had equal authority over their own people, but that "none to have greater Power then the other, Except the Queen of *Pamunkey*, to whom several scattered nations do now again own their ancient Subjection, and are agreed to come in and Plant themselves under her Power and Governme[n]t."

Article XII sought to revive the Powhatan confederacy as a paramount chiefdom with Cockacoeske the preeminent chief. Things did not go smoothly for her or for the confederacy, though. In June 1678, she and her son complained to the governor and Council of State that some Chickahominy had transgressed on their land, and that she could not make them follow her instructions and leave. Later in the month, Cockacoeske dictated a letter to the governor in which she complained, "I am very much dissatisfied about the Rappahannacks, but espetially about the Chickahomineys, who are very disobedient to my Comands; not that they grudge to be under my Subjection, but an Antipathy they have against me for what I did to them." We do not know for certain what she had done that created the "Antipathy." She concluded sourly, "they are a deceitful people." (This is confusing because early records indicate that the Chickahominy had not originally been part of the Powhatan confederacy even though almost every other neighboring tribe was.)

Neither Cockacoeske nor the governor could enforce the subordination of the other tribes to her authority, and thereafter each tribe opened its own line of communication with the governor through its own interpreter. The revived paramount chiefdom never again resembled the formidable and united confederacy that Wahunsonacock had assembled almost a century earlier and that the first invaders encountered in 1607.

Cockacoeske remained werowansqua of the Pamunkey until her death. The exact date and place of her death are not known, but it was probably not long before July 1, 1686, when the tribe's interpreter informed the Council of State that she was "lately dead."

10

Jamestown in 1676

WE KNOW A LITTLE BIT about what Cockacoeske saw when she went to meet the committee of the House of Burgesses in June 1676, because we have an eyewitness description of Jamestown that John Cotton wrote a few months, almost certainly less than a year, after she was in the little capital city. What appears to be the original manuscript narrative, which is missing both its beginning and its ending, is entitled "Narrative of Bacon's Rebellion" and is in the collections of the Virginia Historical Society. An early nineteenth-century transcription, with contractions and abbreviations expanded, spellings corrected, and some errors introduced, is also in the Virginia Historical Society and was prepared for publication as "The Burwell Papers," *Collections of the Massachusetts Historical Society,* 2d ser., 1 (1814): 27–80. From that source, it was later copied into volume one of Peter Force, ed., *Tracts and Other Papers, Relating Principally to the Origin, Settlement, and Progress of the Colonies in North America,* 4 vols. (Washington, D.C., 1836–46), and from Force's text reprinted again in Charles M. Andrews, ed., *Narratives of the Insurrections, 1675–1690* (New York, 1915), 47–98. The nineteenth-century transcription was printed in a more accurate version in *Proceedings of the Massachusetts Historical Society* 9 (1867): 299–324. Because each of the successive reprints of John Cotton's narrative was derived from earlier copies, errors accumulated in the later versions.

Cotton's narrative is one of several contemporary accounts of events of the rebellion, but because he may not have been an eyewitness to more than a few of them, it is not one of the most valuable or reliable. It also contains much evidence of his conscious attempts to impress his readers with his accomplished literary talent and may be of suspect reliability on that account, too. Cotton's wife, Ann Cotton, later composed her own short history of the rebellion based on her husband's original narrative.

John Cotton owned and lived with his wife on a plantation on Queen's Creek in York County, a few miles northeast of Jamestown, but we do not know when or for certain where they were born or when they married. He was apparently related to an early clergyman, also named John Cotton (or Cotten, Clutten, Cutton, Cutting, Cuttinge), and may have been born in Virginia. In June 1676, John Cotton was in Jamestown, perhaps to watch some of the proceedings of the General Assembly, when Cockacoeske was there, and so had a clear memory of the appearance of the capital when he wrote his narrative. John Cotton's account, like many of the narratives that men wrote earlier in the century, is better read aloud to smooth out the spellings and syntax.

"The place on which the Towne is built," Cotton wrote, "is a perfect Peninsulla, or tract of land allmost wholly incompast with water." The peninsula, on the north bank of "the River (Formerly Powhetan, now called James River)," was about three miles long east to west and very narrow for most of its length. At the western end of the peninsula was "a smalle Istmas, tacked to the continent," that is, Jamestown was attached to the mainland by a narrow isthmus that in the early days people called the Neck of Land. To the north of Jamestown was "a deep creeke, rangeing in a cemicircle to the west . . . leaveing in the wholl compass about 5 miles litel more or less" of river and creek shoreline.

Cotton reported that, just as at the time of settlement, the island "is Low ground, full of Marches and swamps, which makes the Aire especially in the Sumer, insalubrirous & unhelty." People in the early days and many later historians blamed the marsh "Aire" or the malaria of the mosquitoes that bred there for the sicknesses that plagued Jamestown during the first decades of English settlement. Cotton complained about it, too. The island "is not at all replenish'd with springs, of fresh water," he explained, "& that which they have in ther wells, brackish, ill sented & penurious, and not gratefull to the stumack; which render the place improper to indure the Commencement of a seige."

The reference to "a seige" suggests that Cotton may have been there again, later in the summer, when the forces of Nathaniel Bacon trapped forces loyal to Governor Sir William Berkeley on the island. Cotton would have then witnessed how precarious existence there was without access to the mainland. It is not clear from the incomplete narrative that Cotton wrote how many episodes of the rebellion he personally witnessed. After Berkeley and his followers left, Bacon's men burned the town.

"The Towne is built much about the middle of the South line," Cotton wrote, by which he meant and explained, "close upon the River, extending east and west, about 3 quarters of a Mile; in which is comprehended some 16 pair howses, most as the church built of Brick, faire and large; and in them about a dozen Famillies (for all the howses are not inhabited) getting there livings by keeping of ordinaries, at extraordinary rates." In the early days, coopers and other artisans as well as merchants and other men plied their trades in Jamestown. That was probably the case in 1676, too, but Cotton did not mention the employment of any residents other than that some or most of them kept ordinaries (inns or taverns), where people who had occasion to do business in offices of the government could sleep and eat when they were in town.

Members of the Council of State, about a dozen prosperous and well-connected men who had lifetime appointments from the king, needed to be in Jamestown frequently in their capacities as executive advisors to the royal governor and as members of the Quarter Court, or General Court as it soon came to be known. Council members also went to Jamestown for meetings of the General Assembly; after 1643 they constituted the upper House of the legislature. And when the assembly met, burgesses traveled to Jamestown from throughout Virginia, as did men and women who had complaints to present or requests to make to the legislators, the governor, or the courts. Perhaps the owners of the ordinaries charged what visitors to Jamestown regarded as exorbitant rates because for some parts of most years, visitors might have been few, and their incomes therefore small. The governor, Sir William Berkeley, owned a large and reportedly flourishing plantation called Greenspring a few miles away. We do not know for certain whether he routinely commuted to the capital or had his own dwelling house there in 1676, as he had during his first administration in the 1640s.

That is it. It is a great pity that Cotton did not go into more detail about the buildings, most of which he noted were brick, or describe the church and the Statehouse in Jamestown. Since the first settlement in 1607, the little town had been the site of a series of progressively larger buildings where

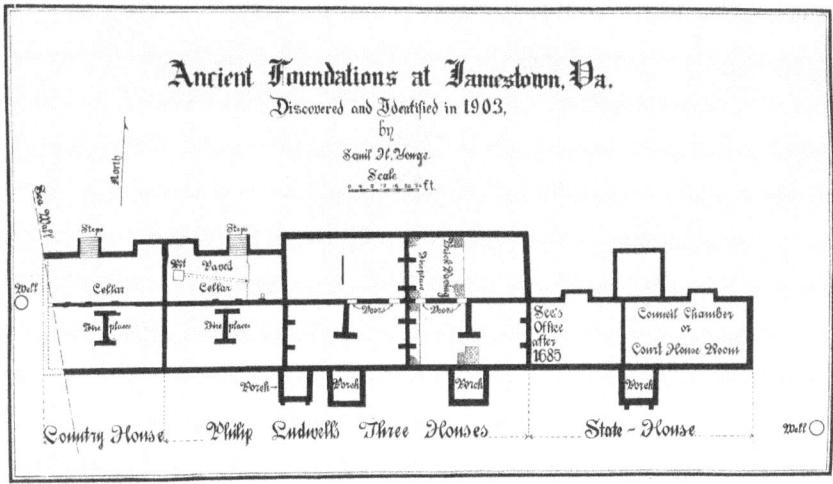

At the beginning of the twentieth century, archaeologist Samuel H. Yonge excavated the foundations of the mid-seventeenth-century Statehouse in Jamestown and published this plan, which indicates how large the building was. (Library of Virginia)

the General Assembly met, the courts held their sessions, and officials like the governor, secretary, and clerks had their offices. In 1676, the Statehouse was probably the largest building in any of the English colonies of North America. Archaeologists have excavated parts of its foundation, which disclosed how large it was. In preparation for the 2007 commemoration of the 400th anniversary of the original settlement there, the Association for the Preservation of Virginia Antiquities (later Preservation Virginia), which owns the site, erected an excellent museum that has on display the results of the archaeological investigations and allows visitors to see exactly how large the building was. It needed to be large. At the time of the rebellion, Virginia was the largest and probably the most populous of the English colonies in North America.

11

The Grievances of the People

Series 1, volume 39, of the archive of the Colonial Office in the National Archives of the United Kingdom, formerly known as the Public Record Office (PRO), contains original signed statements that men in nearly every Virginia county submitted to the royal commissioners of investigation whom King Charles II sent to Virginia late in 1676 to ascertain the causes of the rebellion that Nathaniel Bacon led that year. Two centuries later, agents who worked for the government of Virginia made transcriptions of most of the statements. The transcriptions are in the Library of Virginia, and some of them were published in the *Virginia Magazine of History and Biography* in the 1890s.

Until recently, historians have not taken very seriously the contents of what we usually refer to as the county grievances or have relied solely on the ones that were published or on the official report of the royal commissioners, which has been published as Michael Leroy Oberg, ed., *Samuel Wiseman's Book of Record: The Official Account of Bacon's Rebellion in Virginia* (Lanham, Md., 2005). The commissioners completely ignored the contents of the statements of grievance, which has resulted in serious misunderstandings of the reasons why at the same time that war with First Nations tribes on the frontier seemed imminent, Bacon was able to recruit a large armed force that attacked Governor Sir William Berkeley and produced a brief civil war.

Those statements of grievance disclose widespread dissatisfaction, which amounted to anger in some localities, at the conduct of officers of county governments. It was the behavior of justices of the peace in the counties that attracted disaffected men to join Bacon when he launched his campaign against the governor, not, as had long been believed, widespread dissatisfaction with Berkeley or with the royal government. The men who signed the grievances did not blame Berkeley or Charles II for their tribulations; they blamed the local grandees and their own burgesses for taxing them at too high a rate or inequitably and for letting them have no voice in how local governments functioned in the regulation of their own lives.

Nearly everybody complained that the House of Burgesses voted burgesses large expense allowances that their constituents had to pay, and most of the complaints included grievances against their local justices of the peace who set the annual tax rate, called the levy, too high. Several complained about the exemption from taxation that the General Assembly had allowed to members of the Council of State, most of whom were relatively wealthy but who had to be away from their plantations and at the capital frequently in their multiple roles as legislators, judges, and executive advisors to the governor. Men from most of the counties complained about having to pay taxes to construct a fort that the king had ordered to be built during the most recent Anglo-Dutch War at Point Comfort (it had already begun to fall down) and another that was not ever completed at Jamestown. Taxpayers were also on the hook for even more taxes, because the General Assembly wanted money to buy out the proprietors of the Northern Neck, a large swath of northern Virginia that the king had granted to a few court favorites.

The complaints about taxation contained language that discloses a class consciousness among ordinary white Virginia men. People paid most of the taxes to counties and to parishes (to support the work of the parishes of the Church of England) in the form of poll taxes—taxes on polls, or heads. (Poll taxes were not then tied to the right to vote, as became the case two hundred years later.) Each white male older than sixteen had to pay the poll tax, as did the owner of each enslaved laborer or indentured servant, male or female. People were supposed to pay the taxes in specified amounts of tobacco. Poor white men, artisans, and people who raised little or no tobacco had difficulty paying the taxes, and many of them complained that their tax burden was also relatively higher than that on wealthier men who owned large tracts of land and raised great quantities of tobacco. A few men recommended that the General Assembly require that land, not polls, be taxed, which would relieve the tax burden on a large number of people and increase it on the wealthiest men.

The county poll taxes were the most common grievance. The man who wrote out the grievances of the men from Isle of Wight County put it pithily though clumsily (try reading it aloud): "Whereas ther are some great persons both in honor, rich in estat and have severall ways of gaines and profitts are exempted from paying Leavies and the poor inhabitant being compelld to pay the great taxes, which wee are burdened with having a hogshead or two of tobacco"—a hogshead was a large cask or barrel in which planters packed their crop for shipment to England—"to pay for rent and near two hundred" pounds of tobacco "yearly for Leavies having a wife and two or three children to maintain whether our taxes are not the greater by such favour and privileges granted them which wee desire to be safe of by their paying of Leavies as well as wee," because the members of the council had "noe necessitie from being soe exempted."

Men in Henrico County filed a similar complaint and added that the members of the county court there "are men of a Consanguinity," meaning that they were related to one another, shared the same interests, and looked after their joint interests. The Henrico County men also asked that when the county court and the parish vestry met to set the annual tax levies, "at least six of the Comonalty" be allowed to take part in setting the rate. Men in some other counties made the same demand. The word *commonalty* was going out of usage then in England, but it appeared in several of the statements of grievance. It signified commoners, as distinguished from royalty, nobility, and members of the gentry, a recognition of a class interest or identity among lower-class white men in Virginia.

Men in several counties pointed out that justices of the peace told them that it was none of their business how the county court conducted its—the public's—business. Some men in Surry County complained that justices of the peace "may be obliged"—required—"to render Account in writing what the leavy is for to any that Shall desire it." Some other men in the same county explained, "itt has been the custome of the County Courts att the Laying of the Levy to withdraw into A privat Roome," which concealed from the people what the levy was for and why the men set it at the rate that they did. Men in Northampton County made a recommendation "That our County Records may be free open for Every man to Search and Require Copies as there occasions from time to time shall and may Require . . . paying the Clerk his Just fees."

The men in Nansemond County (the city of Suffolk absorbed the county in 1974) made another complaint about the men who served on the county court, on the parish vestries, and as officers in the county militia. "Yor. Honrs. are sensible," they explained to the commissioners early in 1677, that "there was a rising"—uprising, revolt, rebellion—"in This part of the Country in May last . . . occasion'd by the grevious taxations & burthens wee lay under for many years before." At that time, the commanding officers of the county militia ordered "houses built intitul'd Forts under the pretence of destroying the Heathen"—members of First Nations tribes that had not attacked any English-speaking Virginians in that part of the colony, although others had attacked settlers elsewhere. The Nansemond County men declared that their militia officers used tax money to erect the buildings on their own property and implied that the officers intended to use the buildings for their own private purposes when the threat of a war was gone. At any rate, "the charge of these forts would have gone beyond our ability either to maintain or build."

At the muster of the militia in the county in May 1676, the commanders ordered the men "to assemble together," but the men "roared them down by a generall roar of Commonalty." The men were either very angry or very desperate to risk a charge of mutiny in disobeying their officers at a militia muster. "Yet," the men of Nansemond County continued, "our Militia order'd all manner of necessaryes as Axes, hoos, Halborrds, provisions & the like fitt for the worke & seeing ourselves in this said condition the Heathen hourely expected to come upon us." Because of the "excessive tax likewise that wee did readily account needlesse, and unnecessary," they asked permission from their officers to take their complaints against their local leaders directly to the governor. Surprisingly, the militia commander agreed; or perhaps the "generall roar of Commonalty" so frightened him that he dared not refuse.

The governor was then in the field trying to find and restrain Bacon, so the men appealed instead to his wife, Frances Culpeper Stevens Berkeley, to inform the governor what was wrong and to ask for his assistance. She did so, and the June 1676 session of the General Assembly passed several bills to redress many, but not all, of the complaints. That autumn, though, King Charles II ordered that the assembly reconvene and repeal them all because he mistakenly believed that the only reason that the assembly had passed the laws was because Nathaniel Bacon forced them to do so. The assembly session early in 1677, after the arrival of the royal commissioners, dutifully repealed all of the reform laws.

The boldness of the men in Nansemond County exceeded that of any of the men in the other counties, so far as extant documents indicate, but the other men were bold, too. The intervention of Lady Berkeley seems surprising, but she was a politically astute and well-connected woman and actually traveled to England in the summer of 1676 to explain to the king the causes of the rebellion and to try to excuse her husband's vacillating response to the beginning phases of it. The governor had hoped to prevent conflicts with any of the First Nations tribes, in part because he was deeply engaged in trading with them, but also because it was his job to keep the peace and to protect and meet the needs of the people.

In the end, nothing positive came from the organized protests of white men in nearly every county in Virginia in 1676 and 1677. For the most part, officers of local government subsided into their accustomed methods of doing the public business. Although Bacon's Rebellion was the largest uprising of white Virginians during the colonial period and resulted in the deaths of a great many people, the commonalty gained nothing from their spirited protests and complaints.

Later generations of Virginians appear to have been struck by the rebellion's taking place exactly one century before the American Revolution began. By the end of the eighteenth century, people in Surry County began to refer to a brick mansion house in which some of Bacon's men took refuge after Bacon's death as Bacon's Castle, even though Bacon was never there, and it was not a castle. Early in the nineteenth century, Thomas Jefferson appeared to endorse the view that the cause of the rebellion was similar to the cause of the Revolution, that is, royal government. In histories of Virginia that historians John Daly Burk and Charles Campbell published later in the century, they definitely agreed. Early in the twentieth century, several patriotic women presented to the General Assembly a plaque that echoed that interpretation. It is still mounted in a prominent place in the state Capitol. In 1940, a distinguished professor of history at Princeton University published a romanticized book entitled *Torchbearer of the Revolution: The Story of Bacon's Rebellion and Its Leader* that also depicted Bacon as attempting to reject royal government. All of those interpretations of Bacon's Rebellion as a revolt against royal government were incorrect and utterly incompatible with the surviving documentary evidence, the most compelling of which is the county grievances.

12

A Dead Bastard Child

Accomack County is on the Eastern Shore of Virginia, between the border with Maryland and the Virginia county of Northampton. Pages 159–68, 172, and 183 of the record book entitled Accomack County Wills, Deeds, Orders (1672–82) contain detailed documentation of the county court's investigation in March 1679/80 into the discovery that a young, unmarried woman had given birth to a baby boy and that the body of the dead baby was buried the day after it was born. The county court had responsibility to discover who the father of the child was, because he was undoubtedly guilty of fornication, and also whether the baby was born dead or alive, and if alive, whether it died a natural death or if somebody killed it. The record book also discloses what happened the following August.

The transcription of the testimony offers us an unusual opportunity to listen, as it were, to the actual voices of several seventeenth-century Virginians as the clerk of court recorded them. The testimony indicated that Mary Burton was the mother of the baby; that she was the natural daughter of Sarah Carter (that is, her mother and biological father had not been married); and that Sarah Carter was then married to Paul Carter, who is described as the father-in-law of Mary Burton because he then stood in the eyes of the law in the same relation to Mary Burton as if he had been her biological father. We would call him her stepfather.

The testimony disclosed that sometime in the autumn of 1679, Sarah Carter perceived that her daughter, Mary Burton, was pregnant. Neither woman told anybody else about the pregnancy because it was shameful for an unmarried woman to become pregnant and illegal for her to engage in the fornication that impregnated her. Carter and her husband assisted at the birth of the baby about the middle of January, and she, or she and he—one of several discrepancies in the testimony—buried the body of the baby the next day.

The first entry in the record book contains a transcription of the examination of Paul Carter on "the first Day of March 1679/80." The first question was, "What doe yu. know concerning a Child borne of Mary the Daughter of Sarah the wife of the said Paul?"

He answered "That he doth know that the said Mary had a Man child born of her body and that he & the said Sarah assisted at the birth of the said Child & that he certainly knoweth not whether it were born alive or not & that they did endeavour to preserve the life thereof and that it lay betwixt his wife & her Daughter all night and that the next morning he saw it was dead & he & his Wife buried the said Child but that his Wife carefully washed and dressed it."

Next question, "Doe ye know or have ever heard who was the father thereof reputed?"

He answered, "The said Mary charged one Mr. James Tuck therewith."

Sarah Carter testified next. First question, "What doe you know concerning a Child born of Mary yr Daughter?"

She answered "That about three months since"—three months ago—"being in bed wth her Daughter she perceived her Daughter to be wth Child & charged her therewth who was very unwilling to confess, but at length charged it upon Mr. James Tuck." Sarah Carter also "saith that she assisted at the birth of the said Child & that it was like to dye & did endeavour to preserve it but being dead the next Day she & her husband buried it & that it lay all night in bed betwixt her & her daughter & that it was washed & dressed first."

Next, "The examination of Mary Daughter of the Said Sarah." Mary Burton "Saith That Mr. James Tuck did at first use violence towards her & after she was consenting & that the Said Paul her father in Law did doe in like manner & that both of them lay wth her & that she did Keep it from her Mother untill her Mother did discover the same in manner as aforesaid & that both her Mother & Father in Law assisted her at the birth of the child." (The phrase "in manner as aforesaid" was almost certainly the clerk's interpolation of a legal phrase into the text and not the actual words that Mary Burton used.) She declared that she "supposed the Child to be born alive &

that it lay between her mother & her self all night & that in the morning it was dead & that she thinks her father & Mother buried it & that she thought in her conscience Paul was Father thereto."

The county court had ordered that the body of the baby be exhumed from its shallow grave at the site of an old house that Paul Carter owned and had appointed twelve local women to act as a "jury"—it was not a grand jury or a trial jury but a panel of respectable residents to help the court establish the facts—to oversee the exhumation of the corpse, to "vew the body," and to conduct what was known as a trial by touch to determine whether it was killed and if so, who killed it.

After Paul Carter, Sarah Carter, and Mary Burton gave their testimony, the court heard the report from the jury. The jury members reported that after the baby had been dug up, they had "Caused Sarah the Wife of Paul Carter & Mother of the said Mary to touch handle & Stroake the Childe in wch time we saw no alteration in the body of the Child & afterwards we Called for Paul Carter to touch the sd. Child & immediately whilst he was stroaking the Child the black & soiled places about the body of the Child grew fresh & red so that blud was redy to come through the skin of the Child We also observed the Countenance of the said Paul Carter to alter into very much paleness; the Child also appearing to us to be very much neglected in Severall respects as to the preservation of such an Infant"—it had decayed noticeably since the burial six or more weeks earlier—"& we doe Conclude that if the Child had any violence it was by the throat wch was very black and Continued so though other place wch were black altered to red & fresh Collered," or colored.

English law had for centuries allowed such examinations, called trial by touch, which courts recognized as a legitimate method to determine whether a person had been deliberately killed and if so, who killed the person. Trial by touch rested on widely held firm beliefs in miracles and the power of God. At the time of a trial by touch, if a murderer touched the body of a victim, God would cause the wounds that the murderer inflicted to change color or even bleed. As the jury reported to the Accomack County Court, when Paul Carter handled the body of the dead baby, its wounds changed color, which was therefore good evidence that he had killed the baby. The jury reported that he changed color, too, evidence that he knew that he had been found out. Everybody knew, and courts acknowledged, that trial by touch was good evidence of guilt.

On March 16, the court conducted a second examination and began by asking Paul Carter more questions. He testified that he had helped Mary Burton into bed for the childbirth and that Sarah Carter had placed the baby in the bed with its mother, and that the birth occurred "In the day time in his house about the middle of January."

Asked, "Was the Childe borne dead or alive?" he replied, "I cannot tell."

The court then asked Carter whether his daughter-in-law (stepdaughter) "declared to him who was the Father at the time of her Crying out." The question was based on another old English legal practice and belief, with corresponding religious roots, that at the most dangerous moment of giving birth—"the time of her Crying out"—a woman could not lie and face the prospect of going immediately to Hell if she died giving birth to the child. Midwives in effect acted as officers of the court when at the critical instant that an unmarried woman gave birth they refused to assist in the birth of a baby until the mother of it identified the father. As with the trial by touch, this belief also relied on a widespread assumption that people believed in Heaven and Hell, that at that instant a woman would not—could not—lie, and that they knew that when questioned about who the father was, the answer was good, persuasive evidence in court.

Similarly, courts also recognized as valid the confessions of committing crimes that people made on a deathbed for the very same reason, that the religious beliefs of the time meant that a person in imminent danger of dying would not—could not—lie because that person knew that he or she would automatically go directly to Hell for lying, not to mention as punishment for the crime that the person had confessed to committing.

When the court asked Paul Carter when Mary Burton identified the father, he answered that it was "not until she was brought to Bed and that she said it was James Tucks." Carter also testified that he dug the hole for burying the child at his old house and that his wife placed the body in the shallow grave. When asked why he did not assist Mary Burton before the birth of the child, he stated "That he was altogether ignorant that she was wth. Child" until then.

The court also took additional testimony that day from Sarah Carter. She testified that her daughter "had a bastard Childe born of her body borne in the night about two hours before day"—Paul Carter had just testified that the birth occurred in the daytime—after being in labor "About two howers or two howers & a halfe" and that the baby was born "Dead and it never had any Signs of life in it." That appeared to contradict her earlier testimony that she tried to preserve the life of the baby; but maybe she had then meant that she attempted to revive the baby, or maybe the clerk who recorded the testimony got part of it wrong either then or now.

Sarah Carter's daughter had gone into labor long before daylight on a stormy night, so she did not send for a midwife, neighbor, or anybody to assist. She testified that "she her self cut her blew Apron & put the Child in it & a blanket." She further testified that her husband left the house at the time of the birth; that she placed the dead baby in the bed and lay down on the bed with her daughter, Mary Burton, and the baby "untill sun rise and then she buried it"; "That she her own self" buried it; "& that her husband was absent & knew not where it was buried," but that they later moved the body to a garden.

Next question for Sarah Carter, "Did yu ever examine who got yr. Daughter wth. Childe?" Carter answered "That she did examine her & she owned no Father but James Tuck."

Did Sarah Carter ever "see betwixt yr. husband & Daughter any unusual familliarity or incivillity?" The answer, "one time going to Catch her Mare for going to Mill she came to the old house & there saw her husband hugg & Kiss her Daughter & took up her Daughters Coats up to her Knees & that she rebuked him for it & charged him wth. debauching her Daughter and Paul her husband Said He did her Daughter no harm & so went away."

Had the baby lived, the court would have asked these same questions about paternity. The county court would have needed to know who the father was for two reasons, to prosecute him for fornication, and to make him pay the costs of raising the child. If the court could not establish paternity, then the churchwardens of the local parish would be on the hook for the costs of raising the baby and would increase the parish levy to raise the necessary money. In effect, the innocent residents of the parish would have to pay the costs if the guilty father could not be identified.

The court also took additional testimony from Mary Burton. First question, "Was it in the day or the night that yu were delivered of the bastard Child?" Answer, "In the night," which agreed with Sarah Carter's testimony but contradicted Paul Carter's. She said that she was in labor "An hower or two or thereabout," which was close to what her mother had stated. Mary

Burton, though, misstated the date of birth and gave it as "Some time in the Month of February," not about the middle of January as in all of the other testimony.

The critical question, "Whether was the Child born alive or dead?" Answer, "That it was born alive & she heard it give one Shreek and no more at the birth." She went on to state that the baby was alive when her mother placed it on the bed with them. It is unclear from the next question, "Was the Child alive or dead when yr. mother laid it at yr breast," and the one after that, "What other means was there used beside the breast," whether Mary Burton nursed or attempted to nurse the baby. She testified that she "saw her Mother bring out Water & Sugar to the fire side and offered it to the Child & it would not take it." Would not, or could not? All of which indicated or suggested that she believed that her baby had been born alive.

Asked, "Who doe yu think is the Father of the bastard Child?" Burton answered that "She does verily beleeve that her Father in Law Paul Carter is the Father his having frequently to do doe wth. her & that once in the old house her Mother found him wth. her in his arms wth. hands under her Coats and thinks that her mother comeing hinderd them of any futher action; but that James Tuck had once to doe wth. her."

A grand jury of twelve Accomack County men, having heard all of the testimony, immediately, on that very same day, March 16, indicted "Paul Carter of the sd County aforesaid painter stainer"—court records often indicated the occupation of a person, so we learn that he was a painter and perhaps stained wooden parts of boats or ships to protect them from the water—"not having the fear of God before his eyes but being lead and instigated by the Divell did beget a bastard Child on the body of Mary daughter of Sara wife of the said Paul." The grand jury also "vehemently suspected" that Carter did "villanously murder and destroy the said bastard Child and after the Said murder committed as aforesd. did privily bury the said bastard Child in an old house thereby to hide and conceale the Same and for the further perpetration of the said Crime as aforesd did some time after privily take up & remove the body of the said murdered bastard Child into a Garden place and there allso privily buried the same, ffor all wch. crimes soe committed as aforesaid the said Paul Carter is hereby presented to this worshipful Court that further proceedings may be thereupon had according to the Lawes in that behalfe provided."

The grand jury then indicted "Sarah Wife of Paul Carter of the County aforesaid" and charged that she did "together wth. the said Paul vilanously murder & destroy the sd. bastard Child and after the said murder comitted as aforesd. together wth the said Paul did privilly bury the sd bastard Child in an old house nearby to hide & conceal the same and for the further perpetration of the said Crime."

The grand jury also indicted "Mary the daughter of Sarah Wife of Paul Carter" because she "had a bastard Child born of her body alive begotton by Paul Carter and that after the Death of the said Bastard Child she did conceal that she had a Child."

"This Court," the record continues after the presentation of the grand jury indictments, "doe therefore order that the High Sheriff of the County doe Frthth."—forthwith—"take the bodies of the sd Paul Carter & Sarah his Wife (agt. whom the Suspition is vehement) into his safe Custody" and detain them without bail until he could "deliver them to the high Sheriff of James City so that they be ready to appear before the Hon: Govr. & Councell upon the 4th day of the next Genll: Court there to abide the further tryall." The Accomack County Court also ordered that the sheriff "take into his safe custody the body of the sd Mary untill she give sufficient security to appear at the day & Place aforsd. there allso to abide further tryall."

The General Court, which held all of its sessions in Jamestown, was the only court in Virginia during the colonial period that had jurisdiction to conduct trials of white people accused of committing felonies. The Accomack County Court ordered that the sheriff "impannell six able Men of the County as pt of a Jury & have them also ready at the day & plc aforesaid for the full tryall of the sd accused persons." At the time appointed for the trial before the judges of the General Court, the sheriff of James City County would fill the remaining six seats on the trial jury from what the law called "bystanders," men who happened to be at the site of the trial at the time. The Accomack County Court directed the clerk to copy all of the documents and testimony in the case and forward the record to the General Court before the date for the trial.

For some unrecorded reason, the sheriff evidently did not execute the court directives promptly and apparently let the three indicted people remain at large, even live together in their own house. We know this because on April 27, the General Court "ordered that his Maties. Justices of the Peace of the County of Accomack doe take Effectuall order for the Removall of the sd Mary from the house & being of the sd Paul Carter father in Law to her the sd Mary & place the sd Mary in some Convenient part of the County of Accomack to the intent that the sd Paul Carter & Mary the naturall daughter of Sara the Wife of the sd Paul may not Cohabit as likewise that the sd Paul be constrained from accompanying wth the said Mary the aforesd Justices are desired & Required to Compell the sd Paul to find good security for his due Performance of this order & for his future good behaviour." That is, the court required Paul Carter to post a bond to be of "good behaviour" and stay away from his stepdaughter until the trial, otherwise he would forever forfeit the amount of the bond.

The trials had not yet taken place—we do not know why—when, on August 3, 1680, the clerk of the county court entered into the record book that "by fowel circumstances it may be reasonably presumed the sd Paul Carter is drowned in endeavouring to make his escape by water in a Canoe." The court then ordered that Mary Burton be returned from the safe house where she had lived since the General Court order in April "to her sd mother Sara Carter."

The documents of the case as recorded in the county record book abruptly end at that point. The records of the General Court for the final decades of the seventeenth century and for most of the eighteenth were burned in a fire at the State Court House in Richmond in April 1865 at the end of the American Civil War. We therefore do not know when (or even whether) Sarah Carter and Mary Burton were tried or what the results of the trials were.

One wonders whether residents of Accomack County believed in 1680, as George Percy had believed at the time of the death of Hughe Pryse in the winter of 1609–10, that the drowning of Paul Carter was the method God chose to punish Carter. It is very likely. Religious beliefs of the sort that Percy disclosed when he described the fate of Pryse remained equally strong in Virginia seventy years later. We can plainly see that in the county court's ordering the trial by touch and in the common practice in courts of the time to accept as valid evidence the mother's identification of the father of a child "at the time of her Crying out." In this instance, the trial by touch was good, legal, and persuasive evidence to the grand jury that Paul Carter was both the father and the murderer of the infant "Man child."

13

No Obey

EVERYBODY WHO STUDIES the history of the women of colonial America has encountered the name of Sarah Harrison Blair. Almost nobody else has. Her life was apparently a very unhappy one. At least, it was unhappy after she married James Blair on June 2, 1687, when she was about seventeen years old.

Sarah Harrison was a member of one of the leading landowning families in Virginia, had numerous influential family connections, and must have seemed a good catch to the young clergyman. And Blair must have seemed a very attractive husband at the time they married. At age thirty-two, he was a graduate of Marischal College in Aberdeen, Scotland, and an ordained minister of the Church of England. He had spent two years at a parish in Scotland before he moved to Virginia in 1685, to serve the first of several parishes. In 1690, three years after their marriage, Blair received a commission from the bishop of London to be commissary, the personal representative of the bishop and therefore the most senior clergyman in Virginia, and for most of his long life he was a member of the powerful Council of State. Blair has become famous as one of the founders and the first president of the College of William and Mary, long-time rector beginning in 1710 of Bruton Parish, in Williamsburg, and acting governor with the title president of the council for about eight months beginning in October 1741. In 1722, Blair published a five-volume collection entitled *Our Saviour's Divine Sermon on the Mount* that included 117 sermons that he had composed and delivered on the subject.

When Sarah Harrison married James Blair on that day in 1687, she did something extraordinary, virtually unheard of, the thing that historians have noticed and that gave her the notoriety among them that she has had.

When she and Blair were taking their marriage vows, rather than answer "Yes," or "I will," or "I do" when the minister asked her would she love, honor, and obey her husband in all things, she replied in a firm voice, "No obey." He asked again, and she again replied, "No obey." The minister asked several times, and each time she refused. Apparently, the minister grew frustrated and went ahead with the rest of the ceremony; or perhaps Blair nodded his willingness to proceed without her assent to that one portion of the marriage ceremony. Anyway, they were married that day, and with the assistance of her family connections, he began his rapid ascent within the colonial elite.

James Blair became a well-respected authority on the beatitudes, but he did not always practice what he preached, literally. He was strongly, sometimes violently, opinionated, schemed against people who stood in his way, usually with success—including against three governors—and evidently grew accustomed to having all things his own way. Whether he was already that way when he and Sarah Harrison married or became that way later is not quite clear. Whether it was evident to her when she married him what kind of man he was or would become is also not clear. If she knew or suspected that he was or would become a difficult man to live with, then why did she marry him? It may be that her family pressured her into marrying him. Marriages were not always about love or even compatibility in those days, especially in the high social circle to which she and her family belonged. Wealth, status, important connections, and other factors sometimes influenced choices that people made when they married or when their families played a role in the choice.

It may be that Sarah Harrison's "No obey" response during the wedding ceremony indicates that she had some suspicions about what she was getting into. It may be that she was an unusually self-confident and independent-minded young woman who did not intend to stand in her husband's shadow or always do his bidding. If so, she was not alone among the white women of Virginia. She almost certainly learned later, in 1700, about the ardent courtship by Governor Sir Francis Nicholson of young Lucy Burwell, who at the time was about the same age that Sarah Harrison was, seventeen, when she married James Blair. But Lucy Burwell found Nicholson and his pursuit of her intolerable. Nicholson was even more headstrong in his opinions and ambitions than James Blair, and because they both lived for a time in the new capital city of Williamsburg, it is not surprising that after they cooperated to found the College of William and Mary, Blair and Nicholson had a famous falling-out. Lucy Burwell made a wise choice when she refused to receive Nicholson's advances and enlisted members of her very influential family to force Nicholson to stop his annoying pursuit of her.

Sarah Harrison and Lucy Burwell were undoubtedly not ordinary women at the end of the seventeenth century. Scholars who have studied the lives and actions of Virginia women at that time have perceived that during the last quarter of the century, the social status of white women declined, even among the wealthy class of elite Virginia families to which both Harrison and Burwell belonged. So far as we can tell, white women spoke out less often in public and on public matters; they may have exercised less influence in making decisions that affected their families and children; and it is even possible that their husbands less often named their wives as executrix of their estates when they made their wills or that county courts less often appointed them legal guardians of their own orphaned children. The surviving documentary record for the decades after Sarah Harrison said "No obey" and after Lucy Burwell rejected the annoying public advances of the governor does not preserve as much evidence of such bold and independent behavior as earlier.

Lucy Burwell, after spurning Governor Nicholson, eventually married a member of the prominent Berkeley family and had three daughters and two sons. After her death in 1716, fourteen years after they married, her husband had a loving compliment to her carved on her gravestone, that "She never in all the time she lived with her Husband gave him so much as once cause to be displeased with Her." From that, it is possible to speculate, but not possible to demonstrate, that he had also given her few, if any, causes to be displeased with him.

Sarah Harrison Blair never saw and did not know about the words on that gravestone, which undoubtedly would have made her envious. She had died three years before Lucy Burwell Berkeley died, apparently childless, after she lived most of her life unhappily with the Reverend Commissary Honorable Cantankerous James Blair. She may have relished the absence of her husband during his extended trip to England on business relating to founding the College of William and Mary in the 1690s, but Sarah Harrison Blair was probably a sad and lonely woman, and possibly an alcoholic, at the end of her nearly forty-three years of life.

14

Grace Sherwood Charged with Witchcraft

GRACE SHERWOOD WAS NOT the only Virginian suspected of or charged with practicing witchcraft in colonial Virginia, but she is the only one whose name is now reasonably well known because in the summer of 1706 she was proved to be a witch in a trial by ducking her into water. Her story, which is preserved in the records of Princess Anne County, has attracted the attention of a good many writers, most of whom appear to have known little or nothing about the law of witchcraft, and many of whom have embellished on the few lean facts that the historical record preserves. About the life of Grace Sherwood, we know disappointingly little for certain.

The only other charge of witchcraft in Virginia that consists of more than a very brief mention was in 1626 against a woman whose name was probably Joan Wright, wife of colonist Robert Wright. In the one set of records that mention her, she was identified in a manner that was common for the time as Good Wife (or Goodwife) Wright. Several men and women testified that she had used her powers to injure them or to hinder them in their lawful pursuits. One man stated that she cast a spell on him that prevented him from killing any game with his gun for an entire year. One woman refused to let her act as midwife for her because Good Wife Wright was left-handed and therefore of suspicious character, and claimed that Good Wife Wright later punished her by afflicting her and her infant child with serious, lingering illnesses. Good Wife Wright reportedly foretold the deaths of several people and the deaths of the hens of others. She reportedly threatened to charm a woman into dancing naked in public if she would not supply Good Wife Wright with free firewood. Another told of hearing her relate that when she lived in Hull, England, she had cured her mistress of a disease by casting a hot horseshoe into the woman's fresh urine. And still another person charged that Good Wife Wright, after requesting some plants from a neighbor and being refused, caused all of his plants to die in the night. No record survives that Good Wife Wright was punished, but an absence of evidence from that time period in the history of Virginia is no evidence of an absence.

About Grace Sherwood, we know that she lived in Princess Anne County, in the southeastern corner of Virginia, at the end of the seventeenth century and during the first four decades of the eighteenth. Originally Lower Norfolk County, because it was lower down, or closer to the ocean, than the original Norfolk County from which it was formed, the name of the county was changed to honor Princess Anne of Denmark, next in line to the throne of England after the deaths of King William and Queen Mary, and who became Queen Anne in 1702 after the king and queen both died with no living children. The city of Virginia Beach absorbed the county in 1963.

We do not know for certain when or where Grace Sherwood was born, but she was probably born near where she lived at the time of the witchcraft accusations. We know that she was married to James Sherwood by 1681 when her father, John White, died. She apparently had at least one son by the time that her husband died in 1701. The records concerning the charges of witchcraft brought against her were recorded in the Princess Anne County Order Book 1 (1691–1709). The court records have been printed in whole or in part several times.

In September 1698, Grace and James Sherwood sued two married couples for slander and demanded compensation in the very large amount of £100 because the two couples had "Defamed and abused the said Grace in her good name and reputation saying that she is a Witch and bewitched their piggs to Death and bewitched their Cotton &c." The jury that heard the case ruled in favor of the defendants and against the Sherwoods. The reasons for the verdict are not preserved, but unlike in modern times, truth was not a good defense in a slander or libel case then, so the jurors could have accepted the evidence of the defendants that Grace Sherwood used occult powers to kill the pigs and cause damage to the cotton. The defendants and the court evidently did not seek to prosecute Sherwood for the crime of practicing witchcraft, though.

One of the defendants, Elizabeth Barnes, charged that Grace Sherwood had secretly come to her one night and ridden on her back as you would ride a horse and then assumed the form of a black cat and left by going out through a keyhole in the door. The actions that Barnes described, plus flying through the air and other physically impossible actions, were widely accepted beliefs about the behaviors of witches in the English-speaking world, and perhaps elsewhere, and about their ability to use diabolical means to change their form or persecute honest people.

The famous charge of witchcraft against Grace Sherwood began early in January 1705/6, about a month after she sued Luke Hill and his wife for assault and battery and asked for £50 in damages. Sherwood charged that Hill's wife "had Assaulted Brused Maimed & Barbarously Beaten" Sherwood. The jury awarded Sherwood only twenty shillings—one pound—and made the Hills pay the court costs.

The lean record of the trial, which contains barely one hundred words, does not indicate whether witchcraft played a role in the assault and battery, but it probably did because on January 3, 1705/6, the court ordered Grace Sherwood to appear in court at the insistence of Hill and his wife "in Suspition of witchcraft." Sherwood failed to appear at the next session of court, on February 6, or on the following day. So, on February 7, the justices of the peace, who served as judges of the county court, after a "Long" debate, ordered "that the sd: Grace be here next Court to be Searched" for evidence that she was a witch "by a Jury of women."

A jury consisting entirely of women summoned for such a purpose in a case involving a charge of witchcraft acted much the same as did the jury of women in 1680 who examined the dead body of Mary Burton's illegitimate son, not to determine guilt or innocence, not to settle a civil suit, but to ascertain the facts in a procedure that had long English precedent—in this instance, to search her body for evidence that she was a witch. One such piece of evidence would be a third nipple for suckling the Devil. People believed that witches had such familiar dealings with the Devil. People believed, and courts acknowledged, that such evidence was good, persuasive evidence in a court of law.

At the session of the county court on March 7, 1705/6, Sherwood appeared and consented to be examined. She and the members of the jury retired into a private room where the jury inspected her naked body. Elizabeth Barnes, no less, was the first-named woman in the list of the jury members, which Sherwood probably considered as unfair; and we can certainly state that their past history made it improper that she was one of the women named to examine Sherwood. After the examination, the jury members and Sherwood returned into the courtroom, and the jury reported that "After a Mature Consideration They bring in the verdictt wee of the Jury have Sercht Grace Sherwood & have found Two things like titts wth Severall other Spotts."

The county court record does not clearly indicate whether the jury considered that the "Two things like titts" and the other "Spotts" constituted convincing legal evidence that Sherwood was a real witch or that the justices of the peace concluded that Sherwood was a witch. Three weeks later, though, Luke Hill petitioned the governor and Council of State and reported that the jury had "brought in a Verdict agt the Said Grace"—that she was, indeed, a witch—"but the Court not knowing how to proceed to Judgment thereon," Hill asked "that the attorney Genll. may be directed to prosecute the Said Grace for the same." The governor and the members of the Council of State "Ordered that the petition be referred to Mr. Attorney Genll: to consider and report his opinion to his Excellcy & the council on the first day of the next Genll. Court."

Hill's assertion that the members of the county court did not know how to prosecute a charge of witchcraft, if true, indicates that none of the justices of the peace on the court had a copy of one of the several standard manuals of practice for justices of the peace that were then in print and that explained how to proceed in just such a case. Why? A law that the General Assembly had passed in 1666 required every county court to purchase copies or abstracts of the laws of Parliament and several standard reference works, including one on probate of estates, and specifically including by name Michael Dalton's *The Country Justice: Containing the Practice, Duty and Power of the Justices of the Peace, as well in as out of Their Sessions*, originally published in 1618. In fact, *Country Justice* emphasized the importance of searching the bodies of persons suspected of witchcraft. Why did the court of the county of Princess Anne not order one or more copies? The 1666 law remained in effect until the 1740s. Dalton's *Country Justice* described the duties of English justices of the peace, which by the time of the charges against Sherwood were not the same as the duties of Virginia justices of the peace. With respect to charges of witchcraft, though, the law was exactly the same. Virginia did not have its own law of witchcraft, but the Acte Against Conjuration Witchcrafte and Dealing with Evill and Wicked Spirits that Parliament adopted early in 1603/4, before the settlement-invasion of Virginia, was in effect in the colony.

One other thing: if in fact the members of the Princess Anne County Court did not know how to prosecute a charge of witchcraft, that suggests, but does not prove, that no such recent case was within their knowledge. And that in turn suggests that such cases were probably rare in Virginia at the beginning of the eighteenth century. Whether, or how much, justices of the peace in Princess Anne County, Virginia, knew in 1705 and 1706 about the 1692 witchcraft trials in Salem, Massachusetts, is impossible to know because the trials may have become more famous outside of Massachusetts later than they were at the time.

On April 16, 1706, about three weeks after Attorney General Stevens Thompson received the request to rule on how the county court should proceed with its case against Grace Sherwood, he reported "that the charge or accusation is too general & that the County Court ought to make a further Examination of the matters of fact." If the court found good evidence that she was a witch and had used her powers to injure somebody or somebody's property, then the court should prosecute the alleged crime according to the procedure set out in the criminal code of Virginia that had just been revised in 1705. The attorney general explained that if the members of the county court "thought there was sufficient cause to have (according to that Law) committed her to the Genll prison of this Colony thereby it would have come regularly before the Genll Court." The governor and Council of State sent a copy of the attorney general's opinion to the Princess Anne County Court.

The original report of the attorney general is preserved in Colonial Papers, Record Group 1, Library of Virginia, but it is virtually illegible because the paper turned a dark brown when it was exposed to humidity and sunlight for a long period two centuries later at the 1907 exposition that commemorated the three-hundredth anniversary of the settlement of Jamestown. The clerk of the Council of State copied it into the manuscript journal of the council on the day that Thompson presented his report to the council. The copy that the governor and council sent to the Princess Anne County Court apparently does not survive.

The law that Parliament passed in 1603/4 did not explicitly provide for punishment of people who were proved to be witches, but it clearly provided for punishment if witches were convicted of using occult powers to bring about the death of another person. The penalty was death. The law specified a lesser penalty of one year in jail for any witch convicted for the first time of injury to another person's property. Every quarter during that year the convicted witch had to stand in the pillory for six hours and confess his or her guilt before going back to jail.

On May 2, the Princess Anne County Court conducted a new examination and came to the "Oppinion that there is great Cause of Suspicion" that Grace Sherwood was a witch and may have practiced witchcraft to the injury of Luke Hill and his wife. The court ordered the sheriff to take Sherwood into custody and that the constable search her house and "all Suspicious places Carfully." The court also summoned a second "Able Jury of Women" to attend the next county court meeting.

When the county court next met on June 6 it named a prosecutor for the case, and on the next day, the justices of the peace learned that the women they had ordered to search Sherwood had refused to serve. The court ordered that they be prosecuted for contempt of court and that a second jury of women be summoned. The court also directed that "with her own Consent," Sherwood "be tried in the water by Ducking but the weather being very Rainy & Bad Soe that possibly it might endanger her health," the court postponed the procedure.

Ducking, also known as trial by water, was an old English practice that produced irrefutable proof whether a person was a witch. People believed, and the courts acknowledged, that pure water would not receive a witch, an agent of the Devil. In a trial by water, the sheriff or constable bound the hands and feet of the accused person and lowered him or her into a river or pond. If the person sank—if the water received the person—that proved him or her innocent; if the person did not sink, that proved him or her to be a witch. An innocent person who sank might very well drown in the process, but as Dalton had admonished in his *Country Justice*, it was the responsibility of the people who conducted the trial to endeavor to preserve the life of the accused person. And as the order of the Princess Anne County Court at the previous session of court to postpone the trial because of bad weather indicated, the justices of the peace also tried to protect the life of Grace Sherwood, who remained innocent of the charge of witchcraft until the trial by water proved her to be a witch.

Exactly as with the trial by touch that the female jury conducted on the body of Mary Burton's illegitimate son and the practice of a midwife withholding assistance from an unmarried woman at the time of giving birth until she identified the father, the trial by water was regarded as reliable legal proof. People believed, and the courts acknowledged, that a miracle of God would prove or disprove whether a person was a witch.

On July 10, 1706, Grace Sherwood underwent her trial by water. The sheriff assembled a party of men with their boats to dunk her into water that was deeper than a man was tall to "try her how She Swims Therein." Moreover, the court directed that the men take "Care of her life to preserve her from Drowning." The court also ordered that as soon as the trial was concluded, the sheriff should request "as many Antient & Knowing women as possible he cann to Serch her Carefully For all teats spotts & marks about her body not usuall in Others & that as they Find the Same to make report on Oath To the truth thereof to the Court & further it is ordr that Some women be requested to Shift & Serch her before She goe into the water that She Carry nothing about her to cause any Further Suspicion."

The county court concluded its proceedings against Grace Sherwood that same day. The justices of the peace, after hearing all of the evidence, "to which She could not make any excuse or Little or nothing to say in her own Behalf," agreed with her that she should "be tryed in the water & Likewise to be Serched againe." The court ordered that Sherwood's hands and feet be bound and that she be lowered into the water, where she floated unaided and did not sink. After that, "Five antient weomen" searched her body again. The women reported to the court and "all Declared on Oath that She is not like them nor noe Other woman that they knew of having two things like titts on her private parts of a Black Coller being Blacker than the Rest of her Body." The justices of the peace therefore ordered the sheriff to "take the Sd Grace Into his Costody & to Commit her body to the Common Goal"—jail, also then spelled gaol, goal, and goale—"of this County there to Secure her by irons or otherwise Directed in order for her coming to the Common Goale of the county to bee brought to a Future Tryall there."

The trial would have been held in the General Court in Williamsburg because county courts had no legal authority to try white people accused of crimes. We have no surviving record of an indictment or trial before the General Court; all of the records of the court perished in the State Court House fire in April 1865. We do know that Sherwood was not accused of causing anyone to die, so she could not have been convicted and sentenced to death. If she had been tried and convicted on a lesser offense, as the county court records indicate was the charge against her, she would have been held in the Princess Anne County jail for a year and taken out quarterly and made to stand in the stocks for six hours and confess her guilt.

It is interesting to note that in one of the instances in which the justices of the peace tried to assemble a jury of women to examine the body of Grace Sherwood, the women refused to serve. Why? Did they not believe in witchcraft? Did they not believe that a person who possessed the powers of a witch would necessarily have physical manifestations on her body? Did they simply not wish to take part? It is also interesting that the attorney general had to advise the county court how to proceed. And it is interesting that a private person, Luke Hill, not the sheriff, a constable, or a justice of the peace, initiated the legal process.

And it is most interesting of all to contemplate how anybody could prove that somebody had used witchcraft to kill or injure another person or that person's property. To a surprisingly large extent, people who accused other people of practicing witchcraft and the accused people themselves were often in the same difficult legal circumstances of women who accused men of rape and of the accused men. Judges and juries had to decide whose word to take because there were usually no witnesses to give testimony to having seen a crime or no physical evidence to corroborate either party's testimony. It is very likely that the difficulty of proving charges of witchcraft is what persuaded Parliament in 1736 to repeal the witchcraft law of 1603/4 under the authority of which officials in Princess Anne County struggled with how to proceed against Grace Sherwood.

By a curious coincidence, in that same year, 1736, before news of Parliament's repeal of the law reached Virginia, a Virginia lawyer named George Webb included a summary of the 1603/4 law and a summary of Michael Dalton's entry on witchcraft in his *The Office and Authority of a Justice of Peace*, the first law book ever published in Virginia and the first to explain the responsibilities of justices of the peace in the colony. About the difficulty that accusations of witchcraft posed for judges of the county courts, Webb wrote, "Information of Witchcraft ought not to be received by Justices of the Peace, nor Prosecution awarded thereupon, without strong and apparent Cause, proved by sufficient Witnesses, upon Oath"—the reason being that "Plain and direct Evidence is not to be expected in these Works of Darkness, where no Witnesses are admitted, and therefore we can have only, either by Confession of the Offender, or pregnant and convincing Circumstances, whereupon to found an Indictment, or Conviction."

Grace Sherwood almost certainly returned to the small farm that her late husband had owned, and in 1714 she received a patent, also called a grant, for 145 acres of land in Princess Anne County. She lived to make her mark on a will on August 20, 1733, and died, almost certainly in Princess Anne County, sometime before October 1, 1740, when the county court proved her will and ordered an administrator to settle her meager estate according to the law.

None of the modern scholars who have written about witchcraft in colonial North America believed in witches, but the people about whom they wrote definitely did. In a society of deep and pervasive religious faith, people had inherited traditions and beliefs that explained some otherwise inexplicable natural phenomena and some inexcusable human behavior. They may very well have understood that a belief in God required a belief in the Devil, and that if God could work His will on people on earth, so could the Devil. So many things happened in the world for which causes were not immediately discernable that it was easy to believe that spirits inhabited the world alongside human beings, including evil spirits that the Devil inhabited or animated—witches.

Grace Sherwood's experience has passed from a few meager historical facts into a mixture of history and legend. Witch Duck Creek in the modern city of Virginia Beach is locally recognized as the place where Grace Sherwood underwent her trial by water. Perhaps. Perhaps not. A small waterfowl called a pied-billed grebe that resembles a duck was sometimes known in the olden days as a water witch from its ability to sink quietly and quickly out of sight to feed underwater and then just as suddenly pop up, visible again, on the surface of the water, as if magically. Pied-billed grebes could also have been known locally as witch ducks. They spend winters in coastal and inland Virginia waters to this day.

The legends and myths that people had been propagating about Grace Sherwood for generations became firmly embedded in the local and regional and even statewide folklore. The legend of Grace Sherwood was so widely known as early as 1907 that the state archivist included the attorney general's ruling on how the county court should proceed against her in the three-hundredth anniversary exhibition, where sunlight so badly damaged it as to make it virtually illegible. The legends that accumulated around and derived from the few actual facts had come to be accepted as fact by 2006, and in that year a group of women persuaded Governor Tim Kaine to grant an informal pardon to Grace Sherwood. That same year, a local group commissioned California artist Robert Cunningham to execute a bronze statue of Sherwood, even though no physical description of her exists other than the two juries' vague descriptions of the spots on her body. In 2007, the sponsors installed the statute near where the legends hold that Sherwood lived.

15

Exemplary Punishment for Salvadore and Scipio

THE ORIGINAL MANUSCRIPT OF the executive journals of the Council of State for the years 1705–21 is preserved in a bound manuscript volume in the Library of Virginia as part of Record Group 1 of the archives of Virginia. The contents of the volume, along with all other known surviving volumes of executive council journals from the colonial period, have been published in H. R. McIlwaine, Wilmer L. Hall, and Benjamin L. Hillman, eds., *Executive Journals of the Council of Colonial Virginia*, 6 vols. (Richmond, 1925–66). Page 129 of the manuscript volume contains an order dated April 27, 1710, that will shock most twenty-first-century men and women.

The members of the Council of State, of whom there were usually about a dozen, had lifetime appointments from the king, or from the queen during the reign of Queen Anne from 1702 to 1714. They were all prosperous white men; they were important executive advisors to the governor; they were the members of the upper House of the General Assembly; and they were the judges of the General Court, the highest court in Virginia and the only court with appellate jurisdiction. The General Court had exclusive jurisdiction to conduct trials of white people who were accused of committing felonies. The General Court met in the capital city of Williamsburg after the General Assembly moved the seat of the colonial government there following the October 1698 fire that burned the Statehouse in Jamestown.

Since 1692, trials of enslaved people who were accused of committing felonies were usually conducted in the counties where the crimes were committed in what were called Courts of Oyer and Terminer—literally, to hear and determine the outcome of a case. At each of those trials, a select number of justices of the peace, functioning under a special commission from the

{92}

governor, tried the accused man or woman without a jury and without a right for a convicted person to appeal the verdict for legal reasons. A convicted person could nevertheless ask the governor for a pardon or for clemency.

On April 27, 1710, members of the Council of State, acting in their executive capacity, issued an order for the punishment of two enslaved men, Salvadore and Scipio, who had "been tryed this General Court and found guilty of high Treason." Under Virginia law as codified in 1705, any rebellion, revolt, or other comparable actions on the part of enslaved people, as well as murder or attempted murder of their enslavers, were all classified as treason. The status of enslavers with respect to their enslaved people by that time was almost comparable to the status of the kings and queens with respect to all of their subjects. That the General Court, rather than a county court, tried the two men suggests that authorities had discovered evidence of a serious plot for a rebellion of enslaved people that spread across more than one county. That would have made separate prosecutions in several counties impossible or unwise.

Other records preserved in the Colonial Papers, also part of Record Group 1, in the Library of Virginia include three documents all dated a few weeks before the trial: a letter from Philip Ludwell to Edmund Jenings and the Council of State dated March 19, 1709/10; an order of the president of the council dated March 20, 1709/10; and a letter from the justices of the peace in Surry County to Edmund Jenings dated March 24, 1709/10. The three documents contained information about the identification, capture, and preliminary "Examination, of Severall: Negro and Indian Slaves, Concerned in a Late Dangerous Conspiracy formed and Carried on by great Numbers of the said Negroes and Indians Slaves for making their Escape by force from the Service of their Masters and for the Destroying and cutting off"—killing—"Such of her Majties. Subjects as Should oppose their Designe."

Contrary to what most people later believed, early English Virginians enslaved a great many men and women from First Nations tribes, almost from the very beginning of colonization, and they continued to do so throughout the seventeenth century and into the eighteenth. The terms of enslavement were often limited to a certain number of years, but in June 1676, the General Assembly provided for the lifetime enslavement of Indians captured during the anticipated war with neighboring tribes, perhaps as a means of encouraging poor white men to enlist because, if they survived the war, they might increase their estates and raise their social status by coming into the ownership of an enslaved person. From the comment of a prominent lawyer in the 1770s, we know that a large number of people, perhaps several hundred, successfully sued for their freedom in the eighteenth century because they were descendants of illegally enslaved women from First Nations tribes and according to Virginia law should never have been held in slavery.

It is very probable that Attorney General Stevens Thompson prosecuted the accused men during the trial in the General Court in the spring of 1710. The details are unfortunately not recorded in the records of the executive proceedings of the Council of State, and the judicial records of the General Court for that time were burned in the fire that destroyed the State Court House and its contents in Richmond at the end of the American Civil War in April 1865.

When the Council of State met in Williamsburg on April 27, 1710, the royal governor, George Hamilton, Earl of Orkney, was not present. He had only just been appointed in February 1709/10, and never even contemplated moving to Virginia. In fact, no royal governor ever served in Virginia or even set foot in the colony between the death of Governor Edward Nott in August 1706 and the arrival of Governor Norborne Berkeley, Baron De Botetourt, in October 1768. Queen Anne commissioned Robert Hunter to succeed Nott as governor of Virginia in 1707, but a French fleet captured and imprisoned him, so early in 1710 she commissioned Orkney.

Normally, during the absence of the governor, a lieutenant governor, who had a special commission from the king or queen, served as acting governor and exercised almost all of the powers of the royal governor and was the king's or queen's personal representative in the colony. At the time of Nott's death, though, nobody had a commission to serve as lieutenant governor. Therefore, when Nott died, Edmund Jenings, the senior member of the Council of State in length of service, became acting governor with the title president. Jenings had been a member of the council since 1691 and held the post of president until the arrival of Lieutenant Governor Alexander Spotswood later in 1710. Jenings had a long record of distinguished service. He had been attorney general of Virginia from 1680 until the king appointed him to the Council of State, and he remained a member of the council until 1726.

On April 10, 1710, when the Council of State issued its orders to sentence Salvador and Scipio, President Jenings presided over the meeting, as he had presided along with the other members of the council as judges of the General Court during the trial.

The journal that day recorded that "Salvadore an Indian and Scipio a Negro Slaves have been tryed this General Court and found guilty of high Treason, and Sentence of death passed on them accordingly." The record does not indicate to which tribe Salvador belonged.

Salvador and Scipio being found guilty of treason in the General Court and sentenced to death, the Council of State in its executive capacity directed that in order that "their execution and exemplary punishment may have a due effect for deterring other Slaves from entering into such dangerous Conspiracys It is Ordered that Salvadore be executed (according to the Sentence passed on him) at the Court house of Surry County on the first Tuesday in May, and that his body be disposed of as follows VIZT"—abbreviation of legal Latin that meant to wit, or thus—"his head to be delivered to the Sherif of James City County and by him sett up at the City of Williamsburgh Two of his quarters likewise delivered to the sd Sherif of James City one whereof he is to cause to be sett up at the great guns in James City"—probably on Jamestown island, the original landing site in 1607 and until recently the capital of Virginia—"and the other to deliver to the Sherif of New Kent County to be sett up in the most publick place of the said County, and the other two quarters to be disposed of and sett up as the Justices of the County of Surry shall think fitt to direct."

The council also "ordered that Scipio be executed at the Court house of Gloucester County at the next Court to be held for the said County in May and his body disposed of in manner following VIZT his head and one of his quarters sett up where the Justices of the said County of Gloucester shall think fitt two of his quarters to be delivered to the Sherif of Middlesex one of which he is to cause to be put up in the most publick place of the sd County of Middlesex and the other to cause to be delivered to the Sherif of the County of Lancaster to be sett up in the most publick place of the said County And the Sherif of Gloucester is to cause the other quarter of the said Scipio to be delivered to the Sherif of King and Queen County to be sett up in the most publick place of the said County, And all the said Sherifs are hereby directed and required to cause the several Articles of this order to be duly performed." The order also required that the enumerated counties pay the expenses of the gruesome punishment and public display of the dismembered corpses.

The order to distribute the head and quarters of the two men to several counties for display clearly indicates that the men had been convicted of organizing a conspiracy or rebellion throughout a large area that included at least one county south of the James River, at least three counties north of the river, and at least three other counties northeast of the mouth of the York River. The treatment that the Council of State ordered for the bodies of the two executed men closely resembled how English courts punished the worst criminals. English law required that men who were convicted of treason be hanged, that their entrails be cut out and burned while they were still alive, and that their bodies then be drawn and quartered—four horses tied to the different arms and legs would literally draw the body apart. Women convicted of treason were to be burned alive.

The punishment and dismemberment that the Council of State imposed on the bodies of Salvadore and Scipio in 1710 were of corresponding severity and were intended, as the council stated in its order, to "have a due effect for deterring other Slaves from entering into such dangerous Conspiracys." It was an act of state terrorism, to terrify other people into not doing likewise. Such punishments were more common than we might imagine. A decade earlier, a royal court of vice-admiralty in Virginia had ordered several convicted pirates to be hanged on the coast where ships entering and leaving Chesapeake Bay would see them and that the bodies be left hanging there until they rotted.

The council's order is graphic evidence of just how important slavery had become by then, that "Conspiracys" that threatened slavery were of the utmost seriousness and should be dealt with in a very terrible and frightening public manner—in an "exemplary" manner, which did not mean admirable or excellent, but as an example of what could happen to other enslaved people who did something similar.

Because we have so few surviving records of actions of the General Court during the eighteenth century, and because the records of some of the county courts during the same time are also lost—some in the same fire with the General Court records after they were sent to Richmond during the Civil War for safekeeping—we will never be able to count the number of times that Virginia courts issued sentences that required that the bodies of convicted enslaved people be quartered and hung up on poles in public places. Some such records survive, and rumors of rebellions circulated through most parts of Virginia at one time or another during those decades, which together strongly suggest that people saw rotting body parts of convicted people in some place or other in Virginia from time to time.

The county court in Goochland County, for example, on June 25, 1733, convicted two enslaved men of murdering a white man and "Ordered that the heads & quarters" of the two men "be set up in severall parts of this County." Court records also document payment of 60 pounds of tobacco to the sheriff for "providing Gallow's and Ropes to Hang the Negroes"; 250 pounds of tobacco each for hanging them; and 2,000 pounds of tobacco for transporting and "Setting up the Heads and Quarters of the two Negroes at the places mentioned by order of Court."

16

Drinking More Than Necessary

ON MARCH 21, 1714/15, according to an entry in the record book York County Orders, Wills, Etc., 14:397–98, the York County Court heard "the Complaint of William Cock Esqr: agnst Edward Rippon Ordinary keeper in Williamsburgh for entertaining the Complts: Servt."—a servant of Cock, who made the complaint—"named John Creightong"—or Creighton—"Sufering"—permitting—"him to drink more than was necessary in time of divine Service." Two justices of the peace had suspended Rippon's license to dispense alcoholic drinks, and on March 21, "this Court do hereby Continue the sd. Suspension and the sd: Rippon is further Suspended from retailing any Liquors in his sd. Ordinary untill further order herein & it is ordered that he pay Costs."

Ordinaries, inns, and taverns sold food and drink and often had rooms where travelers could spend the night. Rates that keepers of those establishments charged were closely regulated by law, and each keeper had to have a license from the county court to operate the business. Williamsburg was on the border between York County and James City County, which gave the court of each county jurisdiction within part of the town, which had no municipal government of its own until it received a charter of incorporation and legally became a city in 1723.

The county court order did not specify what the servant drank or enumerate the "Liquors" that Rippon could no longer sell. In *The History and Present State of Virginia*, published in 1705, Virginia native Robert Beverley wrote that Virginians of the time commonly drank "either Wine and Water, Beer, Milk and Water, or Water alone. Their richer sort generally brew their Small-Beer with Malt, which they have from *England*, though

Taverns, inns, and ordinaries in the small towns of colonial Virginia and at the sites of most county courthouses furnished food, drink, and sometimes lodging and fodder for visitors or travelers and their horses. (Drawing by Edwin Austin Abbey, ca. 1885; Art Wood Collection of Caricature and Cartoon, Library of Congress Prints and Photographs Division)

they have as good Barley of their own, as any in the World; but for want of the convenience of Malt-Houses, the Inhabitants take no care to sow it." Small beer was a very low-alcohol beverage that was common in England at the time, too.

"The poorer sort," Beverley continued, "brew their Beer with Mollasses and Bran; with *Indian* Corn Malted by drying in a Stove; with Persimmons dried in Cakes, and baked; with Potatoes; with the green stalks of *Indian* Corn cut small, and bruised," or with pumpkins or other fruits and vegetables, "which some People plant purposely for that use, but this is the least esteem'd, of all the sorts before mention'd."

Before very much later in the century, Virginians brewed great quantities of cider from the juice of apples. By the middle of the century, cider and small beer were the common table drinks in Virginia. Traditionally, it was a responsibility of women in the household to brew or to oversee the brewing of beer and cider for domestic use. People of the time also drank imported perry, a form of cider brewed from the fruits of pear trees.

Robert Beverley also reported in 1705 that Virginians who could afford to do so also drank "*Madera* Wine, which is a Noble strong Wine; and Punch, made either of Rum from the *Caribee* Islands, or Brandy distilled from their Apples, and Peaches; besides *French-Brandy*, Wine, and strong Beer, which they have constantly from *England*." During the seventeenth century, several Virginians had experimented with making wine from native Virginia grapes. Some, such as Governor Sir William Berkeley, boasted about the quality of the wine that they produced, but on the whole Virginia wines do not seem to have been very popular. Brandy became a popular "Strong Drink" in Virginia, and by the end of the eighteenth century some people believed that you could identify the residence of a drunkard by the size of the peach orchard.

The justices of the peace who issued the order to Rippon probably did so for two reasons. One, he had transgressed laws and strong social mores in allowing or enabling a servant to get drunk—whether during a church service or not may not have much mattered. The other was to maintain order and keep the peace. County court documents abound with records of people behaving badly when they were in drink, as the phrase went at the time, even during sessions of the courts or at church services. Back in 1671, the court in Lancaster County prosecuted Richard Price after he drunkenly entered the parish church and did "in a rude irreligious & uncivill manner intrude himself into the seats purposely designated & made use off by his Ma^{ts} Justices of the peace" and then forced himself into the seat reserved for the county sheriff, "to the dishon^r of God Almighty in contempt of his ma^{tis} Magistrates."

In the summer of 1720, the county court in Henrico County holding session at the courthouse was disrupted by "John Bolling coming into Court and behaving himself after a very bad manner to the Justices by calling them Puppies and calling on God to damn them together with other misdemeanours." The court ordered the sheriff to arrest him and scheduled a hearing on his behavior at the next monthly court. At that time, Bolling appeared and acknowledged that "he did behave himself very unduly to the Court, and that he is Sorry for having so done he being at that time very much in drink." The court dismissed the case but ordered him to pay five shillings to the churchwarden "as a fine for his being Drunk."

In 1727 in Essex County, the members of the county court had John Griffin brought before them "for calling them poor rogues in their hearing, and now," while the court was in session, "cursing the Court & striking the Sheriff within the barr of the Court, It is therefore ordered that he be fined five pounds current money for his sd offences" and "that the sd. John be & remain in the Sheriffs Custody 'till he pays the same, & enters into bond with good security in the sum of twenty pounds current money for his good behaviour & then to be discharged paying fees." The next day, much as John Bolling had done, "John Griffin came & humbly beged Pardon of the Court for his misbehaviour & great offences for which he was Yesterday fined the Sum of five pounds . . . he being well known to have always behaved himself with Modesty & Sobriety towards the said Court and all other Persons but that he happened then to be in Drink for which he had been also fined." The court therefore recommended that the governor remit the fine of £5.

At the session of the Westmoreland County Court in May 1739, Richard Patterson entered the courtroom, "and appearing to be Drunk by his Looking in at the Court and Speaking out Loud Come here You Dogs and fight," the court ordered "that he be fined Twenty Shillings"—one pound—"and that he be put into the Stocks there to Remain Till the court Rises and that then he Remain in the Sherifs Custody to be brought before the court Tomorrow Morning (When perhaps he may be Sober) to Enter Into bond with Sufficient Security for his the Said Richard Pattersons Good behaviour &c."

Also in Westmoreland County in the winter of 1744–45, the court fined "Thomas Davis planter" one hundred pounds of tobacco and ordered him to pay fifty pounds of tobacco to the church wardens "for his bidding Benjamin Weeks SubSherif Kiss his Arse in the face of the Court," that is, within the view of the members of the county court. Davis returned to the court in March "in a very Submissive manner & askd pardon for the high offence he had been guilty of & promised for the future to take care never to be guilty of an offence of the Like nature." The court recommended that the fine be remitted.

In each of these instances and in many others that documents preserve, the inebriated men offended the dignity of public officials or men of high social standing who, according to the standards of the time, were always entitled to be treated with respect and with a certain amount of deference. Everybody had a place in the gradations of that hierarchical society. Even respectable gentlemen planters owed respect to justices of the peace, sheriffs, and other officials. In churches, as in the case of Richard Price of Lancaster

County, justices of the peace, sheriffs, and other local notables had reserved seats near the pulpit. Wealthy men sometimes purchased their own pews. In the capital city, the governor, members of the Council of State, other royal appointees, and such dignitaries as the Speaker of the House of Burgesses also had preferred seating near the pulpit. Wealthy families often purchased pews in the most desirable parts of the church and expected that when they were not present, lesser people would not occupy their reserved places.

17

Releese Us out of This Cruell Bondegg

VOLUME 17 OF THE Fulham Palace Papers in the Lambeth Palace Library in London preserves a unique letter from an enslaved Virginian whose name, gender, and place of residence we do not know. The handwriting, the spelling, and the syntax indicate that the writer was barely able to read and write and was not properly educated. The ink is red and faded, possibly made from the berries of pokeweed. The letter is dated "August the forth 1723," with an addition made on September 8, and is addressed to "The Right Raverrand father in god my Lord arch Bishop of Lonnd." It lay in the archive of the bishops of London for more than two and a half centuries, unknown to students of Virginia history or students of slavery in North America, because it had been misfiled among letters from residents of Jamaica; but the first sentence in the letter clearly states that it came from the "Land of verJennia." The letter was published in Thomas N. Ingersoll, ed., "'Releese us out of this Cruell Bondegg': An Appeal from Virginia in 1723," *William and Mary Quarterly*, 3d ser., 51 (1994): 777–82, and it returned to Virginia in 2006 for display at the Virginia Historical Society, in Richmond, in the exhibition *The Episcopal Church in Virginia, 1607–2007*.

The address of the letter informs us that the writer knew enough about the hierarchy of the Church of England, which was the official, established church in Virginia—the church was part of the government of the colony, and the government of the colony was part of the church—to know that the bishop of London had nominal responsibility for all the Anglican churches in North America. Any American who sought to become a priest of the Church of England had to travel to England in order that the bishop of London could ordain him.

The writer of the letter also knew almost exactly the formal way to address a bishop, as Right Reverend Father in God; but the writer mistakenly addressed the letter to the archbishop of London rather than to the bishop, who was not so high an official in the church as an archbishop. Still, it seems pretty remarkable that a scarcely literate enslaved person in Virginia in 1723 would know who to appeal to in all of England and to get the formal style of address almost right. It never hurts now, and probably did not hurt then, to exalt an official by appearing to believe that he holds a higher office than he does, but it could have hurt to demote the addressee by inadvertently giving him a lesser title. For the record, which the writer may or may not have known, in August 1723 Edmund Gibson was the new bishop of London.

As with the texts that English invaders wrote when they described their experiences and observations early in the seventeenth century, it is wise to read this letter from early in the eighteenth century out loud to follow its syntax and to figure out the correct equivalents of badly misspelled words. The letter begins "this coms to sattisfie"—probably meaning to inform—"your honour that there is in this Land of verJennia a Sort of people that is Calld molatters which are Baptised and brouaht up in the way of the Christan faith and followes the wayes and Rulles of the Chrch of England and sum of them has white fathers and sum white mothers and there is in this Land a Law or act which keeps and makes them and there seed SLaves forever—" The long dash often indicated a period, or full stop, or even the end of a paragraph.

The writer was precisely right, with the exception of children of free white mothers. A law of 1662 had made the children of enslaved women lifetime slaves, but a considerable proportion of enslaved Virginians in the eighteenth century had English and First Nations ancestry as well as African ancestry and were lawfully classed as mulattoes, or "molatters," as the writer spelled the word. Some mothers who appeared to be white were in fact legally enslaved women.

Without a mark of punctuation other than the dash, the letter continues, "and most honoured Sir a mongst the Rest of your Charitabell acts and deed wee your humbell and poore partishinners doo begg Sir your aid and assisttancce in this one thing which Lise as I doo understand in your LordShips brest which is that your honour will by the help of our Sufvering"—sovereign—"Lord King George and the Rest of the Rullers will Releese us out of this Cruell Bondegg and this wee beg for Jesus Christs his Sake who has Commaded us to seeke first the kingdom of god and all things shall be addid un to us." The bishop of London had no authority to free anybody in any colony, and it is doubtful that the king did, either, under ordinary circumstances.

Again, the writer knew the formal phrase, "our sovereign lord King George," even if he or she could not spell all the words correctly. The writer's use of the nearly correct modes for referring to the bishop and to the king let us know that even unlettered enslaved men and women—even unlettered free white men and women—knew and understood the conventions of society more thoroughly than a lack of education might initially lead us to suspect. Further, that the writer knew both styles suggests that he or she may have spent time in the vicinity of a court or of a church vestry meeting where those formal phrases would have been in use.

The writer explained that in the case of white fathers and enslaved mothers, "it is to bee notd that one brother is a SLave to another and one Sister to an othe which is quite out of the way and as for mee my selfe I am my brothers SLave but my name is Secrett." People like the writer had white fathers and enslaved mothers and sometimes also had free white half-brothers or half-sisters. That reveals that the writer was not a native of Africa who had been kidnapped and sold into slavery and carried to Virginia aboard a ship of the notorious international slave trading fleet. She or he was a native Virginian and the child of an enslaved woman and a white man. Having written that much, the writer announced that his or her name was a "Secrett," no doubt for fear that somebody might discover the letter before it could reach the bishop, which could likely get the writer into serious trouble with her or his brother-owner.

A new paragraph changes the subject: "and here it is to bee notd againe that wee are commandded to keep holey the Sabbath day and wee doo hardly know when it comes for our task mastrs are as hard with us as the Egypttions was with the Chilldann of Issarall god be marcifll unto us." The complaints continue after another paragraph break: "here follows our Sevarity and Sorrowfull Sarvice we are hard used upon Every account in the first place wee are in Ignorance of our Salvation and in the next place wee are kept out of the Church and matrimony is deenied us."

Some enslavers allowed their enslaved people to attend church, but others did not. The writer knew the basic tenets and language of Protestant

Christianity well enough that we can believe that she or he was fortunate to be allowed to attend church from time to time. The writer was correct about matrimony, too, because from the very beginning early in the seventeenth century through the end of slavery in the 1860s, Virginia law did not recognize marriages between enslaved people, or even between an enslaved person and a free person, as legal, regard their children as legitimate, or provide any legal protections for members of their families; and for three decades by the time the writer wrote to the bishop of London, Virginia law had also prohibited marriages between white Virginians and either free or enslaved Black Virginians or members of First Nations Tribes.

The writer explained the degradation of enslaved people in Virginia graphically: "and to be plain they doo Look no more upon us then if wee ware dogs which I hope when these Strainge Lines comes to your Lord Ships hands will be Looket in to." Following that sentence-long complaint, a sentence-long appeal: "and here wee beg for Jesus Christ his Sake that as your honour do hope for the marcy of god att the day of death and the Redemtion of our Saviour Christ that when this comes to your Lord Ships hands you honour wll Take Sum pitty of us who is your humble butt Sorrowfull portitinors."

Then, "and Sir wee your humble perticners do humblly beg the favour of your Lord Ship that your honour will grant and Settell one thing upon us which is that our Childarn may be broatt up in the way of the Christtian faith and our desire is that they may be Larned the Lords prayer the creed and the ten commandements and that they may appear Every Lord's day att Church before the Curatt to bee Exammond for our desire is that godllines Shoulld abbound among us and wee desire that our Childarn be putt to Scool" so that they could be "Larned to Reed through the Bybell." The line breaks there and obstructs the continuation of the sentence, which concludes, "which is al att prasant with our prayers to god for itts good Success before your honour these from your hmbell Servants in the Lord."

Finally, an apology of the same sort that a great many white men and women of the time inserted into their letters—"my Riting is vary bad I whope yr honour will take the will for the deede"—following which we should add a conjunction such as *but* or *for*, and concluding, "I am but a poore Slave that writt itt and has no other time butt Sunday and hardly that att Sumtimes."

The writer had no opportunity to send the letter to the bishop soon after he or she completed it. We know this because it has a postscript dated

September 8, 1723, also addressed to "my Lord arch bishup." The postscript indicates that the writer lived in deadly fear that somebody in authority would discover the letter and deduce the identity of the writer—of the writers, perhaps, because after the salutation of the postscript, the remainder is in a handwriting that looks to be different, although it may simply be that the pen with which the person wrote the postscript was sharper than the pen with which the writer composed the body of the letter. Before the person wrote the postscript, he or she turned the page 90 degrees clockwise.

The postscript is shocking. It tells us (and told the bishop) about the writer's or the writers' friends' fears for their personal safety as enslaved residents of Virginia and what could happen to them if they were discovered doing something that displeased their enslavers. The postscript reads, "these with care," meaning that the person who wrote the letter and those on whose behalf she or he wrote had to be very careful, for "wee dare nott Subscribe any mans name to this for feare of our masters for if they knew that wee have Sent home to your honour wee Should goo neare to Swing upon the gallass tree"—be hanged from a tree or swing on a gallows. The writer of such a letter and anybody who might have signed it believed that he, she, or they could have been killed as punishment for criticizing the institution of slavery and its consequences for themselves, their families, and their souls.

Historians do not know of the existence of any other similar letter during the colonial period from an enslaved Virginian of such length or such visceral power. Historians do know, however, quite a bit about the conditions under which enslaved Virginians lived in the eighteenth century and enough about the religious instruction that some of them received that we can enlarge on what the "poore Slave" stated. Most of what historians know is from evidence created later in the eighteenth century, but it generally corresponds with what the writer of this letter stated.

For instance, several small schools for children of enslaved Virginians existed in the colony during the 1760s and into the 1770s. Thomas Bray and several associates in England sponsored the schools at the suggestion of Benjamin Franklin. The school in Williamsburg, the only one about which we know very much, functioned for more than a decade and taught about four hundred students to read and write, probably to do some rudimentary arithmetic, and to learn about the Protestant Christianity of the Church of England.

Contrary to what many people, including some historians, believe, it was never unlawful in Virginia to teach Black people, either free or enslaved, to read and write. Nor until 1830 was it ever illegal to open and run a school to teach enslaved people to read and write. Nevertheless, literacy among enslaved Virginians was undoubtedly always very low. As late as 1870, even after the brief operation of Freemen's Bureau schools for the children of enslaved men and women who had become free as a result of the Civil War, only about 10 percent of Black Virginians could read or write or even sign their names. (At that same time, about 40 percent of white Virginians could neither read nor write their names.)

About the religious lives of other enslaved Virginians, the white male directors of the Bray School reported to its British sponsors in 1762, "we think it is a pretty general Practice all over Virginia for Negro Parents to have their Children christened" if they lived "tolerably convenient to the Church or Minister, & some Times a great Number of Adults are baptized together in different Parts of the Country." That was often all that took place, though. "Slaves in this & the neighbouring Colonies are the chief Instruments of Labour," the directors continued, "& we fear that they are treated by too many of their Owners as so many Beasts of Burthen, so little do they consider them as entitled to any of the Privileges of human Nature; & indeed many Owners of Slaves, 'tho they may view them in a different Light & treat them with a great Degree of Tenderness, concern themselves very little or not at all with their Morals, much less do they trouble themselves with their religious Concerns." As soon as the children were old enough to work, their enslavers sent them into the fields or assigned them household labor or other tasks that fully occupied them from early morning rising to late evening bedtime, and many provided no proper religious instruction; some may not have even allowed enslaved people to attend local church services.

The quality and quantity of exposure to Christianity that enslaved Virginians enjoyed undoubtedly varied widely from place to place and from time to time, probably at the whims of individual enslavers or the willingness of clergymen to minister to enslaved people. In the autumn of 1759, a minister of the Church of England reported that one Sunday in his parish when white parents presented their children to be baptized, "some Negroes, as has been constantly the Custom, I believe, all over the Colony, advanced at the same Time to present theirs also." The minister noted that "they behaved modestly & orderly, neither crowding nor jostling their Betters." One of the church wardens, though, a man of importance in the parish, "thought proper to order them to withdraw."

The Black parents and their children, "tho with some seeming Reluctance," began to return to their seats, but the minister "called to them, when near half Way down the Isle, to stop & return." He told them that the church warden had "only intended to keep them at a due Distance from, & to caution them against intermingling with, the white People." That was the etiquette of slavery and also of racial segregation and discrimination later, after the end of slavery. The minister revealed in that part of his account that he shared some of the racist opinions of most white people of the time, that Black people should defer to their "Betters" and as an inferior class of people not intermingle with the white people.

As the Black parents and children began to return to the altar, the church warden announced that what the minister had said was wrong and "That his Meaning was, they should entirely be gone, that, as Warden, it was his Duty to preserve Order in that Place, & that he would not allow whites & Blacks to be baptized together." The minister nevertheless began the baptismal ceremony with the Black families standing where they had paused in the aisle when the church warden told them to stop and begone. The minister baptized the white children and believed himself duty-bound to baptize the Black children, too, but the church warden's orders had been expressed in such strong language (and probably with a loud or threatening voice) that the Black parents withdrew from the church with their children and "carried them all away unbaptized."

At about the same time that the minster and the warden faced off in an Anglican church, Presbyterian minister Samuel Davies concluded a decade-long ministry in Hanover County that was notable for his work to convert and minister to the Black men, women, and children, free and enslaved, who lived thereabouts. He also advocated teaching them to read and write.

For the same reasons that the "poore Slave" adduced, Black people, beginning about the time that Davies conducted services in Hanover County, began to attend services that itinerant Baptist ministers conducted in numerous areas of eastern Virginia. Some, but by no means all, Baptist ministers at the time welcomed Black members into their congregations, and some ministers even began to oppose slavery. So, too, did a few Methodists who then still considered themselves members of the Church of England. The founder of the Methodists, John Wesley, was an early English opponent of slavery. It is no wonder that by the end of the eighteenth century, Baptists and Methodists had made considerable success in ministering to Black Virginians, some free and some enslaved.

Alas, we know nothing for certain about what, if anything, the bishop of London did in response to the 1723 letter from the "poore Slave" in Virginia. Had the bishop done anything that threatened the existence of slavery in North America or even the enslavement of the author(s), we might have some evidence of that activity simply because it would have been extraordinarily unusual.

18

William Byrd and His Vine and Fig Tree

IN JUNE 1726, EXACTLY halfway between Bacon's Rebellion and the Declaration of Independence, William Byrd sat at his desk in his mansion at Westover plantation in Charles City County and wrote a letter to an English earl whom he had met during one of his several extended residences in England. Byrd is one of the most famous people who resided in colonial Virginia, unlike nearly everybody else whose experiences fill these pages. By 1726 Byrd was also among the wealthiest, most influential, and most literary residents of the colony. At the time of his birth, a few months before Bacon's Rebellion broke out, his young namesake father was already making himself wealthy trading with members of First Nations tribes on the frontier and probably selling captured tribal members to tobacco planters as enslaved laborers. When the fifty-two-year-old son wrote his letter in 1726, the family was at the top of colonial society.

Byrd wrote to the earl in a boastful, self-satisfied tone, "We abound in all kinds of provisions, without expence (I mean we who have plantations)." For the information of the earl, who had never seen and may not have known much about Virginia plantations, Byrd explained, "I have a large family of my own, and my doors are open to every body, yet I have no bills to pay, and half-a-crown will rest undisturbed in my pocket for many moons together. Like one of the patriarchs, I have my flocks and my herds, my bond-men, and bond-women, and every soart of trade amongst my own servants, so that I live in a kind of independance on every one, but Providence." The "trade amongst" the enslaved servants that Byrd mentioned probably indicated that he allowed them to raise chickens or other animals or perhaps raise fruits or vegetables that Byrd and the members of his family purchased. Many enslavers allowed their enslaved people to do that. Byrd concluded by adapting a Biblical phrase that several other elite Virginians also used: "we sit securely under our vines, and our fig-trees without any danger to our property."

Byrd distinguished himself and his family from almost everybody else in Virginia with the parenthetical phrase "we who have plantations," which enabled him, as he thought, to live independently of everybody else. By that, Byrd meant that he was the lord of his manor, that he ruled over the members of his family and his scores of enslaved laborers. He also helped rule the colony. Byrd had a lifetime royal appointment to the powerful Council of State, in which capacity he was an influential executive advisor to the royal governor, a member of the upper House of the General Assembly, and a judge of the General Court, the highest court in Virginia. Byrd's wealth and his social and political eminence derived largely from his earnings as owner of large tracts of Virginia land on which he produced tobacco and nearly all of the good things that he ate, and from the profits of which he purchased fine imported clothing, wines, books, and other items of luxurious living that very few other residents of Virginia could enjoy.

Byrd stated that he was independent of "every one," but he was actually utterly dependent on the enslaved men and women who toiled in his fields and enabled his household to function. Although being owner and manager of such a large amount of property and large number of workers was demanding work, Byrd was able to indulge his love of literature and science, and he acquired and enjoyed one of the largest libraries in the colonies. A writer of considerable literary polish, he strove to impress his neighbors and English friends, but he also used his status to exploit the vulnerabilities of serving girls in his household and at the taverns where he stayed when he was in Williamsburg helping to govern the colony. Byrd's sexual appetites and practices are well known because for many years he kept diaries (in a code that he contrived) that recorded not only the state of his health but his sexual exploits with and exploitations of serving women in Virginia and with fine ladies and also with women of the night—whores, he didn't mind calling them—when he was in England.

Despite his sins, Byrd was comfortable in his faith. As a member of the Church of England and believing that in essence he was a good man, a good husband, a good father, a good master, and a good servant of his king, Byrd

William Byrd (1674–1744), of Westover, had copies of this bookplate engraved and printed in England for the books in his library, which was the largest in the colony. (Library of Virginia)

knew that he had succeeded in obtaining all the blessings that a man could covet during a life in Virginia. Byrd was also secure in his belief that his soul would be saved after death. He undoubtedly believed that he was a man to envy, and it is very likely that his friends and neighbors did envy his wealth, his power, and his cultivated mind.

Virginia men and women who were fortunate to live as members of the elite of society looked and acted as if they were entitled to enjoy all the best things of life. With the wealth that Byrd had accumulated when he inherited his father's property and through the labor of other people, he enjoyed a high social standing, and he lived in high style. He even owned his own billiard table and noted once in his diary that after an argument with his wife, they reconciled when he gave her a "flourish"—had sex with her—on the billiard table. When his family later drew on that wealth to rebuild Westover after a fire, the mansion house was one of the largest, most elegant, and most beautiful brick houses in Virginia. Construction of the house and properly furnishing it, though, may have begun the tumble of the family into financial difficulties that the addiction to gambling of Byrd's namesake son exhibited and that eventually ruined the family finances entirely.

It is true that none of the plantation mansions in eighteenth-century Virginia even approached the magnificence of the great country houses and palaces in England, but the Virginia mansions served exactly the same purpose. They filled the landscape with unavoidable evidence that the owners of those mansions were much wealthier than their neighbors and that they were able to live in comparative luxury: to eat, drink, and dress better than everybody else; to have servants or enslaved people to cook, clean, and wait on them; to pay extended visits to family members and friends of their own social class; to marry members of other elite families and augment their wealth and further improve their social standing; to hire private tutors for their children or send some of their sons to England to obtain an education; and to enjoy a much higher social and political status than ordinary white Virginians who in the eighteenth century lived fairly plainly, in much smaller dwellings, and who did their own household and agricultural labor, oftentimes with no assistance or with only one or two hired or enslaved workers.

The big houses set the residents apart from and above everybody else, precisely as English aristocrats set themselves apart from the commoners. A boom in the construction of larger and more elegant mansions in the middle of the eighteenth century, when the Byrd family rebuilt Westover, signaled that the gap in wealth and social status between the very small number of elite families and everybody else was quite conspicuously increasing. And it all rested on the production of tobacco with the labor of enslaved men, women, and children.

Because of his great wealth and high status, Byrd was able to spend several years in England, some of them on business for the governor and Council of State, and he commanded two expeditions to survey the boundary line between Virginia and North Carolina. Byrd did not do any of the actual work of surveying. He was a gentleman who went along to direct the work of the other men and frequently quarrel with his counterparts from North Carolina who he believed were too ignorant or too selfish to see the wisdom of always doing things the way that Byrd demanded. We know all this because Byrd kept detailed records of the expeditions and later employed those records to write an account of the survey of the dividing line. In fact, he wrote two accounts. He circulated one or more manuscript copies of one of them among members of polite society in Virginia and England; and he circulated one or more manuscript copies of the other among close associates who he believed would share his delight in the salacious and risqué episodes and tropes of language that he enjoyed composing and reading.

19

The Air of a City

IN 1728 WHEN WILLIAM BYRD was the senior member of the Virginia commission that met commissioners from North Carolina to begin a survey of the boundary line between the two colonies, he stopped in Norfolk and purchased two kegs of wine and two of rum, 173 pounds of bread, and "several other Conveniencys" to supply the commissioners and surveyors. In one of the two narratives of the expedition that Byrd later composed and circulated among his friends, he wrote that twelve or fourteen oceangoing ships rode at anchor in the harbor of the little city the day he was there. He learned or already knew that residents of Norfolk carried on a brisk commerce with residents of the islands in the West Indies and shipped them beef, pork, flour, and lumber. The ships returned to Norfolk laden with salt, other supplies, and great quantities of rum.

Byrd commented that Norfolk was built on a flat plain on the banks of the Elizabeth River and that the city boasted large warehouses, docks, and wharves as well as straight streets for the merchants, ship carpenters, and the many artisans who resided there and furnished supplies to the ships and sailors who carried on the trade. He concluded from his observations that Norfolk had "the most ayr of a Town of any in Virginia." Another visitor eight years later observed that from all of their international commerce, the residents of Norfolk were "abundantly more refin'd" than Virginians elsewhere.

The port city was still small when the two visitors recorded their opinions. Byrd had lived in London for two extended periods during his life and certainly knew cosmopolitan urban life when he saw it. The name of the other visitor is not recorded, but on the whole he, too, was favorably

This cartouche of the 1751 Fry-Jefferson Map depicts the scene at a Virginia dock where tobacco planters talk with a merchant while enslaved men load hogsheads of tobacco aboard a ship. (Library of Virginia)

impressed. No data survives to admit of a reliable estimation of the size of the population when the men visited the town. By the 1770s, Norfolk had grown to be the eighth-largest city in the thirteen colonies that became the United States in that decade. The population then was about 6,000 people. No other town in Virginia even came close to having so many people in it.

Because Norfolk was the largest and busiest seaport in the colony, it also had the most varied population, but its population of enslaved people was probably a smaller proportion of the population than in the rural parts of Virginia. Across the Elizabeth River from Norfolk, the smaller city of Portsmouth also had merchants, ship chandlers, and artisans and professional men comparable to those in Norfolk. The Gosport neighborhood of Portsmouth at the time that the American Revolution broke out had several very large warehouses that Portsmouth merchant Andrew Sprowle owned. If a contemporary description of his warehouses was accurate and they were constructed of stone, he had to have had it quarried and shipped to Portsmouth because no suitable stone was to be found anywhere thereabouts. The expense of doing so must have been huge. Perhaps they were of locally fired brick, still expensive, but a more common building material. Sprowle's complex of buildings may have been the largest of its kind anywhere in Virginia because he was one of the most active mercantile men in the colony. In the mid-1770s, he chaired the informal association of merchants who met twice a year in Williamsburg to settle accounts with one another and tend to legal and political affairs in the capital.

Norfolk being a city on the Atlantic coast, it was vulnerable to hurricanes and floods. The October 18, 1749, issue of the *Maryland Gazette,* published in Annapolis, contains a long account of a hurricane that struck Norfolk at a time when no issues of the *Virginia Gazette,* which was published in Williamsburg, survive. The captain of the sloop *Hopewell* had taken refuge in Norfolk harbor rather than proceed to his intended destination because "meeting with excessive hard Weather, about 50 Leagues from the Cape"—Cape Henry—"and springing a Leak," he "was obliged to return, and put into *Norfolk* in *Virginia.*" The captain of the *Hopewell* provided the Annapolis printer "a melancholy Account of the Storm which happened very lately and has done incredible Damage near the Mouth of our Bay." The account of the storm reveals not only how strong the wind was and how high the water rose, but its detail of the damage contains much valuable evidence about the landscape and built environment of Norfolk.

The captain's report begins, "On Saturday Evening, the 7th of this Instant"—meaning of the same month—the "Wind began to blow hard, and about one or two in the Morning was very violent at N.E. with Rain, and still kept increasing; but the most violent of the Storm was from ten 'til two on Sunday. The Tide rose 15 Feet perpendicular higher than usual, forcing Ships and other Vessels ashore where the Water was never before known to flow; many of which are now so far from the Water, and some of them loaded, that it will cost as much as they are worth to get them afloat again, if it be practicable: Several new Ships were carried off the Stocks; all the Wharffs, and several Warehouses were carried away. A Warehouse of Col. *Tucker's,* 60 Feet by 30, having in it 90 Pipes of Wine and 40 Hogsheads of Rum on the lower Floor, and a Quantity of Corn and Oats in the Loft, was taken off it's Foundation, carried a Mile and a half from the Place where it stood, and landed upright on the other Side of the River, without any Damage to what was in it; this Warehouse passed by the *Hopewell,* the Eaves of it being about four Feet above Water, and touch'd her Quarter, without doing any Hurt. Wharffs with Anchors, lying on them of 1000 *lb.* Weight, were seen floating on the Water, and were carried away bodily, Stones and Timber together; and the River was almost covered with Lumber, Masts, Yards, Rales, Casks, &c."

"Some Gentlemen now at *Norfolk,*" the relation continues, "who were in *Jamaica* when the last great Hurricane happened there, which destroyed several Men of War, &c. say it was not so violent as this. The Tide kept continually fluxing, and run at a Rate of five Miles an Hour; it overflowed all their Streets, carried some small Craft near a Mile from the ordinary High Water Mark, and left some of them in Corn Fields."

The printer of the Annapolis newspaper also learned—it is not clear whether from the captain of the *Hopewell* or from some other source in Virginia—that at "*Hampton* much Damage is likewise done: A noted Tavern there" had eight feet of water in it, "and a Yawl was paddled through the Passage of the House." A yawl was a small vessel that four or six men propelled with paddles, but it might also have had a mast and a small sail. At the Back River near Hampton, according to the same report, three families drowned, including men, women, and children. Three ships were stranded ashore at the Capes, "and at *Norfolk* very few rode it out," or remained afloat during the storm.

Without the disaster and the report that a Maryland printer published, we would know very little about the storm or about the buildings, warehouses, docks, and other features of the seaport. That an 1,800-square-foot, two-story warehouse full of merchandise of various kinds floated all the way across the Elizabeth River was a remarkable event; but the reported size of the warehouse was remarkable, too, as was the quality of the construction that prevented water from entering and sinking the warehouse. The whole must have weighed as much as or more than a large ship. By law, a pipe was a wooden barrel that held 126 gallons of wine that should have weighed about 1,000 pounds; and a hogshead of rum should have contained 63 gallons and weighed perhaps 500 pounds. It was remarkable, too, that wharves floated away even though loaded with heavy iron anchors and piles of stones that ship captains placed in the lower hulls of their ships to provide ballast and keep a large ship without much heavy cargo upright in a brisk wind or a heavy sea.

Nothing like the city of Norfolk existed anywhere else in Virginia then or for decades thereafter. The smaller port cities of Hampton, Portsmouth, Dumfries, and perhaps Hobb's Hole and the river ports of Richmond, Portsmouth, Petersburg, Fredericksburg, and Alexandria were busy places of trade and waterborne commerce, but Norfolk outshone all of them until the nineteenth century. If the commercial interchange of the city's residents with other places in North America and the world had made them "abundantly more refin'd" than other Virginians who lived on farms or plantations or in small towns, they and the residents of other eighteenth-century cities and towns still had to put up with conditions that a twenty-first-century American would describe as intolerable.

The horses that drew carts and wagons through the streets of Norfolk as men and women carried on their commerce deposited manure everywhere every day. People threw the contents of their chamber pots into the streets, or they dumped the bodies of dead animals into the creeks that penetrated the shoreline of the city. They kept cows and chickens at their houses in town, and some probably kept swine, too. They burned wood to heat their buildings in cold weather, and they burned wood to cook all year long. Because infectious diseases spread more rapidly in towns and cities where people lived packed more closely together than in the countryside, many people of the time regarded the noxious smells as the cause of disease.

Residents of Norfolk later complained that the city council that initially met only once each year did little or nothing to keep the city safe or clean. One of the first ordinances that the council adopted in 1736, shortly after a royal charter created a municipal government for the borough of Norfolk, forbade residents from having wooden chimneys on their houses or places of business and fined any "Inhabitant whose Chimney shall blaise out." The city later purchased a small "water engine" and ordered people to keep leather buckets and hoses, ladders for scrambling onto rooftops to put out fires, and hooks for pulling down burning buildings to prevent the flames and embers from igniting other structures.

After the city of Norfolk burned on January 1, 1776, and was rebuilt after the end of the Revolutionary War, physical descriptions of the city remained much the same. A clever person who was fed up with conditions in

Residents of Norfolk and a few other colonial towns sometimes had fire engines such as this one operated by hand pumps to spray water onto a burning building. (Library of Virginia)

the city placed an advertisement in the local *Va. Chronicle, & General Advertiser* on July 3, 1794, over the signature Peter Police. "STRAYED or STOLEN," it began, "the Two Public FIRE ENGINES, belonging to this Borough: they have not been seen or heard of these nine months; they have no peculiar marks of description—excepting, that the last time they were used they were in very bad order, it is suspected they fled in company with the Overseers of the Streets."

Peter Police appended a note to his advertisement: "WANTED,—A few more thousand loads of FILTH (of any quality) to be distributed, in the most public and frequented parts of the Borough. Fish (if sufficiently stale) will be preferred, as affording a most agreeable flavor: It is hoped, the inhabitants in general will be so obliging as to fling every thing of this nature in front of their houses, particularly in the month of August, a period in which it is highly necessary to use every precaution, to guard against the complaints peculiar to the season." Peter Police almost certainly described the behavior of people of his time and of earlier times because other accounts of urban areas often contain similar descriptions.

An observer about the same time as Peter Police recorded that the residents of Norfolk drank enormous quantities of alcohol because "the water of Norfolk is reckoned very pernicious to the bowels when unmixed with spirit." He and other visitors commented that the city was filthy and full of evil smells. Not long after Peter Police published his announcements, "A Friend to Cleanliness" published a short letter in the *Herald, and Norfolk and Portsmouth Advertiser* of January 31, 1795. "I HAVE been in many Cities, Towns, and Villages in the course of my peregrinations," she or he wrote, "but never passed through so dirty or filthy a town as NORFOLK—the indolence of the magistracy must certainly be the cause; at least it is considered so by every foreigner that I have heard speak on the subject."

Similar descriptions and complaints about American towns and cities can be found in travel accounts and other documents throughout the eighteenth century. Indeed, when reading such sources, what begins to stand out is the rarity of comments, such as those that visitors to Philadelphia often made, about the cleanliness of that city when compared to all others. However refined the residents of Norfolk and other urban places in Virginia may have been or may have considered themselves, their built environment did not always look or smell refined.

20

The Head of Hampton

THE HUNDREDS OF THOUSANDS of original documents preserved in the Local Records Collection at the Library of Virginia include a set entitled Goochland County Free Negro and Slave Records. In that collection is a short note dated August 16, 1739, and signed by justice of the peace George Carrington. "These are to Certifie," it reads in full, "that Samuel Burton John Spears and Henry Sizemore this day brought before me the head of Hampton an outlaw'd Slave belonging to John Owen which said Slave they took up on Fighting Creek, near Collo: Randolphs Quarter, which said Slave they could not take without Killing of him."

A Virginia law enacted in 1723 entitled An Act Directing the Trial of Slaves, Committing Capital Crimes; and for the More Effectual Punishing Conspiracies and Insurrections of Them; and for the Better Government of Negros, Mulattos, and Indians, Bond or Free allowed men to receive compensation from a county if one of their enslaved people escaped from custody before or after conviction of a crime and was "killed or destroied" when somebody attempted to recapture the escapee. Owners of such fugitives or perhaps even justices of the peace could offer rewards for the capture of escapees, which is what the three white men named in the certificate claimed when they asked the justice of the peace to "Certifie" that they had taken Hampton and presented his head as evidence.

The 1723 law and the practices that arose in the capture of people who escaped from justice probably had origins in a law that the General Assembly enacted in 1701 and perhaps in even earlier laws and practices. The 1701 law concerned one person only, named Billy, who had escaped from his enslaver in James City County several years earlier and was rumored to be stealing and either damaging or destroying people's property ever since. The law attainted him—that is, declared him guilty without a trial—and stipulated "That whosoever shall kill or destroy the said negro slave Billy and apprehend and deliver him to justice in this colony and dominion, he, she or they shall be paid and allowed for the same by the publick one thousand pounds of tobacco." The law also declared that if Billy should be killed in an attempt to capture him, his enslaver "shall be paid by the publick four thousand pounds of tobacco, as is provided for a former act for the like cases."

In eighteenth-century Virginia, a county justice of the peace could issue a writ of outlawry and hue and cry that declared that somebody who had escaped from enslavement or from justice and was believed to be dangerous was an outlaw. Being declared an outlaw meant that the person was out of the law, or out of the protection of the law, which is what the word *outlaw* originally meant. The Virginia writ and practice built on two old English practices. Early English courts had declared as outlaws people who failed to appear in court after being summoned several times and denied them any future protections of the law. Originally, those were people involved in civil cases, not criminal cases. Hue and cry was another ancient process for publicizing the escape or elopement of a person, even for a free person who owed service to another as an apprentice or indentured servant. In Virginia, as the Goochland County certificate indicates, Samuel Burton, John Spears, and Henry Sizemore claimed the reward for capturing Hampton. They would not expect to be punished because they could not capture him "without Killing of him." Rather, they expected to be rewarded.

The large body of documents called Local Records in the archives of Virginia consists of city and county government records that the clerks of the localities deposited in the Library of Virginia for safekeeping and to enable people to use them for research. The state's Public Records Act makes clerks of courts and of local governments the sole, legal custodians of the official records that their governing bodies create. If for some reason, such as to remove from a courthouse or city hall bulky files of old records that government officials seldom have occasion to consult, the clerks must deposit them in the Library of Virginia. The law requires the Library of Virginia to make them available to anybody who wishes to read them. These records contain a vast deal more information on an enormous variety of subjects than clerks recorded in the official court order books, deed books, will books, and other bound volumes that are the most familiar records that historians and genealogists ordinarily use in their work. Collections with names like Free Negro and Slave Records can contain many different kinds of documents concerning the ownership, transfer of ownership, or free or enslaved status of individual people or groups of people. Or, as in this instance, a fatal ending to an attempted capture.

Perhaps some researcher with enough curiosity and time could search further into the surviving records of Goochland County, which an act of the General Assembly created in 1728, and locate additional information about the case of "Hampton an outlaw'd Slave." It can surprise even veteran researchers how much more information diligent searching in unfamiliar places can sometimes reveal. These largely unexploited local records, which men and women who wrote county and city histories in the nineteenth and twentieth centuries usually did not have access to, could be employed to enrich our knowledge of many aspects of life in Virginia that we still only vaguely or imperfectly understand.

We can also learn from episodes such as this that sometimes the practices of public officials in Virginia varied from the letter of the law or from practices that arose under the common law in England centuries before anybody in the kingdom ever knew anything about the American continent. Some of those practices, such as Virginia justices of the peace issuing writs of outlawry and hue and cry, created new quasi-legal processes that, like the common law itself, came to be accepted as legitimate through long-accepted usage. It is interesting in this regard to observe that allowing private citizens who had not been specifically deputized to kill an escapee who had been outlawed is not mentioned in George Webb's 1736 book, *The Office and Authority of a Justice of Peace*. The book was the first legal reference work published in Virginia and described the authorities and responsibilities of justices of the peace under the common law and statute law of England and the statute law of Virginia as it existed a mere three years before the death of Hampton, who was not the only person killed during an attempted capture in colonial Virginia.

21

Susannah Sanders Cooper and Her Tavern

IN SEPTEMBER 1744, Susannah Sanders Cooper submitted a petition to the House of Burgesses. She was then about fifty years old, give or take several years, and had lived somewhere in New Kent County, northwest of Williamsburg, for many years. She kept a tavern, or inn, where she provided rooms, dining, and fodder and stables for guests who were traveling through or had gone to the county seat to conduct business. It is likely that her tavern was near the county courthouse where the monthly meetings of the county court took place. Unfortunately for us, the office of the county clerk burned in 1787, which destroyed most of the archive of the county government and deprives us of an ability to reconstruct details of her life or learn more about the tavern.

Cooper had probably been born in York County, near the mouth of the York River. About 1711 she had married a widower named Isles Cooper, which was the beginning of her troubles. The Coopers had a son and may have had a daughter, but about three years after they married, Isles deserted Susannah and moved to North Carolina, where he reportedly married two more times. Both of those marriages were bigamous and therefore illegal because he was still married to Susannah. When and why she later moved to New Kent County and how she began keeping a tavern there are facts lost with the loss of the historical records. But she was a successful businesswoman and purchased land and her tavern and perhaps some enslaved people, too, to assist in serving customers at the tavern.

Because Cooper was legally still married, the property that she acquired was technically her husband's property. The common law of England, which was also the common law of colonial Virginia, decreed that married women, under what the common law called coverture, could not own property. Anything and everything that a woman owned when she married automatically became the property of her husband at the instant of marriage, and anything that she acquired afterward became his property, too.

Some fortunate women who had acquired property, had foresight, and could afford to hire a lawyer—and whose intended husbands were agreeable—negotiated marriage contracts, called separate equitable estates, before the marriage. The contracts placed actual ownership of a woman's property in the hands and under the control of a trustee who was legally bound to use it for her benefit. Her property would therefore be safe. Her husband could not sell it, commit what the common law called waste—cut down timber, sell anything that the property produced, or damage its value in any way—or do anything with the property that the trustee did not authorize, presumably with the agreement of the wife. Moreover, and this may have been the most important reason women wanted to create separate equitable estates before they married, a court could not order that the wife's property be seized by legal process to pay the husband's debts.

Susannah Cooper had no separate estate, so her tavern and all of her other property were constantly vulnerable to the whim of her unfaithful husband or to his creditors. It is likely that her neighbors in New Kent County knew of her legal situation, and because she conducted her business there for several—perhaps many—years, it is evident that they trusted her. Nevertheless, for reasons that we do not know, she decided in September 1744, and not at some earlier time, to submit a petition to the House of Burgesses in an attempt to have her legal vulnerabilities removed.

Petitioning was an ancient right that English kings had long recognized and that was common in the colonies. The process as it existed in Virginia at the time that Cooper submitted her petition required that on court day, when the county court met and a large number of people would be present, she post a notice at the courthouse of her intent to petition and stating the purpose of the petition. That allowed anybody who wished to support or oppose the petition to take action, such as present a counterpetition. The forms of petitions were standardized. From the earliest times when people submitted petitions to the king, petitions were always in the third person and opened with a statement of the humble status of the petitioner and closed with a humble prayer that the petition be granted.

Because the House of Burgesses, which received petitions to the General Assembly, probably would not have accepted one that was not in proper form, most people needed the assistance of an experienced legislator, a lawyer, or a county clerk to follow the customary and legal forms for preparing and presenting petitions. Cooper's petition, along with almost all of the petitions to the General Assembly that people presented before the 1770s, was lost when most of the legislative archive was destroyed during one of the British raids into Virginia during the Revolutionary War.

On Saturday, September 22, 1744, a member of the House of Burgesses, probably one of the two burgesses from New Kent County, submitted Cooper's petition. The summary of it in the official House journal reads, "That Leave may be given to bring in a Bill, to enable her to sue and be sued, as a Feme Sole"—an unmarried woman—"And also to enable her to purchase, sell, and dispose of the Negroes, and other Estate, in the same Manner as a Feme Sole may by Law; or that she may be otherwise relieved as this House, in their Wisdom, shall think reasonable."

The members of the House of Burgesses agreed that the prayer of Cooper was reasonable—one wonders how many burgesses knew her or knew about her legal predicament or may have even stayed at her tavern en route to or from Williamsburg—and ordered that Charles Carter "prepare and bring in a Bill." Carter had quickly emerged as one of the leading members of the House of Burgesses after he was first elected in 1736. He was a major landowner and a younger son of the late Robert "King" Carter, who had been the wealthiest landowner in colonial Virginia.

Carter introduced the bill a few days later, but after a preliminary discussion of it, members of the House of Burgesses referred it to a special committee to investigate and report on the existence of a living husband. When the special committee reported that Isles Cooper was still alive in North Carolina, the House of Burgesses approved the draft bill and scheduled it for a third and final vote on the following day, one month after the legislators received Susannah's petition. On that day, the House of Burgesses passed the bill and sent it to the Council of State, which was the upper House of the General Assembly. The council passed the bill, and on October 25, Lieutenant Governor Sir William Gooch signed An Act, to Enable Susannah Cooper to Sell and Dispose of Her Personal Estate, by Deed or Will, Notwithstanding

Her Husband, Isles Cooper, Shall be Living; and for Other Purposes Therein Mentioned.

The bill that Gooch signed endowed Cooper with legal rights to make contracts, to buy and sell property, to sue and be sued, and to have sole ownership of her property as if she were unmarried or as if "the said Isles Cooper was naturally dead." The common law had denied her those rights because she remained legally married, and he was still alive. In exchange for those benefits, the new law required her to relinquish her dower right, which is not to be confused with a dowery that a bride's family provided to the groom at the time of the wedding to secure his prosperity. By common law, a widow had a dower right to a one-third interest in the estate of her husband to support her after his death and during the remainder of her natural life.

Because the bill endowed Cooper with rights that the common law denied her, the legislators therefore appended to it a clause that the king always required in such circumstances to suspend its effective date pending a decision by the king and his Privy Council whether to approve or disapprove the bill. Gooch forwarded the bill to the Board of Trade in London and requested that the board and the king give their assent to the reasonable law. Gooch asked for a quick approval because, as he explained, "should her Husband return before this Bill is confirmed by His Majesty, all that she has, with great Industry and Honesty gott, since he left her, will be forced from her."

Undoubtedly, the bill produced debate among members of the Board of Trade and later among members of the Privy Council, to which the Board of Trade sent it for final consideration. Nobody took any official action in England, though, until February 1754, nearly a decade after Gooch sent the bill to the Board of Trade. At that time, on the advice of the king's legal counsel, the Privy Council denied the required approval in the name of the king and in effect vetoed the bill that granted Cooper independent ownership and control over the property that by her own endeavor she had acquired. That would have been a radical departure from the patriarchal relationship that English law imposed on married women.

We do not know for certain whether Susannah Cooper was even still alive when news of the decision reached Virginia later that year. In 1751, in a bizarre turn of events, Isles Cooper had sold the New Kent County property to one of his illegitimate North Carolina sons, John Cooper. Thereafter, John

Cooper owned and managed the tavern and the other property that Susannah Cooper had acquired during her years living alone. She might have died before Isles Cooper sold the tavern, but one hopes, if she were still alive at the time of the sale, that his son cared for her properly from the income of the tavern until she died on a date and at a place that the incomplete surviving records do not disclose.

22

One Pistole

LIEUTENANT GOVERNOR ROBERT DINWIDDIE announced in the spring of 1752 that he would thereafter require applicants for grants of what was called "unseated" land—land that white men had not claimed or cultivated according to Virginia law, most of which was in the west—to pay him a fee of one pistole before he would sign the grant, which was also called a patent. Dinwiddie and other colonial governors routinely collected fees for signing official government documents, and some governors of other colonies charged fees for signing land grants. Fee income supplemented the annual salaries of absentee royal governors, out of which they paid a portion to the lieutenant governor who resided in the colony and did all the work as the personal deputy of the king.

Dinwiddie's announcement began a dispute that lasted for several years. Influential members of the House of Burgesses objected that Dinwiddie did not have lawful authority to impose a fee on Virginians, that only the General Assembly, which included elected burgesses, had legitimate right to impose a new fee or tax on Virginians. Dinwiddie and the burgesses hired separate agents to argue their interests before the king and Privy Council in London. The controversy about the pistole fee was an important political event and also produced the earliest-known political slogan in Virginia history. William Stith, a minister of the Church of England and also president of the College of William and Mary, coined it. He angered Dinwiddie at a dinner party by raising his glass to toast "Liberty and property and no Pistole."

Pistole? What was that?

It was a Spanish coin. But Virginia was an English colony. Did pistoles circulate as currency in Virginia then? What would that inform us about daily economic life in mid-eighteenth-century Virginia?

Eighteenth-century Virginians used many kinds of money. English money—that is, pounds, shillings, and pence sterling—furnished the standard for trans-Atlantic commerce. All people valued commodities, merchandise, and trans-Atlantic debts in sterling. English gold and silver coins circulated in Virginia, but most studies of the colonial economy indicate that money of that most valued sort—specie—was often scarce. In daily transactions, eighteenth-century Virginians often exchanged tobacco notes, receipts that tobacco inspectors issued when a planter or a planter's agent carried tobacco to the public warehouse in each county to have it graded and stored until it could be loaded aboard ship. Tobacco notes circulated as an informal paper currency, rather like an IOU that could be signed over to other parties. Tobacco had been such an important commodity since the 1610s that people often stated the value of things in terms of pounds of tobacco and even levied taxes to be paid with specified amounts of tobacco rather than with money.

Spanish coins such as dollars, pistoles, pistareens, and pieces of eight (dollar coins cut into eight equal chips, or bits) also circulated in Virginia. Those coins may have been more common in Virginia than English coins at some times. A pistole was worth £1 2s 6d—one pound, two shillings, and six pennies—when Dinwiddie made his surprise announcement and began a protracted political controversy.

The practice of referring to the value of things in terms of Spanish coins was fairly common during the second and third quarters of the eighteenth century, and with the knowledge that Spanish coins were in circulation in the colony, it is less surprising that Dinwiddie demanded a pistole rather than a sum of English money or a certain number of pounds of tobacco, although people could pay the value of a pistole in any form of money. Incomplete files of Virginia newspapers record the bulk importation of pistoles in 1737, 1739, and 1767, and five bulk importations of pistareens in 1767 and 1768. In 1775 when the Virginia conventions that oversaw the transition of Virginia from an English colony into an independent American state began to issue money to pay the bills, one of the denominations of paper currency that the treasury issued had its value printed on it in three ways: fifteen pence; one shilling and three pence; and, in a misspelling, "A PISTEREEN." In the spring of 1776, an army officer assumed that he did not have to explain what he referred to when he mentioned in a newspaper announcement "the new PISTEREEN BILLS." Congress adopted the familiar Spanish name dollar for the currency of the new United States in 1785.

Paper money of several kinds also circulated in colonial Virginia, perhaps including some bank notes that the Bank of England issued. Before the French and Indian War (or Seven Years' War) that began in the 1750s, several colonial governments issued paper money, and during the war they issued more to pay soldiers and to purchase equipment and supplies. During the war, Virginia issued its first paper money, too. Paper money circulated at a discount. Its sterling value was less than its face value. The legal discount, or exchange rate, for Virginia paper currency at the middle of the eighteenth century was 125. A debt or payment for delivery of merchandise worth £100 sterling required £125 in Virginia currency to pay it.

Paper money from other colonies also circulated in Virginia but often at a greater discount than Virginia paper money. Governments usually allowed people to exchange paper money for gold or silver or to pay their taxes with colonial paper money. The farther away from the colonial government that issued the paper money, though, the greater the difficulty of redeeming it, the greater the risk in receiving it in payment, and therefore the greater the discount on the actual value, the purchasing power, of the note. The face value of a piece of paper money was always below that of sterling, and some of it was below that of Virginia paper currency.

All merchants, tobacco planters, small farmers, and most other men and women were well informed about the different discounts and rates of exchange among English sterling coins and paper money that the Bank of England issued, Spanish coins, various issues of colonial paper currency, and tobacco notes. And to top it all off, rates of exchange between sterling and currency (or current money, as paper notes were usually called then) often varied, and the value of the different kinds of goods and also of tobacco changed, too, which made estimations or calculations of profit or loss, debit or credit complicated and variable.

Sophisticated commercial operators everywhere and even small farmers on the frontier all knew how to evaluate and keep up to date on the fluctuating values of different issues of colonial paper money and tobacco notes. It was so much a part of their daily lives that they could not have imagined how strange and complex it would appear to a twenty-first-century person for whom such multiple and varying monetary values are almost unimaginable. It would be as if people in the United States today were comfortable with simultaneous circulations of United States dollars, Canadian dollars, Mexican pesos, English pounds, Japanese yen, and Euros that sometimes fluctuated in value more or less independently of one another and without warning.

The subject of money in colonial America all by itself gives the lie to common popular assumptions that life was simpler in earlier times. Life was certainly different then, and in many ways, but not necessarily simpler.

23

Lowe Jackson Hanged

THE FIRST NEWSPAPER to be published in Virginia was a four-page weekly that William Parks began printing in 1736. Entitled the *Virginia Gazette*, it included news of arriving and departing ships and reprints of items from newspapers in other colonies as well as from newspapers and learned publications in England and Scotland. The newspaper contained advertisements for the recovery of runaway servants and enslaved laborers; notices of books for sale in the printing office; lists of merchandise in stock in the shops of the little city of Williamsburg; reports on the deaths of prominent Virginians or of wars in Europe; information about crops or cloudbursts; and essays and verse (some of which rose to the dignity of poetry) that Virginians and other English-speaking men and women composed. Unfortunately, many issues of the *Virginia Gazette* do not survive, and for long periods of time we have no copies at all.

Colonial printers exchanged copies of their newspapers with one another, and as a result some very important and interesting accounts from mid-eighteenth-century Virginia were printed or reprinted in newspapers published in Annapolis, Maryland, and in Philadelphia, Pennsylvania. Newspapers from both cities regularly circulated in some areas of northern and eastern Virginia, particularly around Chesapeake Bay. A report that was published in the *Maryland Gazette* in Annapolis on May 10, 1753, bears an April 13, 1753, dateline and was very likely a reprint from the *Virginia Gazette* of that date, which does not survive.

"This Day," the full text of the article reads, "Lowe Jackson, pursuant to his Sentence, was executed at the Gallows near this City. He was drawn on a Sledge from the Prison to the Place of Execution, where he addressed himself to the Spectators, in a very moving and pathetic Speech on the fatal Consequences attending an early Habit of Vice, which had been the Means of bringing him to that shameful and untimely End. He appeared with a Composure of Mind, not frequently attending Men in his unhappy Circumstances, and died in a very penitent Manner. His Body being put into a Coffin, with this Inscription *Mercy! triumph over Justice,* was delivered to his Friends, and it to be interr'd in the county of *Nansemond,* where he was born." (The city of Suffolk absorbed the county of Nansemond in 1974.)

The loss of all the Virginia newspapers from the period as well as the loss of almost all of the eighteenth-century records of the General Court means that we have virtually no other information about Lowe Jackson, including knowledge of the crime for which a jury convicted him at a trial in the General Court. By the middle of the eighteenth century, Parliament had made scores of crimes punishable by death in England. Not all of those laws applied to Virginia, but many English laws enacted before the invasion of 1607 and some of the laws that Parliament passed after that time were in force in Virginia because the General Assembly or the courts had decided to incorporate them into Virginia law.

Virginia had fewer capital crimes when Lowe Jackson was hanged in 1753 than England had, but the number was large. In the 1770s, Thomas Jefferson drafted A Bill for Proportioning Crimes and Punishments Heretofore Capital. He reduced the number from about two dozen or more down to seven for which death remained the mandatory or an alternative punishment.

The hanging of Black or white convicted felons at the gallows in or near Williamsburg or of Black convicted felons at county courthouses occurred in nearly every jurisdiction every few years. Residents of Williamsburg, because the city was the site of all prosecutions of white Virginians, saw more hangings and corporal punishments than any other Virginians witnessed. In May 1765, for instance, on the very day that Patrick Henry made an incendiary speech in defense of the liberties of Americans when the House of Burgesses was considering the resolutions that he introduced to condemn Parliament for passing the Stamp Act, a visitor to Virginia who was on his way to the Capitol passed by the bodies of three men who had that day or the previous day been hanged at the same place where Lowe Jackson died twelve years before. The visitor then made his way to the Capitol and listened to Henry make his famous speech.

The December 15, 1768, edition of the *Virginia Gazette* that Alexander Purdie and John Dixon then published—the city had two newspapers at that time, both titled *Virginia Gazette*—reported that several "criminals were brought to their trials, and received sentence." In fact, the men were accused of committing crimes when they were brought to trial; they were not criminals until convicted, and one of them was, in fact, acquitted. The report is terse and provides no details about any of the men or of the felonies for which they were tried: "Edward Mason, from Amherst, for felony, guilty: Death. Peter Brown, from Lunenburg, for felony, guilty: Death. Richard Pearl, from Spotsylvania, for felony, guilty: Death. Andrew Leitch, from Spotsylvania, for manslaughter, acquitted. George Keale, from Goochland, for felony, guilty: Burnt in the hand. George Charge, from Frederick, for felony, guilty: Burnt in the hand." Following the string of six trials that day, three men hanged.

Hanging convicted criminals, much the same as dismembering the bodies of Salvadore and Scipio had been in 1710, was supposed to make other people think seriously about their behavior and take pains to avoid being guilty of any of the numerous offenses for which hanging—all hanging then was public—was the means of punishment. Hanging and lesser physical punishments—almost always public—such as cutting off ears, branding with a hot iron, cutting a letter into the face or hand—in the case of Hester Prynne in Nathaniel Hawthorne's novel *The Scarlet Letter*, a red letter A, for Adulterer—also served as visible warnings to people against committing serious infractions of the law and also in some instances to warn people against associating with a person who had already violated the law and whose physical scars informed people that they had been convicted.

It is very likely, too, that public humiliations such as the whipping that William Mills suffered in 1628 for robbing his master's store were painful as well. And the stripes that a whipping inflicted on the body often lasted a lifetime. Painful though whipping was, the punishment very seldom actually killed a convicted person. In the winter of 1751–52 in the frontier county of Augusta, a man named John Smith was charged with theft, but the county court decided that "the Goods by him taken are of Small Value and the sd. Smith praying for Corporal Punishment, It is Considered by the Court that for the sd Offence he receive on his bare Back at the Public Whipping post of this County thirty five Lashes well Laid on and it is said to the Sheriff that

Execution thereof be done Immediatly, and that he be remanded back to the Goal of this County there to remain until he Enter into Recognizance for his good behaviour for a twelve month & now Coming in the Sum of Fifty pounds with two Securities in the Sum of Twenty five Pounds Each."

Smith and the men who posted bond for him would forfeit the amount of the bond if he committed any offense at all during the following twelve months. Even for what evidently amounted to a minor crime, Smith paid with public infliction of painful permanent stripes on his back rather than risk some even more painful or disfiguring punishment if he had been tried and found guilty.

In the same county in May 1768, an enslaved man named Tom was tried for stealing one dark bay horse and bridle, two beaver hats, one "Large Bag of the price of Two Shillings," one rifle, one pair of stockings, and one book. The court found him "not Guilty of the said Charge unless the Stockings he Confessed to." For confessing to taking the stockings, the court "ordered that the Sheriff take him to the Whiping Post and there to receive Thirty nine Lashes and to have his Ear Cropt"—cut off—"and that the Execution thereof be done Immediately." Losing one's ear signaled for life that the person had been convicted of a crime.

Small wonder, then, that twelve years earlier, Margaret Campbell, also of Augusta County, "made Oath that the left Ear of her Son James Beard about Eight years old was Bit of by a Horse, Which is on her Motion Ordered to be Certified." She put it on record that her young son was not a convicted felon, which is what his physical appearance for the rest of his life suggested, but the victim of an interaction with a farm animal.

One other thing that the newspaper report of the hanging of Lowe Jackson in 1753 suggests is the importance of tales of repentance that people could read or hear and cause them to think about their responsibility for their own future actions. Such narratives already filled novels and plays for readers of the English language and probably provided clergymen with meat for their sermons about good, moral, Christian behavior.

24

Long and Painful Service During the War with France

On May 28, 1754, a company of soldiers from Virginia under the command of a young militia colonel, George Washington, encountered a small party of French soldiers and some of their allies from one of the First Nations tribes east of Fort Duquesne, the French fortification at what is now Pittsburgh.

The previous autumn, Lieutenant Governor Robert Dinwiddie had sent Washington into what is now northeastern Ohio to order that the French withdraw from the territory that Virginia claimed under the authority of the royal charters that had created the colony. Under those charters, Virginia claimed all of what became the Midwest and a large part of the unexplored west all the way to the Pacific Ocean. Washington's mission did not achieve its objective, so early in 1754 Dinwiddie ordered Washington west again. The colonel marched at the head of a small party of militiamen through southern Pennsylvania toward the French fort. The French defeated Washington in May, and his small party took refuge not far away at the Great Meadows in a makeshift fortification that they called Fort Necessity.

On July 3, after the French attacked the fort, Washington had to surrender his force to save the men who had survived. One of the men under Washington's command that day was Timothy Conway, who in 1774, twenty years later, petitioned the General Assembly for financial relief from the wounds that he received during the ensuing war between Great Britain and France, which in Britain was called the Seven Years' War and in the American colonies the French and Indian War. Conway's undated petition with an accompanying enclosure from a lieutenant under whom he served that confirmed what Conway stated was presented to the House of Burgesses on May 17, 1774, and is preserved in the Colonial Papers, Petitions, Record Group 1, Library of Virginia.

During the colonial period and until after the Civil War, Virginia did not have departments of government to which people could appeal for assistance or for a redress of a grievance. They petitioned the General Assembly for relief or, as Susannah Cooper had done in 1744, for passage of a special law on their behalf. As with Cooper's petition, Conway's is in the formal third person, but unlike her petition, which indicates that she had enjoyed considerable success under serious legal disabilities, his petition contains a story of patriotic dedication and severe and painful loss.

Conway's petition recited that he was "at the Battle of the meadows under the Command of Colo. George Washington, Received a wound through the wrist of his Right arm, which greatly endangered his Life, and was therefore discharged the Service."

Several months later, and "Struggling under every difficulty Consequent of his distressed Circumstance, his wound having discharged several peices of Shatter'd Bone, and thinking himself, so much Recovered, that he Could again serve his Country," Conway reenlisted "into the Ranging Company Commanded by Capt. John Ashbey in the year 1755, in which service he Continued about eighteen month, when the sd. Company were disbanded." Rangers were small parties of scouts or guides who usually moved about and operated at a distance from the main body of an army—in that case, the large British expedition that General Edward Braddock commanded in a second failed attempt to capture Fort Duquesne. On that expedition, the French and their allies attacked again, not far from the Great Meadows, and killed the general. Colonel Washington was present and heroically saved the remainder of the men and guided them home.

Timothy Conway, his petition continued, "then inlisted again into the Virginia Regiment, and Continued in that service, in Capt Waggoners Company till after General Forbeses Campaign, in the year 1758," when the British defeated the French and renamed the site of the French fort Pittsburgh, for William Pitt, also known as the "Great Commoner," who was then the king's first minister.

The petition concluded: "The many hardships your Peititioner Suffered during that long and Painfull Service Occasioned his wound to Break out into an ulcer which was thought incurable and was again discharged the service." Conway complained (politely) to the General Assembly that he had never "Received the Smallest assistance, or support, from his Country, and it is with Reluctance that he Sues for assistance at this time, but being now under the weight of old age and unable to Labour for support of Life," he had no other option.

When a petition such as Conway's reached the House of Burgesses, somebody read it aloud—probably one of the burgesses from the petitioner's county of residence—and the Speaker of the House almost always referred it to the appropriate committee, in this case, to the Committee of Claims. At every session of the assembly, the Committee of Claims considered numerous petitions on a wide variety of subjects. If the request of a petition seemed reasonable, the committee would so report to the full House. Some petitions, as Susannah Cooper's, resulted in the burgesses ordering one or more of their members to draft a bill to grant the petitioner's request. Petitions on which the Committee of Claims reported favorably did not always result in the drafting and enactment of a law as Cooper's did. Instead, if the full House of Burgesses accepted and agreed with the committee's recommendation, the House ordered it to be recorded in what they called the Book of Claims, which provided the treasurer of Virginia warrant to pay the sum of money that the committee had decided that the petitioner should receive.

Conway received nothing. Not because he was not deserving, but because one of the political controversies that led to independence occurred in May 1774 during that session of the General Assembly, and the royal governor abruptly dissolved the assembly—put it out of business—before it concluded its work. The busy committee had not completed its review of Conway's petition or come to a decision about his claim. If Conway had petitioned one or more years earlier, he almost certainly would have received a sum of money in compensation or perhaps a smaller annual sum to support him in his crippled old age.

Nobody who petitioned the General Assembly in 1774 received any relief. A few of those other petitions also survive, including several from people with claims that also stemmed from the Battle of Great Meadows in 1754. Archer Dent, according to his petition, "Served as a Private Soldier in the Virginia Regiment Commanded by Colo. Washington upwards of Seven years; that whilst he was in his Majesties Service he received three Different Wounds which has Disabled him in such a Manner as to render him

Incapable of supporting himself, and that he is at this time Destitute of the Common Necessary's of Life." The docketing on Dent's petition indicates that the Committee of Claims completed its review of the petition and prepared to recommend to the full House that he be "Allowed £25 present Relief and £5 per Annum during Life."

John Fraser was also at Fort Necessity in 1754 at the time of the Battle of Great Meadows. He was a resident of Pennsylvania and had since died, but in 1774 his widow, Jane Fraser, petitioned the General Assembly of Virginia for relief, for financial compensation. Her petition reported that her "said husband had been concerned for many years in a trade with the Indians on the River Ohio, where he was in the Month of June 1754, when he received Intelligence that hostilities were Commenced or likely to take place between this Colony & the said Indians, and thought it prudent to retire from that Countrey with his effects."

John Fraser "Accordingly set off with his goods carrd. by sevl. Horses to Return to Pensylvania, & on his way, met with this Colony Troops" under the command of George Washington, who "expecting an Attack from the Enemy, pressed the sd. John Fraser's horses to be emploied in bringing some stores and a partie of men from Mr. Christopher Gists, & also in bringing Amunition & Provisions from Col. Cresaps to the sd. Meadows for Protection of the Forces, in consequence of which the sd. John Fraser was detained at the Meadows, until the Battle happened at that place & the Virga. Troops Capitulated, when all the sd. John Frasers goods were taken & Plundered by the Enemy (A particular account of which, taken the day before the sd. Engagemt. amounting to £2252.4 is hereto annexed) and were totally lost to him." The "particular account" does not survive. The sum named is surprisingly large for a man engaged in trade with Ohio Valley tribes. Perhaps he had more than a few valuable horses with him.

Jane Fraser's petition continued, "the sd. John Fraser soon after came to the City of Wms.burg to Petition for a Recompense for his said losses, the event of which yr. Petr."—your petitioner—"is wholly unacquainted with," but she recalled that he had been offered half the stated value of his horses and goods. Thereafter, she continued, "the said John Fraser being of a dilatory disposition, never concerned himself further in the sd. Claim during his life, Nor should yr. petr. have undertaken this long and fatiguing Journey, or troubled this Honble House on the Subject"—she had traveled all the way from somewhere in Pennsylvania to Williamsburg to present the petition and perhaps speak on behalf of her claim—"but that she hath been lately called on by two Merchts. in Philadelphia for about seven hundred & fifty pounds, now due for the Purchase of part of the sd. goods, wch. she cannot discharge, without the total ruin of her self & seven young children."

Jane Fraser also received nothing. Her petition reached the House of Burgesses on May 25, 1774, the day before the governor dissolved the assembly, so the Committee of Claims never even had time to begin considering it.

Soldiers and sailors who are killed or wounded are not the only casualties in war. Their wives and widows as well as their children and orphans are also casualties and have to live with the loss of a husband and father and of the income that he is no longer able to earn to support them. It is entirely possible that more women and children than men could be classified as casualties of war.

The raids that members of First Nations tribes conducted against frontier settlers during the Seven Years' War cost the lives and livelihoods of hundreds of white Virginians, who in return sought out and killed some of the people who had attacked them or killed anybody they suspected of being dangerous. Virginians fled from large swathes of the northwestern settlements during the war and consequently suffered in other ways than the soldiers and members of their families. The fighting dragged on in various parts of North America and between France and Great Britain in other parts of the world until the two nations concluded a peace in 1763. One article of that treaty required the French to cede to Great Britain all of its mainland claims in North America east of the Mississippi River. In effect, that treaty between those two kingdoms made the Mississippi River, beyond which was New Spain, the western boundary of Virginia.

25

All Was Not Tobacco

IN 1764 AND 1765, Lord Adam Gordon, a British army officer, made a tour of the American colonies. Early in the latter year he spent a few days in Virginia. "Norfolk," he wrote in his journal, "is the Port of most traffick in Virginia, it contains above four hundred houses, has depth of Water for a Forty Gun Ship, or more, and conveniences of every kind for heaving down, and fitting out large Vessels, also a very fine Rope-Walk." A manuscript copy of the journal is in the King's Manuscripts in the British Library in London, 213, folios 1–69, and a transcription of that copy is in the Library of Congress. It has been published as "Journal of an Officer's [Lord Adam Gordon's] Travels in America and the West Indies, 1764–1765," in Newton D. Mereness, ed., *Travels in the American Colonies* (New York, 1916), 367–453, quotation on 406, with the bracketed words as part of the title.

Norfolk harbor was and is famous for having sufficiently deep water for oceangoing ships and is now the home port of what is purported to be the largest fleet of naval vessels in the world. That in 1765 it had "conveniences of every kind for heaving down, and fitting out large Vessels" means that it had a dry dock for taking large ships out of the water so that workmen could scrape off barnacles and repair hulls by resting the ships on the keel and one side and then on the keel and the other side—heaving down, or careening the ship, it was called. Norfolk also had "a very fine Rope-Walk" from which men wove threads or strings of hemp fibers into long and strong ropes that all sailing ships used for adjusting the rigging or tying the ship up to a pier. Virginia farmers grew hemp for sale to England but also for making rope for local use and for sailing ships.

Norfolk had all of the necessary skilled workmen for those various tasks, as well as for "fitting out" large ships. Ship chandlers supplied butts of fresh water and barrels of salt pork, salt beef, and ship biscuit, the hard-baked bread that could be packed in barrels and was a staple of the diet of eighteenth-century sailors. Virginia and North Carolina farmers regularly sold livestock to agents who transported the animals to Norfolk for slaughter and to be salted down and packed in barrels for transport elsewhere or to feed the crews of commercial and naval vessels.

Inasmuch as we know from the ship captain's report of the hurricane of 1749 that "Several new Ships were carried off the Stocks" during that storm, Norfolk also had the skilled people and access to the essential materials to build large sailing ships. Norfolk was probably the only place in Virginia in the middle of the eighteenth century where men constructed ships capable of engaging in trans-Atlantic trade, but men constructed smaller ships in many other places in the colony.

Building and repairing large ships required many laborers and skilled craftsmen to shape timbers and planks and experienced shipwrights to direct the labor of men who did the work. Shipbuilding required able blacksmiths to make or repair the various iron fittings that large, complex ships required. All of those facilities depended on hired white men or hired or enslaved Black men to do much of the actual labor. It may be, too, that Norfolk had one or more factories that produced canvas for the sails, although perhaps local shipfitters or ship chandlers sent orders to factories in England or elsewhere to import the necessary sailcloth for the different sizes and riggings of ships.

In addition, men had to cut down trees elsewhere and float or drag them to the site of construction, where other men would saw or shape them to fit, both of which were exacting and difficult labor. Other men hauled up from North Carolina barrels of pitch, or tar, which they had boiled from the sap of pine trees. Shipwrights used the tar to caulk the seams of wooden watercraft of all sizes and to tar the rope lines to protect them from salt spray. Still other men, called coopers, made the barrels to hold the food and drink for the crew and to contain the cargo, and still others filled water butts with the tannin-rich water of the Great Dismal Swamp, which though dark and unappetizing in appearance did not breed dangerous populations of disease-bearing organisms in hot weather.

At some of the smaller ports in mid-eighteenth-century Virginia, ship captains would probably have been able to purchase supplies such as barrels, casks of salt beef or pork, casks of small beer or rum for the sailors to drink, and maybe even ship biscuit. The availability of those supplies in turn indicates that Virginia families raised ample quantities of beef and pork or produced small beer or maybe even baked ship biscuit for sale to the ship captains.

We know for certain that the importance of fishing and short-distance trade among small places along the rivers and within Chesapeake Bay required many kinds of watercraft, each of which skilled people constructed by hand from locally available timber, cordage, iron ship fittings, and canvas. The variety of sailing ships of domestic manufacture in Virginia was probably quite wide even without counting mid-sized and large vessels built elsewhere that engaged in coastal or trans-Atlantic trading.

The colonial Virginia landscape was consequently a varied one with many highly skilled workmen, not an endless succession of the tobacco plantations for which the colony was famous. Men worked at small to medium-sized ironworks in several parts of the colony to smelt iron ore and cast it into blocks, called pigs, for the use of blacksmiths or to send by wagon or cart to one of the towns or cities where smiths could manufacture iron ship fittings or other implements. The ironworks, in turn, relied on other working men to extract the ore from the earth, others to cut timber and turn it into charcoal, and still others who fired the furnaces and tended them until the molten iron drained out and cooled into pigs. Nearly every household required cooking implements of iron, as well as vessels or utensils of pewter or pottery, and every farmer required iron tools with which to work the soil.

Small market towns dotted the countryside of Virginia by the middle of the eighteenth century, and in those places as well as on the larger plantations blacksmiths made agricultural and household implements that farmers and plantation workers needed. Wheelwrights practiced the fine craft of making wooden wheels or constructed and repaired wagons and carts. Carters drove carts and wagons to transport items of merchandise and agricultural produce to local or distant markets. Men cut and shaped masts and other heavy timbers for shipment through Norfolk to the West Indies, and still other men in Virginia as well as in North Carolina barreled tar—called naval stores—for sale to ship chandlers or for export through Norfolk.

In Henrico and Chesterfield Counties, near the market town of Richmond, men dug soft, high-sulfur coal from shallow surface mines for use in small industries and for sale. One of the entrepreneurial mine owners, Samuel Du-Val, advertised for sale as far away as Rhode Island that the coal from his mines was as good as any that could be shipped in from Newcastle, England. In small households and on large plantations, people spun wool, flax, or cotton into thread, wove thread into cloth, and sewed cloth into garments. Before the American Revolution, large planters imported fine clothing from England, but they also purchased coarse cloth for fabricating clothing for enslaved laborers. In short, the countryside as well as the small towns and larger ports provided work and livelihoods for thousands of people who seldom or never worked in a tobacco field.

Many free and enslaved men worked in agricultural fields without producing a single pound of tobacco, and many free and enslaved women also did work that was essential to their families and to the economy without working in a tobacco field. In areas of northern and interior Virginia where the soil was less suitable for profitable tobacco production than in the older regions of southeastern Virginia, a good many eighteenth-century planters (including George Washington) gave up on tobacco cultivation and raised small grains such as wheat, oats, barley, or corn—what they often still called Indian corn because when English-speaking people of the time referred to corn, they usually meant small grains generally. Customs records indicate that exports of small grains through the one port of Norfolk from 1768 to 1772 had a total value of £130,000 sterling.

It never had been all tobacco. Many Virginia planters experimented with various other crops than tobacco to diversify the Virginia economy, even during the seventeenth century. Some seventeenth-century Virginians produced potash for export. They caught a wide variety of fish and preserved them with salt—Washington did that in the eighteenth century, too, as well as constructed and operated a distillery. Some seventeenth-century Virginians, including Governor Sir William Berkeley, harvested native grapes and made wine that they boasted was of good quality. Berkeley also cultivated mulberry trees and imported larvae of the silkworm (called silkworm seed) to produce silk in Virginia. He actually presented a sample of silk that he had produced to King Charles II in the 1660s.

So did another Virginia planter, Edward Digges, who served briefly as governor in the 1650s, between Berkeley's two administrations. Digges was renowned for the high quality of the sweet-scented tobacco that he produced on his York County plantation, and he sold it for so high a price that he became even more wealthy than he already was when he moved to Virginia. He was fortunate to reside in the very best part of Virginia for growing the most prized strain of tobacco.

For several years, Digges also produced silk in some abundance. He distributed silkworm seed to other planters and encouraged them to begin production on their own plantations. He imported two skilled Armenian silk workers from the Ottoman Empire and by 1654 was regarded as the premier producer of silk in Virginia. To a collection entitled *The Reformed Virginian Silk-Worm* that was published in London in 1655, a friend contributed a report from Digges and even included a poem that lauded his achievements. Digges presented Charles II with more and better-quality silk than Berkeley did. Digges was equally at home and equally well known in London as in Virginia. In December 1660, a few months after Charles II took the throne, he appointed Digges to the Council of Foreign Plantations, the forerunner of the Board of Trade that during the first two-thirds of the eighteenth century directed colonial affairs for the king.

It was never all tobacco. The Virginia countryside exhibited hundreds of examples of small industry and many other and varied enterprises.

26

John Wayles's Neighbors and His Families

JOHN WAYLES LIVED on his large plantation in Charles City County, not far from Williamsburg and not far from Westover, the seat of the wealthy Byrd family. Wayles had a family, he planted tobacco, and he acquired several large properties in the Blue Ridge Mountains, but he supplemented his income by collecting debts that men in his extended neighborhood owed to the English mercantile firm of Farrell and Jones. On August 30, 1766, after more than a year of financial difficulties that political and economic crises generated, Wayles reported to Farrell and Jones on the problems that the Virginia men who owed them money then faced. The letter is in Treasury Class 79, Bundle 30, in the National Archives of the United Kingdom, formerly known as the Public Record Office (PRO), with other documents relating to the claim of J. T. Warre, surviving partner of Farrell and Jones, against the executors of the estates of John Wayles and Richard Randolph. John M. Hemphill II discovered and published the letter with abbreviations and contracts expanded as "John Wayles Rates His Neighbours," *Virginia Magazine of History and Biography* 66 (1958): 302–6.

Wayles reported to Farrell and Jones that their creditors had numerous difficulties in paying their debts to one another as well as to their English business associates. One especially prominent local resident actually went about "Armed to protect himself from the Sheriff." He feared that the sheriff might any day appear with a court order to seize some or all of his property to pay his back taxes or to pay the men from whom he had borrowed money or purchased enslaved laborers or other valuable commodities on credit. For such information as that, Wayles's letter is intrinsically interesting; but it is also interesting because in one paragraph he vividly described the rapid and impressive recent rise in the social status and elegant lifestyles in the residences of the local elites and disclosed one of the reasons why they were all or nearly all deeply in debt.

"Within these 25 Years," Wayles explained, "£1000. due to a merch^t was looked upon as a Sum imense and never to be got over. Ten times that sum is now spoke of with Indifference & thought no great burthen on some Estates. Indeed in that Series of time Property is become more Valuable & many Estates have increased more then tenfold, But then Luxury & expensive living have gone hand in hand with the increase of wealth. In 1740 I don't remember to have seen such a thing as a turkey Carpet in the Country"—a carpet manufactured in Turkey and imported into Virginia, probably through England—"except a small thing in a bed chamber, Now nothing are so common as Turkey or Wilton Carpetts"—carpets made with a fine weave. "All this is in great measure owing to the Cred^t which the Planters have had from England & which has enabled them to Improve their Estates to the pitch they are Arrivd at, tho' many are ignorant of the true Cause."

Wayles continued, "In 1740. no man on this River"—on the banks of the James River—"made 100 hh^d of tobacco"—hogsheads were the large wooden casks that tobacco planters packed with as much as 1,000 pounds of tobacco for shipment to and sale in England—"now not less then six exceed that Number." If mercantile houses such as Farrell and Jones had difficulty collecting the money that they had extended to the planters in the form of credit, Wayles explained, it was the fault of the merchants for extending credit beyond the abilities of many planters to pay, especially after many of them had spent lavishly to build and furnish their large, new mansion houses.

The easy credit that Wayles described, which English mercantile firms made available to Virginia planters in exchange for the profits that the merchants anticipated from the sale of Virginia tobacco, had enabled planters to purchase increased numbers of enslaved people from Africa or from their neighbors; buy expensive carpets, furniture, and clothing from England; and put up large new mansion houses. Most of the largest and best known of the plantation mansions in Virginia date from the middle decades of the eighteenth century, such as the rebuilt Westover (the Byrd family), Shirley (the Carter family), and Berkeley (the Harrison family) in Wayles's own Charles City County; Carter's Grove (the Burwell family) in James City County; and Rosewell (the Page family) in Gloucester County.

The mansion at Shirley Plantation, in Charles City County, was probably begun in the 1720s at the beginning of the great boom in construction of plantation mansions in Virginia. (Library of Virginia)

Virginia tobacco planters often had difficulty paying their debts to British mercantile firms. Either a bad year when the tobacco crop failed or another year when they harvested so much tobacco that the price per pound fell sharply could force planters to seek an extension of credit from the mercantile houses that marketed their tobacco in England. In good years, planters might make a profit, but all agriculture was risky, and planters seldom enjoyed a long run of good weather, bountiful (but not too bountiful) crops, and high prices.

The strains of being in a long-term condition of debtor gave many Virginia families constant aggravation. The debts that planters incurred in participating in the tobacco trade and as a consequence of their increasingly plush style of living plagued some Virginia families for decades. The debts became an issue in the new state's politics during and after the American Revolution. Thomas Jefferson later condemned the merchants because "These debts had become hereditary from father to son for many generations, so that the planters were a species of property annexed to certain mercantile houses in London." Indeed, Wayles's letter to the firm of Farrell and Jones survives because after the American Revolution it was evidence in a claim that the surviving partner of the firm filed against the estates of Wayles and another very prominent local planter.

Thomas Jefferson knew as much as anybody about planter indebtedness. He was a debtor, too, all of his adult life. He actually knew in detail about the debts of Wayles's estate. On the first day of January 1772, Jefferson married Wayles's young, widowed daughter, Martha Wayles Skelton, who inherited much of the Wayles estate and a very large number of Wayles's enslaved people when her father died in the next year. One of those enslaved people was also one of Wayles's own daughters, Sally, half-sister to Jefferson's new wife. Wayles apparently had about half a dozen children with an enslaved woman, Elizabeth, or Betty, Hemings, whose father was reportedly a white ship captain named Hemings who was engaged either in the tobacco trade or in the slave trade or perhaps both.

Sally Hemings was a newborn baby when Martha Jefferson inherited her. That is to say, when Thomas Jefferson inherited her because he and Martha Wayles Skelton apparently executed no separate equitable estate before they married. When Martha Jefferson died in 1782, Thomas Jefferson came into full possession of her father's several thousand acres of land and enslaved people, including his late wife's half-sister, and £4,000 of debts.

Long after the death of Martha Jefferson, Thomas Jefferson and Sally Hemings apparently had several, perhaps as many as seven, children. Some of them lived in slavery at Jefferson's Monticello or at his rural retreat, Poplar Forest, until his death in 1826, but some of them left and had such light-colored skin that they moved out of Virginia and passed as white people.

27

The Candidates

ROBERT MUNFORD WROTE a play in 1770 and entitled it *The Candidates; or, the Humours of a Virginia Election, A Comedy*. It is short and unsophisticated, has three acts, and is generally regarded as one of the earliest comic plays in American literature. It depicts an election for members of the House of Burgesses late in the colonial period. Munford was then in his thirties, was a veteran of the war with France, and had represented Mecklenburg County, Virginia, on the border with North Carolina, in the House of Burgesses for five years. He remained a burgess through 1775. Munford's son published the play, another that Munford wrote about 1777, and several poems in 1798, about fifteen years after Robert Munford died. We have no evidence that anybody ever performed *The Candidates* during Munford's life.

The main characters in *The Candidates* are all caricatures: Mr. Worthy—who decides to leave the legislature but later changes his mind—Mr. Wou'dbe, Mr. Strutabout, Mr. Smallhopes, and Sir John Toddy, the local ne'er-do-well who squandered his promise. The local electoral politics that Munford described may or may not have been an accurate representation of exactly how elections for members of the House of Burgesses were conducted late in the colonial period. It seems reasonable to conclude that in general it probably was. Through numerous references to the play in twentieth-century scholarship, *The Candidates* has contributed to the modern popular image of public life in eighteenth-century Virginia.

More importantly, the truly remarkable group of national leaders from Virginia who gained fame during and after the American Revolution—George Washington, Peyton Randolph, James Monroe, John Marshall,

James Madison, Richard Henry Lee, Thomas Jefferson, and Patrick Henry—appeared to prove that public life in colonial Virginia had been a superior school for the art of statecraft. It was. A much larger second tier of state leaders who gained lesser fame included men who in other times or places would probably have become better known and retained their fame longer if they had not labored in the shadows of the first tier.

Our national and state historical memories give credit to those men and to the political education and experience that they gained in Virginia for creating the American system of representative democracy. If we look closely at the political world in which they came to maturity, though, we see that it did not at all resemble what we like to imagine, and it was not a prototype for what came later. Colonial Virginians did not enjoy a democratic society or a democratic politics. The society was highly stratified socially and economically, and its politics and political institutions both reflected and created that stratification.

Members of the House of Burgesses were the only elected public officers in the colony. The king and his London bureaucracy appointed the governor, the members of his Council of State (who served as his executive advisors, as members of the upper House of the General Assembly, and as judges of the highest and only appellate court in Virginia), as well as many other important public officers, such as the attorney general. Elections for burgesses did not happen on a regular or predictable schedule. The royal governor or his deputy, the lieutenant governor, decided when to hold elections and also called the assembly into session when he thought it wise or necessary. During the eighteenth century, elections took place at roughly three- to five-year intervals, and the assembly only occasionally met, usually for short sessions, not annually or on any other schedule.

Government and politics were not at all democratic. To the extent that they were even representative, they represented almost exclusively the class of prosperous tobacco planters. Virginia's 1736 election law permitted only adult, white males who owned a certain minimum amount of land to vote—one hundred acres of land or fifty acres of land and a house in the countryside, or a lot or part of a lot in either of the two incorporated cities, Williamsburg and Norfolk. No women, no members of First Nations Tribes, and no poor people of any race or place could ever vote.

Only about two-thirds to three-quarters of adult white male Virginians may have owned enough land to qualify to vote for members of the House of Burgesses, and at any given election about half to three-quarters of qualified men actually voted. That was a pretty small portion of the whole number of adults in Virginia. And they voted by voice vote, not by secret ballot. Elections took place on what was called court day, the day each month when the county court met and a large number of people could be expected at the courthouse. The sheriff conducted the election and tallied the votes. The candidates stood beside or behind him as men came forward and announced out loud who they voted for.

The 1736 law made it an offense punishable with expulsion from the House of Burgesses for a candidate to endorse or oppose in public any proposal for enacting a new law, repealing an old one, or amending any law. There were no campaigns as we understand them. Voters made their choices based on their knowledge of the talents and social standings of the candidates, as was the case in Munford's play. Politics was very personal and local. It is likely that, also as in Munford's play, following the election, victorious candidates and the voters, too, expected that burgesses would exercise their best judgment on the propositions that the General Assembly considered independent of what their constituents believed.

Voters in each county were entitled to elect two members; voters in Williamsburg, Norfolk, and on Jamestown Island were entitled to elect one each; and the president and professors of the College of William and Mary were also entitled to elect one. Moreover, a man could vote in any or all counties and cities in which he owned the minimum necessary amount of real estate. (George Washington first won election to the House of Burgesses in July 1758 in Frederick County, where he owned land, not in Fairfax County, where he lived.) The apportionment of representation in the legislature reflected the belief that representatives represented their constituents and also the property that they and the voters owned.

Election day probably resembled a fair or a lively market day more than a solemn civic occasion. The 1736 law made it illegal to bribe or pay voters to vote for any candidate, but it had become customary long before Robert Munford's time for candidates to put out large quantities of alcoholic drink for everybody who attended on election day. George Washington spent a large sum of money to treat the people who assembled at the courthouse in Winchester when he was a candidate for the House of Burgesses in Frederick County in 1758; and a few years later, an observer described another candidate "swilling the planters with Bumbo" (rum punch) near Petersburg. A newspaper reported in December 1768 that at an election in New Kent County, "a man who had drank a little too freely, and rode a young and skittish horse, in attempting to mount, received two kicks, which in a few hours put an end to his life." As if such events were so common as scarcely to be worth reporting in detail, the newspaper report concluded, "We have heard of one or two more deaths at the different elections."

Nobody ever elected the justices of the peace who formed the county courts and ran the county governments. The governor, in the name of the king, commissioned justices of the peace. The justices named many local officials and made recommendations to the governor of men to fill vacant seats on the court. During the second half of the seventeenth century and all of the eighteenth century, governors regularly selected new justices of the peace from those lists, so the county courts had been, for more than a century before Munford wrote *The Candidates,* undemocratic, unelected little county oligarchies who in effect selected their own successors.

The only other institution of local government, the parishes of the Church of England, operated in almost exactly the same way, except that vestrymen actually appointed men to vacant seats on the vestry. Occasionally, though, when a board of vestrymen became hopelessly dysfunctional, people petitioned the General Assembly to pass a special law to dissolve the sitting vestry and order an election of new members, but that did not happen very often.

Virginia tobacco planters—white, male Virginia tobacco planters—dominated government and society at all levels. It was they who received appointments to the county court or to a parish vestry. It was they who served in the House of Burgesses. It was the elite of them who were able to contrive royal appointments to the Council of State or wield sufficient influence that the royal bureaucracy in London rewarded them with a lucrative appointment as a customs officer, or as clerk of the House of Burgesses or of one of the royal courts. Lists of members of county courts, parish vestries, and the House of Burgesses clearly indicate that each county had its own elite small political population that ran the affairs of both church and state. They were the Virginia counterparts, on a smaller scale, of the British class of landed aristocrats. That is not at all clear in *The Candidates*.

In almost no way did the institutions and practices of government and politics in colonial Virginia predict the evolution of a system of representative democracy in the United States in the nineteenth century, even if we like to look backward in time and imagine that Washington, Jefferson, Henry, and the other men who founded the United States desired that to happen. Until almost the last minute—certainly not until the last year—they did not desire to change anything in their political system, which guaranteed them alone the ability to live the good life of prosperous, white, male Virginia tobacco planters who were loyal subjects of the king.

The Candidates contains nothing noteworthy about the first stirrings of colonial resentment against Parliament and George III that eventually led to independence. It is not about politics or public affairs. It is entirely about human foibles, something like a comedy of manners, with aspirants for the House of Burgesses and a few voters as the principal characters.

Robert Munford became very uneasy with some of the changes in Virginia that independence set off beginning in 1776. In 1777, he wrote another play, *The Patriots*, in which he used some of his characters to illuminate what he believed were destructive changes in politics, society, and gender roles that he blamed on the political ferment that led to independence or that independence unleashed. In 1775 he ceased to serve in the General Assembly.

Perhaps, as Mr. Worthy had done at the opening of *The Candidates*, Munford decided that he had served long enough in the legislature. In the spring of 1779, though, voters of Mecklenburg County elected him to the House of Delegates, and they reelected him in 1780. Perhaps, as with Mr. Worthy toward the end of *The Candidates*, some events in local politics persuaded him to change his mind and made him willing to serve again; or perhaps he reentered public life in hopes of controlling or limiting the changes that disturbed him.

28

George's Marked Face and Broken English

GEORGE TWICE RAN AWAY from the plantation in Albemarle County, in the foothills of the Blue Ridge Mountains, where he was an enslaved laborer. The owner of the plantation lived far to the southeast, in Williamsburg, and hired overseers or farm managers to run the several tobacco plantations that he owned in different parts of Virginia. As a resident of Williamsburg, the owner found it easy to place an advertisement in the local *Virginia Gazette* to request that whoever found George and another man who ran away with him in 1767 return them to the plantation in Albemarle County. George ran away again in 1771, and the owner again advertised for his capture and return.

Advertisements for the capture and return of enslaved men and women who had run away from their enslavers or of indentured or hired laborers who had run away from their masters or employers appeared in almost every issue of the surviving copies of colonial Virginia newspapers. We have no way to know how many people ran away from enslavers or employers who did not place advertisements in Virginia newspapers. Men and women who lived at a distance from Williamsburg probably had fewer opportunities than other Virginians to place notices in the newspaper, and people who occasionally read a newspaper in northern or northwestern or southwestern Virginia not only received old news, they probably read about people who had escaped a long time ago from an area remote from their own residences.

The advertisements are valuable sources for learning about the appearance of enslaved people. The *Virginia Gazette* of November 2, 1739, reported, for instance, that "a Negro Man, suppos'd to be a Runaway" and then being confined in a county jail was "about 5 Feet 10 Inches high" and was wearing

APRIL 16, 1767.

RUN AWAY from the subfcriber, near *Williamfburg*, laft *Saturday* night, a Negro fellow named **BOB**, about 5 feet 7 inches high, about 26 years of age, was burnt when young, by which he has a fcar on the wrift of his right hand, the thumb of his left hand burnt off, and the hand turns in; had on a double breafted dark coloured frieze jacket, and yellow cotton breeches. He was lately brought home from *Hartford* county in *North Carolina*, where he has been harboured for three years paft by one *Van Pelt*, who lives on *Chinkopin* creek; he paffed for a freeman, by the name of *Edward* or *Edmund Tamar*, and has got a wife there. He is an extraordinary fawer, a tolerable good carpenter and currier, pretends to make fhoes, and is a very good failor. He has been gone for eight years, a part of which time he lived in *Charleftown, South Carolina*. He can read and write; and, as he is a very artful fellow, will probably forge a pafs. All mafters of veffels are hereby cautioned from carrying him out of the colony, and any perfon from employing him. Whoever apprehends the faid fellow, and conveys him to me, fhall have 3 l. reward, if taken in this colony; if in *North Carolina*, 5 l. and if in any other province, 10 l.

WILLIAM TREBELL.

Advertisements such as this from the April 17, 1767, issue of the *Virginia Gazette*, which Alexander Purdie and John Dixon published in Williamsburg, inform historians of how enslaved people and indentured servants were clothed. (Library of Virginia)

"a Cotton Jacket, and a red Wastecoat under it, an old Crocus Shirt, a Pair of old Crocus Breeches, and a very good Pair of Shoes and Stockings; he is a new Negro, and can't speak *English;* his Name is understood to be *Tom.*" The word *crocus* probably meant yellow.

The first advertisement for George in 1767 described him as "a tall slim Negro fellow" who was "marked on the face as the *Gold Coast* slaves generally are." The second advertisement revealed that he "speaks broken *English.*" George's facial markings and broken English indicate that he was a native of Africa and, like the "new Negro" Tom and thousands of other men, women, and children, had been kidnapped, sold to a dealer, sold again to a captain of a slave trading ship, somewhere along the line given an English name, transported across the Atlantic Ocean to Virginia, and then sold to another agent or to the owner of the plantation who marched him 100 or 150 miles from the seaport where he had landed to the plantation in Albemarle County.

Forcible importation of men, women, and children from Africa was at its height in Virginia during the first three-quarters of the eighteenth century. Customs records document that between 1698 and 1775, white Virginians purchased more than 70,000 natives of Africa who arrived aboard the slave trading ships, but the actual number was undoubtedly much larger. As Adam Smith pointed out in 1776 in his *Wealth of Nations* and as the editors of the online *Trans-Atlantic Slave Trade Database* concluded more than two hundred years later, for numerous reasons customs records were not always reliable, and for the slave trade they probably underestimated the actual number by 20 percent or more. And for the years 1725–69, including some years during which importations were probably the largest, about one-fourth of all Virginia customs records do not even survive; and the ones that survive do not enumerate the enslaved people whom shippers smuggled past customs officers or bribed officers not to record. The total number of men, women, and children imported directly from Africa whom white Virginians purchased during the first three-quarters of the eighteenth century was certainly far in excess of 100,000.

In the 1767 advertisement for the return of George and his companion, the plantation owner added, "I hope wherever these fellows may be apprehended that they will receive such moderate correction as will deter them from running away for the future." He thereby authorized anybody who captured either man to punish him, presumably by whipping him or by taking him to the sheriff in the county where he was apprehended to have him whipped—lashed with a long leather whip that usually left on the victim's back painful, sometimes bloody, and often permanent scars, called stripes. All enslavement ultimately rested on coercion and violence or the threat of violence—it had to include violence because repeated threats without any actual violence would have become totally ineffective.

The presence of those thousands of forced immigrants meant that the sound world of eighteenth-century Virginia was a jumble of dozens of languages and dialects. Even white people spoke many different versions of English, depending on where in England, Scotland, or Ireland they or their ancestors had come from; a few immigrants from Germany resided in northern and northwestern Virginia then, too; and most members of First Nations tribes probably still retained their own languages. The numerous languages and dialects of Africa further complicated the sound world of Virginia and also complicated the work of white men and women who directed the labor of recently imported enslaved people. Many of the enslaved people may have had difficulty understanding the commands of their enslavers or overseers. Under that circumstance, a frustrated or impatient overseer, master, or mistress might resort to physical punishment more often than ordinary to compel obedience.

The best estimates, derived from a wide variety of sources, many of them also estimates, indicate that in 1770, on the eve of independence, between 450,000 and 500,000 people lived in Virginia. In 1790, when the first federal census recorded that more than 800,000 people lived in the state, about three-eighths of them, 300,000 human beings, were enslaved. Because the international slave trade had almost come to a halt during the American Revolution, and because of a large influx of white people from other places in North America and from Europe, the proportion of enslaved Virginians was probably higher in 1770 than it was in 1790. The population of enslaved natives of Virginia continued to increase naturally, but it is clear in many instances that those native Virginians knew about the experiences of their ancestors and preserved those memories for generations.

29

The Great Fresh of 1771 and Its Consequences

THE SURVIVING DOCUMENTARY RECORD of colonial Virginia contains several accounts of very severe floods and hurricanes. Those storms killed people, destroyed ships and buildings, and damaged property. We will never know how many people, ships, or buildings were lost or the consequences for most of the people who survived. Most records and accounts of inundations are too brief or too general to provide much reliable information. The account of the 1749 hurricane is one of the best, but the accounts of the great flood of 1771 are more detailed. It was the worst flood in the recorded history of Virginia.

At the end of May 1771, a low pressure system moved slowly northeast up the Blue Ridge Mountains and dumped a tremendous amount of rain in the western Carolinas and Virginia. The resulting flood produced what one man called "the most extraordinary Overflowings of our different Rivers, that had been known in the Memory of Man." The Rappahannock, James, and Appomattox Rivers all rose higher than anybody could remember, forty feet vertically in some of the narrow channels of the James River, higher even than members of First Nations tribes knew about from their ancestral traditions.

Alexander Purdie and John Dixon published eyewitness accounts of the flood in their Williamsburg *Virginia Gazette* on June 6, 1771, and Richard Bland, who lived near Jordan's Point, downriver from Petersburg and Hopewell, wrote a long description of it, too. (Richard Bland to Thomas Adams, August 1, 1771, Adams Family Papers, Virginia Historical Society, and printed in *Virginia Magazine of History and Biography* 5 [1898]: 128–29.)

The flood washed away houses and barns, drowned people and livestock, and even swept oceangoing ships out of the rivers onto previously dry farmland. Silt covered fields in some places as much as ten feet deep. In other places, rotting mounds of trees, uprooted crops, dead farm animals, and decaying human bodies created an intolerable stench and threatened an epidemic of contagious disease. Newspaper reports of the "Great Fresh," as it soon came to be called, were reprinted in other colonies, in England and Scotland, and even in Germany. It was a spectacular disaster. "A waggish Blade at Richmond," one Virginia newspaper reported not long after the flood, "said it was his Opinion Old Nick had bored a hole through the Mountains, and let in the South Sea"—an old term for the Pacific Ocean—"upon us."

The floodwater damaged or destroyed more than 3 million pounds of tobacco that planters and merchants had stored in six of the colony's numerous public warehouses. To provide compensation for the owners of the damaged or ruined tobacco that was in the colony's custody, an emergency session of the General Assembly met in July. Legislators then debated how best to compensate the planters and merchants. The treasurer of Virginia, Robert Carter Nicholas, who was also a member of the House of Burgesses, summarized what happened this way: the legislators, "after considering maturely every Proposal, that was offered," concluded "that nothing would enable them, except a farther Emission of Paper Money, to do the Sufferers that speedy Justice, they had a right to expect." The assembly therefore voted to issue £30,000 in paper money, "the smallest Sum, that could answer that Purpose."

A natural disaster like a major flood (or even an unnatural disaster) can have many unanticipated consequences. At the time of the flood, it is unlikely that anybody anticipated that paper money would again become a major subject of political discussion. Paper currency had created serious problems in Virginia since the French and Indian (Seven Years') War and in other colonies before, during, and after the war. During the war, the General Assembly had issued the first paper currency in Virginia's history to pay soldiers and purchase supplies. Paper currency then was not a permanent money. It was more like a temporary loan that individuals extended to the government when it purchased supplies or paid soldiers during the war with France, and the government later repaid the loan when it allowed those people to pay their taxes with the paper money. Because the previous treasurer had allowed too much of that paper currency to remain in circulation after he should have destroyed the bills when people paid taxes with them, he inadvertently contributed to the greatest financial crisis ever, which came to light shortly after his death in the spring of 1766.

Opposition to paper money continued long after the war with France and the disclosure of the scandal. Paper money was not at all like specie (gold and silver coins) of known and stable value. Paper money could change in value, it was sometimes difficult to redeem, and many people did not know whether to trust it. Tobacco planters were accustomed to long-term commercial relationships with British merchants who kept ledgers of credit and debit that planters usually felt comfortable with because they knew and trusted the men who kept them. Small planters had similar relationships with local merchants or the subagents of Scottish tobacco trading firms. So, too, blacksmiths, coopers, wheelwrights, shopkeepers, and other men and women engaged in manufacturing or commerce. All commercial relationships required a certain level of trust in other people as well as in the laws and practices of trade. In that respect, commerce was very much personal.

Paper money, however, was totally impersonal; it was not gold or silver and had no stable, intrinsic value. No element of trust inhered in paper money apart from the promise of the government that issued it to redeem it in specie on some future day. The past record of several New England colonies did not give anybody much confidence, and the recent treasury scandal seriously eroded such confidence as had existed in Virginia.

With the colony at peace after the end of the war in 1763, nobody anticipated a necessity to issue new paper money. In 1769, though, the king required Virginia to pay for marking the boundary in the southwest between Virginia and the Cherokee. The General Assembly voted to issue £10,000 in currency to cover the cost and to enable the government to function during a shortfall in the amount of revenue that the treasury received.

The surprise flood in 1771 made more paper money necessary, but a year and a half later, on January 29, 1773, another surprise forced the treasurer to make a stunning public announcement. "IT is with infinite Concern," he began, "that I find there is *immediate* Occasion to caution the Publick against several very pernicious and therefore the more dangerous Forgeries of many of the FIVE POUND BILLS emitted in *November* 1769 and *July* 1771." The 1771 bills were printed on a "peculiar Sort of Paper" with delicate artwork that the treasurer had hoped would be difficult to imitate. The engraver of the counterfeiting plates, probably Petersburg silversmith Benjamin Woodward, evidently succeeded very well.

The treasurer eventually identified very subtle differences between the original bills and the counterfeit bills. The only way to identify some of the counterfeits was by touch, to feel the imperfect imitation of the watermark on the back. "The counterfeits are so exquisitely done," the treasurer privately lamented to a friend, "that they have deceived the most penetrating Geniuses amongst us; it cost a select Committee & myself two Days Examination before we could fix any certain Criteria to distinguish the good from the forged Bills."

Somehow—the surviving documents do not clearly indicate how or why—the supposed counterfeiters were acquitted at a trial in the General Court and got away with it. Counterfeiting remained a problem for years thereafter in Virginia and elsewhere. Public debates about paper money continued in Virginia right up to the eve of the American Revolution. Then, the states and the new national government both issued large quantities of paper currency that lost much of its value through inflation. The national currency depreciated to such an extent that the phrases "not worth a continental" and "not worth a continental dollar" permanently entered the English language, and people did not then require any explanation to understand what they meant.

In another unanticipated and indirect way, the Great Fresh played its small role in the events that led up to the American Revolution. In the emergency 1773 session of the General Assembly, burgesses re-created an old Committee of Correspondence at the same time that they dealt with the crisis that counterfeiters had created. One of the purposes of the new committee was to coordinate intercolonial attempts to put all counterfeiters out of business, but that was not the only motivation or necessarily even the most important one.

The previous year, some men in Rhode Island had burned a royal revenue cutter that was there to enforce various British customs laws. In response, the king created a special court of vice-admiralty in Boston with power to transport to England for trial there anybody it suspected of complicity in the event. The new court reminded people of a section in the Stamp Act of 1765 that had authorized a vice-admiralty court in Nova Scotia to try people in that colony from any of the other colonies who were accused of violating it. Some burgesses called to mind the 1534 Act for the Trial of Treasons Committed Out of the King's Dominions, which could have made people who publicly opposed laws or practices of the British government vulnerable to transportation to England to be tried for treason, a crime that carried a gruesome death penalty. Leading Virginia politicians had by then been publicly objecting to British policies for almost a decade, and some of them undoubtedly felt themselves vulnerable.

Under those circumstances, Thomas Jefferson, Richard Henry Lee, Patrick Henry, and a few other burgesses drafted the motion to form a new Committee of Correspondence. The resolution passed and authorized the committee "to obtain the most early and Authentic intelligence of all such acts and *Resolutions* of the *British Parliament,* or proceedings of Administration, as may relate to, or affect the British Colonies in America, and to keep up and maintain a Correspondence and Communication with our Sister Colonies, respecting these important Considerations." That committee and other committees in the other colonies played a critical role in coordinating American responses to the series of threats that led the committees in the summer of 1774 to summon into being the First Continental Congress.

30

Patrick Lunan Exposed

At the October 1771 session of the General Court in the Capitol in Williamsburg, the judges of the court—the new governor, John Murray, Fourth Earl of Dunmore, who had just arrived in Virginia a few weeks earlier, together with the members of the Council of State—heard some of the best lawyers in Virginia argue a case of prime importance. The evidence presented in *Godwin et al. v. Lunan* could have made some of the judges squirm in their seats or look out into the audience for fear that ladies or youngsters were there listening. The evidence described the shockingly indecent behavior of a clergyman.

We know about the event because one of the colony's top lawyers, Thomas Jefferson, was there and took notes on the arguments of counsel or, more likely, borrowed written copies of their arguments and copied or abstracted them for future reference. Jefferson sometimes took notes on arguments that lawyers made in court, even in cases in which he participated. After his death, his grandson Thomas Jefferson Randolph published the copies that Jefferson made from other people's notes when he studied law and his own notes that he made while he practiced before the General Court. The volume was printed in 1829 and entitled *Reports of Cases Determined in the General Court of Virginia. From 1730, to 1740; and from 1768, to 1772*. The notes on *Godwin et al. v. Lunan* are on pages 96–108.

The case that included the indecent evidence pitted the vestrymen of the Upper Parish in Nansemond County (in 1974 the city of Suffolk absorbed the county) against the parish minister, Patrick Lunan. The vestrymen tried to fire him, but he would not go. They then sued him in the General Court to force his resignation.

The evidence presented to the court, as Jefferson recorded it, stated that Lunan "was much addicted to drunkenness, in so much, as to be often drunk at church, and unable to go through divine service, or to baptize or marry those who attended for those purposes; that he officiated in ridiculous apparel unbecoming a priest; that he was a common disturber of the peace, and often quarrelling and fighting; that he was a common and profane swearer; that on the 10th of July 1767, and at other times, he exposed his private parts to view in public companies, and solicited negro and other women to fornication and adultery with him." The lawyer for the vestrymen also stated that Lunan "had declared he did not believe in the revealed religion of Christ, and cared not of what religion he was so he got the tobacco, nor what became of the flock so that he could get the fleece." That was about as serious as charges against any clergyman could be.

Lunan coveted "the tobacco," which was his salary. By law every minister of the Church of England received 16,000 pounds of tobacco and cask as his annual salary. Each parish in Virginia also had a glebe, which consisted of a plantation from the supplemental earnings of which the minister could live in the dwelling house in a style proper for an important member and leader of the community. The lewd behavior described in court is shocking, even today, but at that time, for a clergyman not to "believe in the revealed religion of Christ" or to care no more about his flock—his parishioners—except to "get the fleece" was probably just as shocking.

The institutions and practices of the Church of England had evolved in Virginia from a rudimentary form early in the seventeenth century to become a distinctive Church of Virginia by the eighteenth century. Until the disestablishment of the church in 1786, the Church of England was an integral part of the government of Virginia, and the government of Virginia was also a part of the church, much as church and state had been united with each other during the English Reformation when the king became the official head of the English church.

Most of the parishes of the Church of England in eastern Virginia were smaller than any of the counties, and parishes were therefore the most local units of government in the colony. As with some of the responsibilities of the church in England, Virginia parishes had responsibilities that are now regarded in the United States as civil and not religious, such as keeping official registers of births, marriages, and deaths, and sharing with county courts responsibility to identify and care for orphans and the poor. Vestrymen and churchwardens also had legal responsibilities as part of their official duties to report to the county court for prosecution moral offenses such as adultery, fornication, swearing, and non-attendance at church, each of which was a crime. As an integral part of the colonial government, the church exercised essential responsibilities for protecting the moral and religious health of the community.

Beginning in 1662, the General Assembly invested churchwardens with the task of assembling the parish residents every fourth year to walk all property boundaries and renew boundary markers in order that all property be rendered secure and that disputes about property lines not disrupt the community. Processioning, or beating the bounds, as the practice was known, continued in many localities well into the nineteenth century. Several times during the seventeenth century and again in 1728 when legislators tried to reduce tobacco production in order to raise the price per pound, they empowered churchwardens or vestrymen to enforce limits on the number of plants each laborer could tend. That the legislature imposed those responsibilities on parish officials and not on justices of the peace, constables, or sheriffs indicates how important the parish communities and officials were.

Vestries taxed everybody in the parish, not just active members of the Church of England, to pay for the civil and religious responsibilities of the parish and to construct and keep in repair churches and chapels of ease for parishioners who lived too far from the parish church to attend services there regularly. In the eighteenth century, parish vestries generally imposed heavier taxes on the residents of the parish to pay for the civil and religious responsibilities of the church than justices of the peace imposed to pay for operating the county governments and keeping the peace.

Laymen—vestrymen, churchwardens, and clerks of the vestry—enjoyed almost complete control over the parish and the church, comparable to the control that justices of the peace and the county courts exercised in civic affairs. During the middle decades of the seventeenth century, vestrymen acquired authority to fill vacancies in their number, which made vestries self-appointed boards (much like the county courts) without oversight of a bishop or of the parishioners. As early as 1643, or perhaps even earlier, the General Assembly empowered vestries to appoint clergymen, a responsibility that lay parish officers in England never exercised. Virginia vestrymen employed and dismissed ministers in ways with no counterparts in the ecclesiastical laws and practices of England.

The earliest governors may have sometimes inducted ministers, as bishops always did in England, but for the most part vestrymen employed clergymen without an induction. Properly inducted clergymen had a common law property right to their jobs—called a cure—but no eighteenth-century Virginia clergyman ever had that right because no bishop ever resided in—or even visited—the colony to induct them. This was the main issue that the lawyers disagreed about in the case of Patrick Lunan of the Upper Parish of Nansemond County in 1771: what right did Lunan have to his job, and who, if anybody, had authority to deprive him of that right?

The organization and functioning of the church in eighteenth-century Virginia more nearly resembled the Church of Scotland or the congregational churches in New England than it resembled the Church of England in England. The system as it evolved in the seventeenth century suited the planters and local leaders who served on parish vestries in the eighteenth century very well because it allowed them control over all church affairs; and the church and its moral teachings were of fundamental importance to the version of English culture that Virginians created in their portion of North America. As Richard Bland, a General Court lawyer, burgess, and the keenest student of the colony's laws and history, explained when he presented his arguments during the hearing of Patrick Lunan's case, in all the world the Virginia church was *sui generis,* one of a kind.

In spite of the testimony in court in that case, the vestrymen's suit failed because the judges and lawyers could not agree on who had jurisdiction—the vestry, the governor, the General Court, or the commissary, who was the bishop of London's personal representative in the colony. Eventually, the vestrymen dipped into the parish treasury and used tax money that the vestry had collected from the parish residents to pay Patrick Lunan to relinquish his post—to buy him out, or pay him to begone.

The Lunan case used to be cited in scholarship about Virginia late in the colonial period to make a point that the clergymen of the Church of England were then too few in number, inept, or even injurious to the church, which in turn has been cited as a reason why at the time of *Godwin et al. v. Lunan,* Baptist and Presbyterian ministers were seducing large numbers of members of the Church of England into their congregations. Scholarship

St. Stephen's Episcopal Church, in New Kent County, shown here in an 1862 drawing, has probably remained substantially unchanged in exterior appearance since the 1740s. (Library of Virginia)

published late in the twentieth century and early in the twenty-first, though, demonstrates that there were enough good clergymen in Virginia and so few truly incompetent ones (Lunan was unique, not representative) that the ministries of those clergymen were not the prime reason why Baptists and Presbyterians succeeded in the aftermath of the Great Awakening in converting members of the established church to their own denominations.

31

Subversive Religious Doctrines

ON THE EVE OF INDEPENDENCE, the religious culture of Virginia was in flux. Religion is a subject that historians once believed did not matter very much to colonial Virginians. In the 1760s and 1770s, though, devoted Virginia members of the Church of England were suspicious of, or even hostile to, the new evangelical movement that had its roots in the Great Awakening that had swept through New England and also touched Virginia and some other southern colonies. Baptist ministers successfully enticed members of Anglican churches away and embraced them in their Baptist congregations. A smaller group within the Church of England, Methodists who still considered themselves Anglicans, also challenged the status quo, and a notable proportion of Presbyterians in northern and western Virginia had been growing for many years.

Protestant men and women who dissented from some of the teachings and practices of the Church of England were generally lumped together under the term dissenters. The Baptists and Presbyterians, in particular, introduced a larger measure of Calvinism into Virginia culture during the middle decades of the eighteenth century than the first colonists had brought with them to the colony at the beginning of the seventeenth. Worried Anglicans disapproved and challenged them.

On February 20, 1772, the Williamsburg *Virginia Gazette* that Alexander Purdie and John Dixon published printed a long, unsigned "ADDRESS to the ANABAPTISTS *imprisoned in* CAROLINE *County, August 8, 1771.*" It has been attributed to Attorney General John Randolph without any reasons assigned, but some internal evidence suggests that the author may have been one of the county's lawyers.

The address affirmed in strong language that under English and Virginia law, Protestants had a right to believe what they wanted and to practice their religion as they wished, but that "every Member of a Community is obliged to submit to such Laws as are made for the Good of the Whole, however contrary to his Inclination or Interest, which he must give up to the Opinion or Interest of a Majority." People's private opinions on matters of religion, the author went on, were "not the Objects of Law or Government; while they keep those to themselves, they may enjoy them without Interruption from the civil Magistrate. But if they go about publickly preaching and inculcating their Errours, raising Factions tending to disturb the publick Peace, or utter Doctrines which in their Nature are subversive of all Religion or Morality, they become obnoxious," and the perpetrators became liable to "civil Punishment."

At the time of the publication of the "ADDRESS," members of the House of Burgesses were debating the provisions of a bill to enlarge the scope of religious toleration in Virginia. Back in 1699, the General Assembly had incorporated the essence of the English Act of Toleration into Virginia law, which exempted some Protestant dissenters such as Quakers and Presbyterians from the penalties and punishments that England had imposed on Catholics and other dissenters during the reigns of Henry VIII and Elizabeth I. The 1699 Virginia law required dissenting ministers to obtain a license from the governor to erect a meetinghouse and prohibited them from preaching anywhere else. During the years immediately preceding the American Revolution, justices of the peace and sheriffs in several counties harassed, persecuted, or even jailed Baptist ministers who refused to apply for licenses or to follow the Virginia law strictly.

The preamble to the bill that the Committee for Religion introduced in the House of Burgesses early in 1772 and that was printed in William Rind's *Virginia Gazette* of March 26, 1772, stated that in order "to give Ease and Quiet to scrupulous Consciences in the Exercise of Religion . . . all his Majesty's Protestant Subjects dissenting from the Church of England, within this Dominion, shall have and enjoy the full and free Exercise of their Religion, without Molestation or Danger, or incurring any Penalty whatsoever." The chair of the committee later explained that the consensus of opinion among the burgesses was "that the Toleration should be made more extensive here than it was in England."

Nevertheless, the bill contained restrictions on dissenting ministers and congregations. Each minister and each congregation had to apply to the local county court for permission to have a meetinghouse; members could not meet and ministers could not preach or teach anywhere else; they could not hold meetings at night; and they could not lock doors or windows to prevent magistrates or law enforcement officers from monitoring their meetings. The restrictions in the bill were very much like those that had been in the 1699 law but were more detailed. The draft bill explicitly retained a provision in an existing law that prohibited enslaved people from attending services of dissenting churches.

Because of differences of opinion on several features of the bill, it never came to a vote in the House of Burgesses. The most influential burgesses who supported the bill were unwilling to relinquish the privileged status that the Church of England enjoyed in Virginia. They appear to have been willing to tolerate Protestant dissenters so long as the dissenters remained a quiet minority and so long as the established church could continue to minister to the governing majority.

The promise of religious liberty in the preamble to the 1772 toleration bill and in the opening phrases of the "ADDRESS" was couched in language that no dissenter was likely to find objectionable, although some of the restrictions in the bill certainly were. What was most objectionable was that, as the "ADDRESS" clearly stated, "civil Magistrates"—sheriffs, constables, and justices of the peace, who were not elected and therefore did not necessarily represent the "Majority" of people in the community—had wide legal discretion to decide which beliefs, practices, or actions could "disturb the publick Peace" or which doctrines were "in their Nature . . . subversive of all Religion or Morality" and therefore "obnoxious" and liable to land a person in jail. In short, the laws of England and Virginia—which might or might not have represented the opinions of a "Majority" of the people in the colony—did not grant permission for anybody to do or to say anything in public about religion that some sheriff or justice of the peace believed was objectionable. And that was the most serious of all of the grievances that dissenters had because the vague criteria for legal action left local government officials free to harass, punish, or imprison them. The bill that the House of Burgesses considered in 1772 did, too.

Dissenters also had other grievances. No marriage in Virginia was legal unless a minister of the Church of England performed it. Children of parents who married in their own Baptist, Presbyterian, or Lutheran churches, or in Quaker, Mennonite, or Church of the Brethren meetinghouses, would therefore be legally illegitimate, which imposed numerous serious legal disabilities on them. Moreover, all taxpayers in the colony paid taxes—called tithes, even though parish vestries did not set them at one-tenth of the person's wealth or income—to their local parish to pay for both the civil and religious work of the parishes of the Church of England.

The American Revolution changed all of that, but in the years immediately before independence, the political power of members of the Church of England remained too strong for dissenters to make any headway in the campaign that they had just begun to enlarge their own religious liberty. That churchmen in Virginia reacted strenuously to the equally strenuous dissenters indicates that both were deeply concerned about preserving their religious beliefs and practicing in their own denominations and churches.

32

Robin v. Hardaway

ONE DAY IN OCTOBER 1988 in the Virginia State Library and Archives (later the Library of Virginia), I was consulting with a librarian who was cataloging several old law books that the library had just purchased from a private dealer. I was in part responsible for the purchase because I had been researching the history of the library that the colonial Council of State acquired before the American Revolution and what became of the books afterwards. The library was also known at the time as the General Court library. In the 1840s, the General Assembly authorized the transfer of some law books to Lewisburg, in Greenbrier County, where the Supreme Court of Appeals held an annual western session in addition to its regular sessions in Richmond. After 1863, when Greenbrier County became one of the counties in the new state of West Virginia, the books became the property of the new state. The books came on the market in the 1980s, and the Virginia State Library and Archives purchased them. Some of them contained the bookplate of the Council of State.

When the cataloguer picked up volume two of John Tracy Atkins, *Reports of Cases Argued and Determined in the High Court of Chancery in the Time of Lord Chancellor Hardwicke, With Notes and References*, 3 vols. (London, 1765–68), a small slip of paper fell out. I immediately knew what the document was and that it contained information that was new to historians of Virginia. The paper is now in the archives of Virginia with the Records of the General Court, Record Group 104, accession number 33,700, in the Library of Virginia in Richmond.

The document is a copy of a verdict that a jury returned in the case *Robin v. Hardaway* on May 2, 1772, following a trial in the General Court. During the

{176}

colonial period, the General Court was the highest court in Virginia and the only court with appellate jurisdiction. Almost all of the records of the General Court between the 1670s and the American Revolution were destroyed in the fire that burned the State Court House in Richmond at the end of the American Civil War in April 1865, so every surviving scrap is valuable.

I knew about *Robin v. Hardaway* because I had recently studied the arguments that the lawyers had made to the judges before the jury trial so that the court could decide which of several old Virginia laws applied. Thomas Jefferson, a General Court lawyer who was not engaged on either side in the case, apparently obtained copies of the written arguments of counsel and copied or abstracted them and filed them with his notes on other cases. The notes that Jefferson made are too long and detailed for him to have made them while the lawyers presented oral arguments about which of several old Virginia laws governed the case. One of Jefferson's grandsons later compiled and published the notes and others that Jefferson had made when he was studying law and practicing before the General Court in *Reports of Cases Determined in the General Court of Virginia. From 1730, to 1740; and from 1768, to 1772*, ed. Thomas Jefferson Randolph (Charlottesville, 1829). *Robin v. Hardaway* is on pages 109–23. Whether the arguments that Jefferson recorded were part of an appeal from an adverse ruling of the Dinwiddie County Court or part of a case that the General Court heard on original jurisdiction is not clear because the colonial records of the Dinwiddie County Court are also lost.

Robin v. Hardaway was an important case, particularly for understanding how enslavement of members of First Nations tribes had been treated in seventeenth- and eighteenth-century Virginia law. As Jefferson prefaced his notes from the lawyers' arguments, the twelve plaintiffs who brought the case charged that they were all "descendants of Indian women brought into this country by traders, at several times, between the years 1682 and 1748 and by them sold as slaves under an act of the General Assembly made in 1682. The question therefore was, when that act was repealed, and whether it ever was?" If the 1682 law had been repealed, the enslavement of the women was illegal if the women had entered Virginia after the repeal, and the plaintiffs in the case were therefore entitled to their freedom.

Seventeenth-century Virginia laws had treated enslaved people of African and First Nations ancestry in much the same way for many purposes, but the laws had imposed limitations that changed from time to time concerning when and how English Virginians could acquire or how long they could hold members of First Nations tribes in slavery. Those differences were at the heart of the arguments of counsel in *Robin v. Hardaway*. The lawyers' arguments focused on whether changes made to the law of 1682 in 1684 or in 1691 or by the revised slavery law that the assembly adopted in 1705 effectively repealed the 1682 law even without containing explicit language to that effect.

The legal issues were complicated because of the different stipulations in those laws about when or how enslaved people entered Virginia, who sold them to Virginians, and who bought them. Those complications were evidently what most interested Thomas Jefferson and motivated him to preserve the long legal arguments. What most interested me, though, were the implications of some of the explanations that the lawyers for the plaintiffs and the defendant employed to explain the meaning of the contested laws.

The lawyer who represented Robin and his fellow plaintiffs was Thomson Mason, who had attended one of the prestigious Inns of Court in London, where he was called to the bar. He then returned to Virginia, served in the House of Burgesses, and was an active member of the General Court bar, the select group of Virginia attorneys who practiced exclusively before the colony's highest court. Mason was the younger brother of the more famous George Mason, who in 1776 prepared the first drafts of the Virginia Declaration of Rights and the first Constitution of Virginia. George Mason also served in the Constitutional Convention of 1787 and in the Virginia Ratification Convention of 1789. Members of the Mason family had been prominent in the northern part of Virginia for decades and remained prominent in the public life of Virginia until the Civil War.

Richard Bland was the lawyer for John Hardaway, the Dinwiddie County resident and defendant who claimed legal ownership of the plaintiffs. Bland had served in the House of Burgesses for thirty years by then and also spent many hours studying old records in the Capitol or in the office of the secretary of the colony in Williamsburg. He also acquired other records that he kept at his plantation residence in Prince George County. (Thomas Jefferson later purchased those original records from Bland's estate, and they survive in the Thomas Jefferson Papers, Library of Congress.) Bland knew more than anybody else about Virginia's history and its legal records. In 1774, an acquaintance remarked that Bland had "something of the look of musty old

Parch[men]ts w'ch he handeleth and studieth much." All that reading may have ruined his eyesight. We know that he wore eyeglasses because another man once referred to him as "Spectacle Dick."

In 1772, Mason and Bland expressed differing opinions about slavery and the laws of slavery as they had evolved in Virginia during the previous century and a half. Their differences revealed perceptions that not only influenced how they interpreted the old Virginia laws but also offered a preview of the differing ideas about slavery in the new republic that the American Revolution unleashed.

Thomson Mason maintained in his opening argument that the 1682 law that authorized enslavement of members of First Nations tribes under some conditions was "originally void in itself, because it was contrary to natural right"; that the significant changes that the 1684 law made virtually repealed it; but that if the law of 1684 did not in fact repeal the act, other alterations contained in the law of 1691 did; "And if by neither of those," then "it was actually repealed in 1705."

Mason's reliance on "natural right," or natural law, appears to have been an innovation, but so few learned discussions of the Virginia law of slavery survive from the time that we cannot state categorically how he developed the idea or whether he developed it on his own. It should perhaps not be surprising that Mason made that argument. By stating that slavery under certain circumstances violated "natural right," Mason alluded to an interpretation that English law did not recognize the concept of people as property, and that therefore slavery could only exist within a country (or a colony) by the clear sanction of statute law, which was then often called positive law.

Many nations nevertheless acknowledged the existence of slavery on the ground that it was more humane to enslave people who were captured in battle than to kill them. Many Englishmen also seem to have shared that belief and even brought back to England people they had purchased from enslavers in the Mediterranean or Africa. If, as Mason argued at length, the English invasion of North America did not constitute a just defensive war against the original inhabitants, then Englishmen were not justified under international standards or English law in enslaving those original inhabitants as permanent prisoners of war or in enslaving their descendants.

Mason even went so far as to draw a parallel between the enslavement of some members of First Nations tribes and the protests that he and many other influential public men had been making in Virginia and elsewhere in the colonies about acts of Parliament that taxed residents of the colonies who were not represented in Parliament. Those men often argued that Parliament was attempting to enslave free Americans without their consent. Mason stated, according to Jefferson's notes, "The Indians of every denomination were free, and independent of us; they were not subject to our empire; not represented in our legislature; they derived no protection from our laws, nor could be subjected to their bonds. If natural right, independence, defect of representation, and disavowal of protection, are not sufficient to keep them from the coercion of our laws, on what other principles can we justify our opposition to some late acts of power exercised over us by the British legislature?"

That was not Mason's main point, though. He went beyond traditional methods of analyzing law and rested his case in part on natural law, on the unfairness or injustice with which Virginia had treated the enslaved people who sued for their freedom. "The laws of nature are the laws of God," Mason declared. "A legislature must not obstruct our obedience to him from whose punishments they cannot protect us. All human constitutions which contradict his laws, we are in conscience bound to disobey." Following that theoretical argument, Mason then discovered in the laws of 1684, 1691, and 1705 no positive legislative action that justified holding the plaintiffs in slavery if they had entered Virginia and been sold into slavery under the conditions that the law of 1682 permitted.

Mason disclosed one other very interesting thing during his argument on behalf of the enslaved plaintiffs. He explained that for decades Virginia lawyers and judges had believed that the 1684 law had in effect repealed the 1682 law, and that under that belief, "hundreds of the descendants of Indians have obtained their freedom, on actions brought in this court" because they or their female ancestors had been imported into Virginia and sold as enslaved people after 1684.

That was singularly important. A Virginia law of 1662 that remained in effect until 1865 stipulated that at the moment of birth, the child of an enslaved woman became the property of the person who owned the mother. All of the children of an illegally enslaved woman were therefore entitled to their freedom, and all of the children of her daughters and their female descendants were also entitled to their freedom. All of the plaintiffs in

Robin v. Hardaway believed that they were entitled to be free because they descended directly through female lines from one or another of the illegally enslaved "Indian women."

Richard Bland, the principal counsel for John Hardaway, gained a posthumous reputation as an opponent of slavery, perhaps because of misinterpretation of some remarks that Thomas Jefferson made in 1814 about a bill that Bland introduced in the House of Burgesses early in the 1770s "for certain moderate extensions of the protection of the laws to these people," as Jefferson described it. During the debate, as Jefferson recalled, Bland "was denounced as an enemy to his country, & was treated with the grossest indecorum." It is not clear what bill Jefferson referred to or whether it passed in its original or in an amended version, but it definitely did not look to the abolition of slavery.

Jefferson recorded that Bland began his argument on behalf of Hardaway and his claim to legal ownership of the plaintiffs by asserting that "societies of men could not subsist unless there were a subordination of one to another, and that from the highest to the lowest degree. That this was conformable with the general scheme of the Creator, observable in other parts of his great work, where no chasm was to be discovered, but the several links run imperceptibly into one another. That in this subordination the department of slaves must be filled by some, or there would be a defect in the scale of order."

Like Mason, Bland also described the laws of 1684, 1691, and 1705 in detail, but Bland came to the conclusion that because the laws of 1684 and 1691 did not clearly and explicitly repeal the law of 1682, the original law remained in force. Bland also argued that the relevant portions of the 1705 revision of the Virginia slave code differed so little in essence from the 1682 law that it probably did not clearly repeal that law, either.

As for Mason's novel assertion that natural law should have invalidated the 1682 law from the beginning, Bland declared that the law of 1682 and earlier ones that Mason "so much complained of, were founded on principles of self-defence, and may be considered as proofs of the humanity of our ancestors, who substituted this punishment on the Indian captives, instead of those cruel deaths they inflicted on ours." That was precisely the same argument for the legality of slavery that lay at the base of the international recognition of the just right of slavery as a result of warfare. Bland, however, sought to praise, or at least to excuse, the Virginia laws with a faint damn: "But certain it is, they are much less unjust than the laws making slaves of negroes, inhabitants of Africa" who "can never injure our properties or disturb our peace," unlike the members of First Nations tribes, who he stated "were perpetually invading both." Regardless of whatever Bland thought about the initial enslavement of natives of Africa and of the practice of Virginia men and women continuing to hold them and their descendants in slavery, he believed that the Virginia laws that enslaved them and also members of First Nations tribes were justifiable.

Richard Bland's defense of Hardaway's legal right to own the people he held in slavery was better advocacy than Thomson Mason's according to legal practices of the time and only deviated from them in the instance of his rebutting Mason's claim of a natural law right to a presumption of freedom. Bland's legal reasoning resembled the legal and political arguments that defenders of slavery employed after the American Revolution when slavery as it had evolved in North America came under attack. Bland did not say anything, so far as Jefferson's notes indicate, that questioned the propriety of or seriously undermined slavery except to acknowledge that in some respects the original enslavement of Africans might have been less easily justified than the enslavement of members of First Nations tribes. Bland did not suggest that the laws that permitted Virginians to buy and sell people with African or First Nations ancestry were to be questioned.

In fact, Richard Bland's very first remarks about the necessity for somebody to fill the "department of slaves" lest there be "a defect in the scale of order" appear to suggest that Bland was not inclined, as Mason may have been, to have any doubts about the propriety of slavery or to require additional positive law sanctions to impose or retain slavery. Bland apparently regarded slavery as a naturally occurring phenomenon, as part of the Creator's plan, and therefore he accepted it without question. Bland was a religious man and a close student of the Bible, which contains many references to, and no condemnations of, slavery as it was practiced in ancient times, so that would not be in the least surprising.

Bland might not have felt strongly impelled to question the existence, morality, or legality of slavery or too closely examine the belief systems that it had generated among his class of Virginia ladies and gentlemen. He and they relied on slavery too much, both in the management of their households and to produce tobacco, their principal cash crop, to be often tempted to question or to doubt the propriety of the basis of their prosperity and status. Evidence suggests that during Bland's lifetime (he died in October 1776), very few white Virginians openly expressed serious reservations about the morality or propriety of slavery. The same considerations later applied when the morality of slavery or the compatibility of slavery with the bases of the new democratic republic that the American Revolution created stimulated opposition to the institution.

Thomas Jefferson concluded his note on the arguments of counsel in *Robin v. Hardaway* with "The court adjudged that neither of the acts of 1684 or 1691, repealed that of 1682, but that it was repealed by the act of 1705." Jefferson recorded nothing about the jury trial that followed. The jury heard evidence after the judges had decided that the 1705 law in effect repealed the 1682 law to establish when and under what circumstances the female ancestor of each of the twelve plaintiffs who sued for their freedom entered Virginia, who purchased them, who may have purchased or inherited them in the meantime, and also to prove that the plaintiffs were, in fact, descendants of the original women through the female line of descent.

The copy of the verdict that we found in Atkins's *Reports*, which John Brown made when he was the clerk of the postwar court from 1781 to 1794, contains some more information. It disclosed that an enslaved man named Robin, together with seven other enslaved men (Daniel, Cuffie, Isham, Moses, Peter, Davy, and Ned) and four enslaved women (Hannah, Judy, Autry, and Silvia), had sued John Hardaway, of Dinwiddie County, for illegally holding them in slavery on the grounds that they were all descendants through the female line of women who were originally members of a First Nations tribe somewhere outside of Virginia. On May 2, 1772, the General Court jury declared that Robin and the other plaintiffs were "free and not Slaves" and awarded each of the twelve people one shilling in damages from the defendant, John Hardaway, as well as full compensation for their expenses in bringing the lawsuit.

That meant that Hardaway had to pay all of the court costs and fees that clerks charged as well as the bill that Richard Bland submitted to him for representing him. Hardaway may also have had to pay the bill that Thomson

Mason submitted for representing the plaintiffs. Since 1711, a standing rule of the General Court had entitled people who sued for their freedom on the ground of illegal enslavement to have the benefit of legal counsel. An old English rule that Virginians usually applied required the losing party in a civil suit to pay all costs, including the fee of the victorious lawyer.

The financial award to the freed plaintiffs was a less-than-negligible monetary compensation for having been improperly held in slavery all of their lives, but they could thereafter live as free men and women. The finding of freedom also indicates to us that the female ancestors of the plaintiffs who then received their freedom did not arrive in Virginia until 1705 or later because according to the ruling of the General Court, they would have been legally enslaved under the act of 1682 if they had arrived between that year and 1705.

For the twelve plaintiffs, the jury verdict was a life-changing event of the first order of importance, never to be forgotten. For the historian, the verdict is interesting, but because no other original record from the case survives, it is also disappointing. From the verdict we do not learn anything about the identities of the plaintiffs' ancestors or the circumstances under which they became enslaved in Virginia. We do not even learn the surnames of the twelve people. From the beginning of slavery in Virginia until its abolition in 1865, white people routinely and deliberately omitted surnames from both public and private references to enslaved people, which denied enslaved people one essential human trait, knowledge of their family heritages.

From other sources, though, we can learn some details about the ancestor of one of the plaintiffs and about others of her descendants. Better-documented court cases later in several Virginia counties and one in a Kentucky county disclose that one of the "Indian women" had been a member of an Apalachee tribe in Florida before being pressed into slavery somehow about 1705 and later sold, perhaps to a trader and by him to a Virginian. We know her by the name of Judith, or Judy, Coleman, even though we do not know whether she initially called herself by that name or received that name from Francis Coleman, the Virginian who had purchased her. The defendant Hannah, who obtained her freedom along with Robin and ten other people in May 1772, was her descendant. About three dozen other descendants of

Judith Coleman successfully sued for their freedom, but they all remained illegally enslaved until they won their freedom suits, some of them not until the nineteenth century.

We still do not know anything about the enslaved ancestors of the other plaintiffs in *Robin v. Hardaway* or, without their family names, what eventually became of them.

33

New Virginias in the West

IN SEPTEMBER 1774, a large number of volunteers marched from what is now the southwestern portion of Virginia northward to the upper Ohio Valley to take part in a campaign against the Shawnee. A militia officer who remained at home grumbled that the men under his command prided themselves so much on their self-reliance and personal independence that he and the other officers had to persuade the militiamen what to do. The officers could not order the men about, he wrote in a letter, because "Every Dog Doeth acording to freedoms of his own Will." Not long thereafter, another man in the same portion of Virginia explained, "Mountains has always been friendly to liberty," as if it were the mountains, not the beliefs and the social and economic conditions of people, that produced their intense desire for personal liberty.

William Doak, the militia officer, addressed his September 22, 1774, letter to William Preston, the county lieutenant, or commanding officer, of the county militia. The letter survives in the Lyman C. Draper MSS, 3QQ101, State Historical Society of Wisconsin, where Draper's huge collection of manuscripts relating to the eighteenth- and nineteenth-century frontier is preserved in volumes that Draper sequenced with letters of the alphabet. At first glance, it appears that Doak insulted his men with his "Every Dog Doeth acording to freedoms of his own Will," but that appears to have been a variation on a colloquial saying that meant that each person acted from his own volition and not under instructions or coercion from anybody else, the very definition of independence.

By the time Doak wrote his complaining letter, English-speaking people had been residing in the valleys of that part of Virginia for more than two decades. The original pioneer settlers and their children grew up self-reliant. They had no choice. They were far away, perhaps a day of riding or even more of walking, from courthouses, taverns, or market towns and had to rely on themselves and on their neighbors for protection from potentially hostile members of First Nations tribes who resented the incursion onto their ancestral hunting grounds.

In the valleys west of the Blue Ridge Mountains, settlement patterns and social structures developed differently during the second century of the colony than they had during the first century of English settlement that began on the coast and spread to the eastern slope of the mountains. In the east, settlers initially established their farms and plantations on the banks of the major rivers or on the shore of Chesapeake Bay, but as time progressed and the number of English people increased, they created small market towns and a few larger seaport towns. In the southwest, though, people established few plantations, and they created a few small towns at the sites of courthouses, country churches, and perhaps at the scattered taverns that enterprising people built along what they began to call the Great Wagon Road. The road stretched along a route that members of First Nations tribes had used for generations and that linked the backcountry, beyond the Blue Ridge, to south-central Pennsylvania in the northeast and to the valleys of western North Carolina in the southwest.

The landscape was not suitable for the large-scale commercial agriculture and plantations of the sort that eastern tobacco planters established. The western farmers tilled their own small plots. They and the few men who accumulated large landholdings (like those of Colonel William Preston) never developed so stratified a society as east of the mountains. Even the largest landholdings were modest compared to some in the east, and mansion houses were less numerous and also smaller in the west than in the east. The social and political structures evolved to be more democratic—or less undemocratic—than in the east—so much so that Captain Doak had to persuade the militiamen under his command and could not order them to do their parts in preparing for their community's self-defense.

To the northeast in the long series of valleys through which the Great Wagon Road ran, settlement began even earlier than in the southwest, but the society there also evolved to be more democratic—or less undemocratic—than in the east. Enterprising speculators obtained large grants of frontier land from the governor and Council of State and with the encouragement of the British government organized parties of immigrants to settle in the valleys of the Shenandoah and Potomac Rivers. The land barons, some of whom lived in the east, grew wealthy sponsoring the settlement and sale of the land. One of the land barons, Jost Hite, was particularly active and effective in recruiting immigrants from the German principalities and also from settlements that Germans had already established in Pennsylvania. They were and are incorrectly called Pennsylvania Dutch, which did not mean Dutchmen, or people from the Netherlands, but was a corruption of Pennsylvania Deutsch, *Deutsch* being the German word for German.

The Germans created an agricultural landscape quite different from what people created in other portions of Virginia. Germans built little market towns throughout the valley, with churches, farms, and settlements that did not so much encourage everybody to act "acording to freedoms of his own Will" as to focus people in communities. The sense of local community was probably stronger there than it was farther east, and even though English-speaking and German-speaking people lived near one another and routinely interacted with one another, the descendants of German immigrants preserved much of their language and culture rather than merge themselves fully into the dominant English culture.

Germans were very numerous in the Shenandoah Valley. Early in the first recruitment of volunteers to fight in the war for independence, a Lutheran minister, who was also an ordained minister in the Church of England in the Shenandoah Valley, became colonel of a regiment that had so many officers and enlisted men from the German settlements that it was called the German Regiment. Later, in 1795, the state government commissioned a Philadelphia printer to issue a compilation of Virginia tax laws in the German language for use in the Shenandoah Valley and adjacent mountains. Still later, in the nineteenth century, a German-language printing house flourished in the valley, and men, women, and children read and spoke German in some communities even into the twentieth century.

Despite the many differences between the society that developed in the southwest and the society that developed in the Shenandoah Valley, the two shared some important characteristics. Not until the second quarter of the nineteenth century did the white people in either place introduce slavery on a large scale. In fact, large-scale commercial agriculture had a hard time

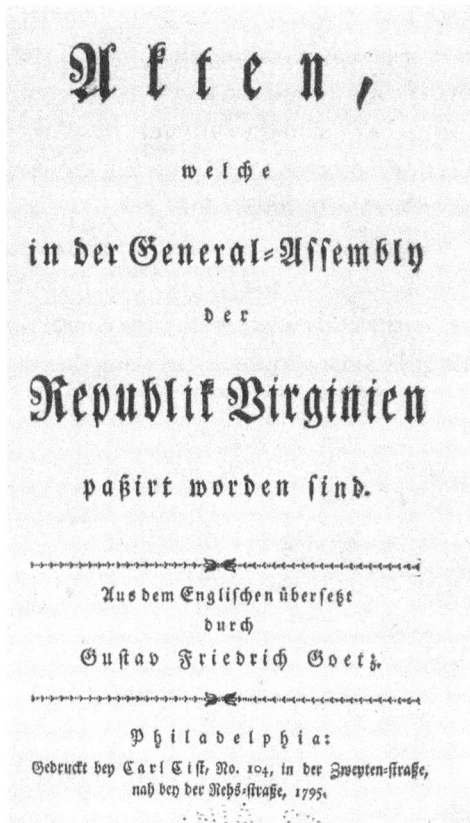

Title page of the German-language edition of Virginia tax laws that the state government had published in Philadelphia in 1795 for use in the Blue Ridge Mountains and Shenandoah Valley, where German-speaking Virginians had lived for decades. (Library of Virginia)

getting established, but when it did in the nineteenth century, the valleys of western Virginia, especially the Shenandoah Valley, flourished. From the very beginning and for decades thereafter, Virginians west of the Blue Ridge maintained their main avenues of commerce via the Great Wagon Road and river connections with Philadelphia and Baltimore rather than to the same extent that large planters and small farmers east of the Blue Ridge did with Alexandria, Fredericksburg, Richmond, Petersburg, or Norfolk. It is perhaps symbolic that the Virginia colonel of the German Regiment in the American Revolution, John Peter Gabriel Muhlenberg, was a brother of the Pennsylvania congressman who was the first Speaker of the United States House of Representatives, Frederick Augustus Muhlenberg.

An elite class of social and political leaders emerged during the eighteenth century west of the Blue Ridge, but it was neither so wealthy nor so dominant as the elite class east of the Blue Ridge. In the east, the dominant families had surnames like Robinson, Randolph, Mason, Harrison, Digges, Corbin, Cary, Carter, Cabell, or Burwell. The Scots-Irish and German immigrant origins of the western elite are to be seen in the surnames of a few of the most important families, like Zane, Vanmeter, Stuart, Russell, Preston, McDowell, Hite, Crockett, Christian, Campbell, and Breckinridge.

Before the fight for independence began, which set off a revolution in Virginia, the colony had changed so much in so many ways that it could never have become again like it was in the early days, even if the American Revolution had not made more changes or made those changes long-lasting or even permanent.

SUGGESTED READING

Chapter 1. Alien Invasion

Horn, James. *A Land as God Made It: Jamestown and the Birth of America*. New York: Basic Books, 2005.
Kupperman, Karen Ordahl. *The Jamestown Project*. Cambridge: Belknap Press of Harvard University Press, 2007.
Rountree, Helen C. *The Powhatan Indians of Virginia: Their Traditional Culture*. Norman: University of Oklahoma Press, 1989.
The Complete Works of Captain John Smith (1580–1631). Edited by Philip L. Barbour. 3 vols. Chapel Hill: University of North Carolina Press for the Institute of Early American History and Culture, 1986. The volumes contain both Smith's recollections and excerpts from other narratives.
Vaughan, Alden T. *Transatlantic Encounters: American Indians in Britain, 1500–1776*. Cambridge: Cambridge University Press, 2006.

Chapter 2. The Werowansqua of Appamattuck Meets the Alien Invaders

Fausz, J. Frederick. "The Invasion of Virginia: Indians, Colonialism, and the Conquest of Cant: A Review Essay on Anglo-Indian Relations in the Chesapeake." *Virginia Magazine of History and Biography* 95 (1987): 133–56.
Gleach, Frederic W. *Powhatan's World and Colonial Virginia: A Conflict of Cultures*. Lincoln: University of Nebraska Press, 1997.
Horn, James. *A Land as God Made It: Jamestown and the Birth of America*. New York: Basic Books, 2005.
Kupperman, Karen Ordahl. *The Jamestown Project*. Cambridge: Belknap Press of Harvard University Press, 2007.
Rountree, Helen C. *The Powhatan Indians of Virginia: Their Traditional Culture*. Norman: University of Oklahoma Press, 1989.

Rountree, Helen C., and E. Randolph Turner III. *Before and After Jamestown: Virginia's Powhatans and Their Predecessors*. Gainesville: University Press of Florida, 2002.

Townsend, Camilla. *Pocahontas and the Powhatan Dilemma: An American Portrait*. New York: Hill and Wang, 2004.

Chapter 3. Hughe Pryse and the Loss of Faith

Bond, Edward L. *Damned Souls in a Tobacco Colony: Religion in Seventeenth-Century Virginia*. Macon, Ga.: Mercer University Press, 2000.

Fausz, J. Frederick. "An 'Abundance of Blood Shed on Both Sides': England's First Indian War, 1609–1614." *Virginia Magazine of History and Biography* 98 (1990): 3–56.

Horn, James. *A Land as God Made It: Jamestown and the Birth of America*. New York: Basic Books, 2005.

Kupperman, Karen Ordahl. *The Jamestown Project*. Cambridge: Belknap Press of Harvard University Press, 2007.

Tarter, Brent. "Evidence of Religion in Seventeenth-Century Virginia." In *From Jamestown to Jefferson: The Evolution of Religious Freedom in Virginia*, edited by Paul Rasor and Richard E. Bond, 17–42. Charlottesville: University of Virginia Press, 2011.

Tarter, Brent. "Reflections on the Church of England in Colonial Virginia." *Virginia Magazine of History and Biography* 112 (2004): 338–71.

Chapter 4. Lawes Divine, Morall and Martiall

Flaherty, David H., ed. *For the Colony in Virginea Britannia, Lawes Divine, Morall and Martiall, Etc., Compiled by William Strachey*. Charlottesville: University Press of Virginia for the Association for the Preservation of Virginia Antiquities, 1969. The book includes an informative introduction and the full text.

Konig, David Thomas. "'Dale's Laws' and the Non-Common Law Origins of Criminal Justice in Virginia." *American Journal of Legal History* 26 (1982): 354–75. Reprinted in Eric H. Monkkonen, ed., *Crime & Justice in American History*. Vol. 1, *The Colonies and Early Republic*. 368–98. Westport, Conn.: Meckler, 1991.

Prince, Walter F. "The First Criminal Code of Virginia." *Annual Report of the American Historical Association for the Year 1899* (Washington, D.C.: American Historical Association, 1900). 1:311–63.

Tarter, Brent. "Lawes Divine, Morall and Martiall." Virginia Humanities' online *Encyclopedia Virginia*.

Chapter 5. Richard Bucke, the Book of Common Prayer, and the Bible

Billings, Warren M. *A Little Parliament: The Virginia General Assembly in the Seventeenth Century*. Richmond: Library of Virginia, 2004.

Bond, Edward L. *Damned Souls in a Tobacco Colony: Religion in Seventeenth-Century Virginia.* Macon, Ga.: Macon University Press, 2000.
Hecht, Irene, and *Dictionary of Virginia Biography.* "Richard Bucke (1581 or 1582–ca. 1624)." Virginia Humanities' online *Encyclopedia Virginia.*
Kukla, Jon. *Political Institutions in Virginia, 1619–1660.* New York: Garland, 1989.
Tarter, Brent. *The Grandees of Government: The Origins and Persistence of Undemocratic Politics in Virginia.* Charlottesville: University of Virginia Press, 2013.

Chapter 6. Thefts from Edward Grindon's Warehouse

Billings, Warren M. "Pleading, Procedure, and Practice: The Meaning of Due Process of Law in Seventeenth-Century Virginia." *Journal of Southern History* 47 (1981): 569–84.
Carson, Cary, Joanne Bowen, Willie Graham, Martha McCartney, and Lorena Walsh. "New World, Real World: Improvising English Culture in Seventeenth-Century Virginia." *Journal of Southern History* 74 (2008): 31–88.
Horn, James P. P. *Adapting to a New World: English Society in the Seventeenth-Century Chesapeake.* Chapel Hill: University of North Carolina Press for the Institute of Early American History and Culture, 1994.
Pagan, John Ruston. *Anne Orthwood's Bastard: Sex and Law in Early Virginia.* New York: Oxford University Press, 2003.
Perry, James R. *The Formation of a Society on Virginia's Eastern Shore, 1615–1655.* Chapel Hill: University of North Carolina Press for the Institute of Early American History and Culture, 1990.
Potter, Jennifer. *The Jamestown Brides: The Story of England's "Maids for Virginia."* Oxford: Oxford University Press, 2019.
Tarter, Brent. *Virginians and Their Histories.* Charlottesville: University of Virginia Press, 2020.
Tate, Thad W., and David L. Ammerman, eds. *The Chesapeake in the Seventeenth Century: Essays on Anglo-American Society.* Chapel Hill: University of North Carolina Press for the Institute of Early American History and Culture, 1979.

Chapter 7. Anthony Johnson's Enslaved Man

Breen, T. H., and Stephen Innes. *"Myne Owne Ground": Race and Freedom on Virginia's Eastern Shore, 1640–1676.* New York: Oxford University Press, 1980. This work has the most thorough account of Anthony and Mary Johnson.
Coombs, John C. "Beyond the 'Origins Debate': Rethinking the Rise of Virginia Slavery." In *Early Modern Virginia: Reconsidering the Old Dominion,* edited by Douglas Bradburn and John C. Coombs, 207–38. Charlottesville: University of Virginia Press, 2011.
Coombs, John C. "'Others Not Christians in the Service of the English': Interpreting the Status of Africans and African Americans in Early Virginia." *Virginia Magazine of History and Biography* 127 (2019): 213–38.
Deal, Joseph Douglas. *Race and Class in Colonial Virginia: Indians, Englishmen, and Africans on the Eastern Shore during the Seventeenth Century.* New York: Garland, 1993.

Goetz, Rebecca Anne. *The Baptism of Early Virginia: How Christianity Created Race.* Baltimore: Johns Hopkins University Press, 2012.
O'Malley, Gregory E. *Final Passages: The Intercolonial Slave Trade in British America, 1619–1807.* Chapel Hill: University of North Carolina Press for the Omohundro Institute of Early American History and Culture, 2014.
Parent, Anthony S. *Foul Means: The Formation of a Slave Society in Virginia, 1660–1740.* Chapel Hill: University of North Carolina Press for the Omohundro Institute of Early American History and Culture, 2003.
Suranyi, Anna. *Indentured Servitude: Unfree Labour and Citizenship in the British Colonies.* Montreal: McGill-Queen's University Press, 2021.

Chapter 8. Elizabeth Key and the Law of Slavery
About Elizabeth Key

Billings, Warren M. "The Cases of Fernando and Elizabeth Key: A Note on the Status of Blacks in Seventeenth-Century Virginia." *William and Mary Quarterly,* 3d ser., 30 (1973): 467–74.
Tarter, Brent, and *Dictionary of Virginia Biography.* "Elizabeth Key (fl. 1655–1660)." Virginia Humanities' online *Encyclopedia Virginia.*

About Slavery in Seventeenth-Century Virginia

Billings, Warren M. "The Law of Servants and Slaves in Seventeenth-Century Virginia." *Virginia Magazine of History and Biography* 99 (1991): 45–62.
Breen, T. H., and Stephen Innes. *"Myne Owne Ground": Race and Freedom on Virginia's Eastern Shore, 1640–1676.* New York: Oxford University Press, 1980.
Coombs, John C. "Beyond the 'Origins Debate': Rethinking the Rise of Virginia Slavery." In *Early Modern Virginia: Reconsidering the Old Dominion,* edited by Douglas Bradburn and John C. Coombs, 207–38. Charlottesville: University of Virginia Press, 2011.
Deal, Joseph Douglas. *Race and Class in Colonial Virginia: Indians, Englishmen, and Africans on the Eastern Shore during the Seventeenth Century.* New York: Garland, 1993.
Goetz, Rebecca Anne. *The Baptism of Early Virginia: How Christianity Created Race.* Baltimore: Johns Hopkins University Press, 2012.
Morgan, Edmund S. *American Slavery, American Freedom: The Ordeal of Colonial Virginia.* New York: Norton, 1975.
Parent, Anthony S. *Foul Means: The Formation of a Slave Society in Virginia, 1660–1740.* Chapel Hill: University of North Carolina Press for the Omohundro Institute of Early American History and Culture, 2003.
Vaughan, Alden T. "The Origins Debate: Slavery and Racism in Seventeenth-Century Virginia." *Virginia Magazine of History and Biography* 97 (1989): 311–54.
Walsh, Lorena S. *Motives of Honor, Pleasure, and Profit: Plantation Management in the Colonial Chesapeake, 1607–1763.* Chapel Hill: University of North Carolina Press for the Omohundro Institute of Early American History and Culture, 2010.

Chapter 9. Cockacoeske and the Fate of the Powhatan Confederacy

"Articles of Peace (the Treaty of Middle Plantation)." Virginia Humanities' online *Encyclopedia Virginia*.

McCartney, Martha W., and *Dictionary of Virginia Biography*. "Cockacoeske (d. by July 1, 1686)." Virginia Humanities' online *Encyclopedia Virginia*.

Negrin, Hayley. "Cockacoeske's Rebellion: Nathaniel Bacon, Indigenous Slavery, and Sovereignty in Early Virginia." *William and Mary Quarterly*, 3d ser., 80 (2023): 49–86.

Rice, James D. *Tales from a Revolution: Bacon's Rebellion and the Transformation of Early America*. New York: Oxford University Press, 2012.

Washburn, Wilcomb E. *The Governor and the Rebel: A History of Bacon's Rebellion in Virginia*. Chapel Hill: University of North Carolina Press for the Institute of Early American History and Culture, 1957. This work corrected and superseded Thomas Jefferson Wertenbaker's romanticized *Torchbearer of the Revolution: The Story of Bacon's Rebellion and Its Leader*. Princeton: Princeton University Press, 1940.

Chapter 10. Jamestown in 1676

Bernard, Virginia, and *Dictionary of Virginia Biography*. "Ann Cotton (fl. 1650s–1670s)." Virginia Humanities' online *Encyclopedia Virginia*.

Bernard, Virginia, and *Dictionary of Virginia Biography*. "John Cotton (d. after October 24, 1683)." Virginia Humanities' online *Encyclopedia Virginia*.

Kelso, William M. *Jamestown: The Buried Truth*. 2d ed., rev. Charlottesville: University of Virginia Press, 2017.

Washburn, Wilcomb E. *The Governor and the Rebel: A History of Bacon's Rebellion in Virginia*. Chapel Hill: University of North Carolina Press for the Institute of Early American History and Culture, 1957. This work corrected and superseded Thomas Jefferson Wertenbaker's romanticized *Torchbearer of the Revolution: The Story of Bacon's Rebellion and Its Leader*. Princeton: Princeton University Press, 1940.

Chapter 11. The Grievances of the People

Billings, Warren M. *Sir William Berkeley and the Forging of Colonial Virginia*. Baton Rouge: Louisiana State University Press, 2004.

Tarter, Brent. "Bacon's Rebellion, the Grievances of the People, and the Political Culture of Seventeenth-Century Virginia." *Virginia Magazine of History and Biography* 119 (2011): 3–41.

Tarter, Brent, and *Dictionary of Virginia Biography*. "Nathaniel Bacon (1647–1676)." Virginia Humanities' online *Encyclopedia Virginia*.

Thompson, Peter. "The Thief, the Householders, and the Commons: Languages of Class in Seventeenth-Century Virginia." *William and Mary Quarterly*, 3d ser., 63 (2006): 253–80.

Washburn, Wilcomb E. *The Governor and the Rebel: A History of Bacon's Rebellion in Virginia*. Chapel Hill: University of North Carolina Press for the Institute of Early American History and Culture, 1957. This work corrected and superseded Thomas Jefferson Wertenbaker's romanticized *Torchbearer of the Revolution: The Story of Bacon's Rebellion and Its Leader*. Princeton: Princeton University Press, 1940.

Chapter 12. A Dead Bastard Child

Bond, Edward L. "Source of Knowledge, Source of Power: The Supernatural World of English Virginia, 1607–1624." *Virginia Magazine of History and Biography* 108 (2000): 105–38.
Hoffer, Peter Charles, and William B. Scott, eds. *Criminal Proceedings in Colonial Virginia: Fines, Examination of Criminals, Trials of Slaves, Etc., from March 1710 to 1754*. Athens: University of Georgia Press for the American Historical Association, 1984.
Horn, James P. P. *Adapting to a New World: English Society in the Seventeenth Century Chesapeake*. Chapel Hill: University of North Carolina Press for the Institute of Early American History and Culture, 1994.
Pagan, John Ruston. *Anne Orthwood's Bastard: Sex and Law in Early Virginia*. New York: Oxford University Press, 2003.
Perry, James R. *The Formation of a Society on Virginia's Eastern Shore, 1615–1655*. Chapel Hill: University of North Carolina Press for the Institute of Early American History and Culture, 1990.
Rankin, Hugh F. *Criminal Trial Proceedings in the General Court of Colonial Virginia*. Charlottesville: University Press of Virginia for the Colonial Williamsburg Foundation, 1965.

Chapter 13. No Obey

Bond, Edward L. "Anglican Theology and Devotion in James Blair's Virginia, 1685–1743." *Virginia Magazine of History and Biography* (1996): 313–40.
Brown, Kathleen M. *Good Wives, Nasty Wenches, and Anxious Patriarchs: Gender, Race, and Power in Colonial Virginia*. Chapel Hill: University of North Carolina Press for the Institute of Early American History and Culture, 1996.
Brown, Kathleen M., and *Dictionary of Virginia Biography*. "Lucy Burwell (1683–1716)." Virginia Humanities' online *Encyclopedia Virginia*.
Downey, Fairfax. "The Governor Goes A-Wooing: The Swashbuckling Courtship of Nicholson of Virginia, 1699–1705." *Virginia Magazine of History and Biography* 55 (1947): 6–19.
Evans, Emory G. *"A Topping People": The Rise and Decline of Virginia's Old Political Elite, 1680–1790*. Charlottesville: University of Virginia Press, 2009.
Legg, Polly Cary. "The Governor's 'Extacy of Trouble.'" *William and Mary Quarterly*, 2d ser., 22 (1942): 389–98.
Snyder, Terri L. *Brabbling Women: Disorderly Speech and the Law in Early Virginia*. Ithaca, N.Y.: Cornell University Press, 2003.
Tate, Thad W., and *Dictionary of Virginia Biography*. "James Blair (ca. 1655–1743)." Virginia Humanities' online *Encyclopedia Virginia*.

Chapter 14. Grace Sherwood Charged with Witchcraft

"An Acte against Conjuration Witchcrafte and dealing with evill and wicked Spirits." Virginia Humanities' online *Encyclopedia Virginia*.
Bond, Edward L. "Source of Knowledge, Source of Power: The Supernatural World of English Virginia, 1607–1624." *Virginia Magazine of History and Biography* 108 (2000): 105–38.
Games, Alison F. *Witchcraft in Early North America*. New York: Rowman and Littlefield, 2010.
Godbeer, Richard. *The Devil's Dominion: Magic and Religion in Early New England*. Cambridge: Cambridge University Press, 1992.
Karlsen, Carol F. *The Devil in the Shape of a Woman: Witchcraft in Colonial New England*. New York: W. W. Norton and Co., 1987.
Kierner, Cynthia A. "Grace Sherwood, The Virginia Witch." In *Virginia Women: Their Lives and Times*, edited by Cynthia A. Kierner and Sandra G. Treadway. 2 vols., vol. 1. Athens: University of Georgia Press, 2015–16.
Moore, Scott O. *The Witch of Pungo: Grace Sherwood in Virginia History and Legend*. Charlottesville: Rivanna Press of the University Press of Virginia, 2024. Moore includes thorough accounts of how various legends concerning Sherwood came to be popularly believed.
Witkowski, Monica, and Caitlin Newman. "Witchcraft in Colonial Virginia." Virginia Humanities' online *Encyclopedia Virginia*.

Chapter 15. Exemplary Punishment for Salvadore and Scipio

Aptheker, Herbert. *American Negro Slave Revolts*. New York: Columbia University Press, 1943. This work has been reprinted several times.
Deal, Joseph Douglas. *Race and Class in Colonial Virginia: Indians, Englishmen, and Africans on the Eastern Shore during the Seventeenth Century*. New York: Garland, 1993.
Gallay, Alan, ed. *Indian Slavery in Colonial America*. Lincoln: University of Nebraska Press, 2009.
Gallay, Alan. *The Indian Slave Trade: The Rise of the English Empire in the American South, 1670–1717*. New Haven: Yale University Press, 2002.
Schwarz, Philip J. *Twice Condemned: Slaves and the Criminal Laws of Virginia, 1705–1865*. Baton Rouge: Louisiana State University Press, 1988.
Shefveland, Kristalyn Marie. *Anglo-Native Virginia: Trade, Conversion, and Indian Slavery in the Old Dominion, 1646–1722*. Athens: University of Georgia Press, 2016.

Chapter 16. Drinking More Than Necessary

Cargil, Amanda. "What Did the Founding Fathers Eat and Drink as They Started a Revolution?" Online *Smithsonian Magazine*. July 2018.
Crews, Ed, and Dave Doody. "Drinking in Colonial America: Rattle-Skull, Stonewall, Bogus, Blackstrap, Bombo, Mimbo, Whistle Belly, Syllabub, Sling, Toddy, and Flip." Online *Colonial Williamsburg Journal*. 2007.
Green, Emma. "Colonial Americans Drank Roughly Three Times as Much as Americans Do Now." Online *Atlantic*. 2015.

Hansard, Gregory J. *Virginia Cider: A Guide from Colonial Days to Craft's Golden Age.* Charlottesville: University of Virginia Press, 2024.

Meacham, Sarah Hand. *Every Home a Distillery: Alcohol, Gender, and Technology in the Colonial Chesapeake.* Baltimore: Johns Hopkins University Press, 2009.

Chapter 17. Releese Us out of This Cruell Bondegg

Bly, Antonio T. "In Pursuit of Letters: A History of the Bray School for Enslaved Children in Colonial Virginia." *History of Education Quarterly* 51 (2011): 425–59.

Forret, Jeff. *Race Relations at the Margins: Slaves and Poor Whites in the Antebellum Southern Countryside.* Louisiana State University Press, 2000.

Fountain, Daniel L. *Slavery, Civil War, and Salvation: African American Slaves and Christianity, 1830–1870.* Louisiana State University Press, 2010. Both Forret and Fountain questioned how well enslaved people in the United States understood the Christianity that they learned in the nineteenth century.

Meyers, Terry L. "Benjamin Franklin, the College of William and Mary, and the Williamsburg Bray School." *Anglican and Episcopal History* 79 (2020): 368–93.

Nelson, John K. *A Blessed Company: Parishes, Parsons, and Parishioners in Anglican Virginia, 1690–1776.* Chapel Hill: University of North Carolina Press, 1959. The book contains a chapter on the church's ministry to free and enslaved Black Virginians.

Pilcher, George William. *Samuel Davies: Apostle of Dissent in Colonial Virginia.* Knoxville: University of Tennessee Press, 1971.

Richards, Jeffrey H. "Samuel Davies and the Transatlantic Campaign for Slave Literacy in Virginia." *Virginia Magazine of History and Biography* 111 (2003): 333–78.

Whitley, W. Bland, and *Dictionary of Virginia Biography.* "Samuel Davies (1723–1761)." Virginia Humanities' online *Encyclopedia Virginia.*

Chapter 18. William Byrd and His Vine and Fig Tree

Berland, Kevin, ed. *The Dividing Line Histories of William Byrd II of Westover.* Chapel Hill: University of North Carolina Press for the Omohundro Institute of Early American History and Culture, 2013.

Evans, Emory G. *"A Topping People": The Rise and Decline of Virginia's Old Political Elite, 1680–1790.* Charlottesville: University of Virginia Press, 2009.

Hayes, Kevin J. *The Library of William Byrd of Westover.* Madison, Wis.: Madison House and the Library Company of Philadelphia, 1997.

Lockridge, Kenneth A. *The Diary and Life of William Byrd II of Virginia, 1674–1744.* Chapel Hill: University of North Carolina Press for the Institute of Early American History and Culture, 1987.

Long, Thomas. "William Byrd (1674–1744)." Virginia Humanities' online *Encyclopedia Virginia.*

Marambaud, Pierre. *William Byrd II of Westover, 1674–1744.* Charlottesville: University Press of Virginia, 1971.

Mooney, Barbara Burlison. *Prodigy Houses of Virginia: Architecture and the Native Elite.* Charlottesville: University of Virginia Press, 2008.

Musselwhite, Paul. *Urban Dreams, Rural Communities: The Rise of Plantation Society in the Chesapeake.* Chicago: University of Chicago Press, 2019.

Quitt, Martin, and *Dictionary of Virginia Biography.* "Byrd, William (1674–1744)." Virginia Humanities' online *Encyclopedia Virginia.*

Rozbicki, Michal J. *The Complete Colonial Gentleman: Cultural Legitimacy in Plantation Society.* Charlottesville: University Press of Virginia, 1998.

Rozbicki, Michal J. *Culture and Liberty in the Age of the American Revolution.* Charlottesville: University of Virginia Press, 2011.

Smith, Daniel Blake. *Inside the Great House: Family Life in Eighteenth-Century Virginia.* Ithaca, N.Y.: Cornell University Press, 1980.

Todd, Dennis. *Patriarchy in Peril: William Byrd II and Slavery in Early Virginia.* Knoxville: University of Tennessee Press, 2023.

Winner, Lauren F. *A Cheerful and Comfortable Faith: Anglican Religious Practice in the Elite Households of Eighteenth-Century Virginia.* New Haven: Yale University Press, 2010.

Chapter 19. The Air of a City

Berland, Kevin, ed. *The Dividing Line Histories of William Byrd II of Westover.* Chapel Hill: University of North Carolina Press for the Omohundro Institute of Early American History and Culture, 2013.

Parramore, Thomas C., Peter C. Stewart, and Tommy Bogger. *Norfolk, The First Four Centuries.* Charlottesville: University Press of Virginia, 1994.

Tarter, Brent, ed. *The Order Book and Related Papers of the Common Hall of the Borough of Norfolk, Virginia, 1736–1798.* Introduction, 3–32. Richmond: Virginia State Library, 1979.

Chapter 20. The Head of Hampton

Billings, Warren M. "A Virginia Original: George Webb's *Office and Authority of a Justice of Peace.*" In *"Esteemed Bookes of Lawe" and the Legal Culture of Early Virginia,* edited by Warren M. Billings and Brent Tarter, 157–77. Charlottesville: University of Virginia Press, 2017.

Schwarz, Philip J. *Slave Laws in Virginia.* Athens: University of Georgia Studies in the Legal History of the South, 1969.

Schwarz, Philip J. *Twice Condemned: Slaves and the Criminal Laws of Virginia, 1705–1865.* Baton Rouge: Louisiana State University Press, 1988.

Stubbs, Tristan. *Masters of Violence: The Plantation Overseers of Eighteenth-Century Virginia, South Carolina, and Georgia.* Columbia: University of South Carolina Press, 2018.

Chapter 21. Susannah Sanders Cooper and Her Tavern

Bailey, Raymond C. *Popular Influence upon Public Policy: Petitioning in Eighteenth-Century Virginia.* Westport, Conn.: Greenwood Press, 1979.

Salmon, Marylynn. *Women and the Law of Property in Early America*. Chapel Hill: University of North Carolina Press, 1986.

Sturtz, Linda L., and *Dictionary of Virginia Biography*. "Susannah Sanders Cooper (d. after June 9, 1751)." Virginia Humanities' online *Encyclopedia Virginia*.

Sturtz, Linda L. *Within Her Power: Propertied Women in Colonial Virginia*. New York: Routledge, 2002.

Tarter, Brent. "When Kind and Thrifty Husbands Are Not Enough: Some Thoughts on the Legal Status of Women in Virginia." *Magazine of Virginia Genealogy* 33 (1995): 79–101.

Chapter 22. One Pistole

Ernst, Joseph Albert. "The Robinson Scandal Revivius: Money, Debts, and Politics in Revolutionary Virginia." *Virginia Magazine of History and Biography* 77 (1969): 146–71. Ernst's article treats Virginia paper currency and exchange rates in depth.

Greene, Jack P., ed. "The Case of the Pistole Fee: The Report of a Hearing on the Pistole Fee Dispute before the Privy Council, June 18, 1754." *Virginia Magazine of History and Biography* 66 (1958): 399–422.

McCusker, John J. *Money and Exchange in Europe and America, 1600–1775: A Handbook*. Chapel Hill: University of North Carolina Press for the Institute of Early American History and Culture, 1978.

"Paper Money in Colonial Virginia." *William and Mary Quarterly*, 1st ser., 20 (1912): 227–62. The article reprints two very long letters that treasurer Robert Carter Nicholas published in 1773 to explain the history of paper money in Virginia since the 1750s.

Sen, Tinni, Turk McCleskey, and Atin Basuchoudhary. "When Good Little Debts Went Bad: Civil Litigation on a Virginia Frontier, 1745–1755." *Journal of Interdisciplinary History* 46 (2015): 60–89.

Tarter, Brent. "Dinwiddie, Robert (3 October 1692–27 July 1770)." In *American National Biography*, edited by John A. Garraty and Mark C. Carnes. 24 vols., vol. 6, 620–21. New York: Oxford University Press, 1999.

Chapter 23. Lowe Jackson Hanged

Rankin, Hugh F. *Criminal Trial Proceedings in the General Court of Colonial Virginia*. Charlottesville: University Press of Virginia for the Colonial Williamsburg Foundation, 1965.

Roeber, A. Greg. *Faithful Magistrates and Republican Lawyers: Creators of Virginia Legal Culture, 1680–1810*. Chapel Hill: University of North Carolina Press, 1981.

Chapter 24. Long and Painful Service During the War with France

Anderson, Fred. *Crucible of War: The Seven Years' War and the Fate of Empire in British North America, 1754–1766*. New York: Knopf, 2000.

Bailey, Raymond C. *Popular Influence upon Public Policy: Petitioning in Eighteenth-Century Virginia.* Westport, Conn.: Greenwood Press, 1979.

Griffith, Lucille Blanche. *The Virginia House of Burgesses, 1750–1774.* Rev. ed. University: University of Alabama Press, 1970.

Hofstra, Warren R., ed. *Cultures in Conflict: The Seven Years' War in North America.* Lanham, Md:. Rowman and Littlefield, 2007.

Ward, Matthew C. *Breaking the Backcountry: The Seven Years' War in Virginia and Pennsylvania, 1754–1765.* Pittsburgh: University of Pittsburgh Press, 2003.

Chapter 25. All Was Not Tobacco

Billings, Warren M. *Sir William Berkeley and the Forging of Colonial Virginia.* Baton Rouge: Louisiana State University Press, 2004.

Farmer, Charles J. *In the Absence of Towns: Settlement and Country Trade in Southside Virginia, 1730–1800.* Lanham, Md.: Rowman and Littlefield, 1993.

Hendricks, Christopher E. *The Backcountry Towns of Colonial Virginia.* Knoxville: University of Tennessee Press, 2006.

Herndon, G. Melville. "The Story of Hemp in Colonial Virginia" (PhD., University of Michigan, 1959). Bound photocopy of typescript, Library of Virginia.

Hofstra, Warren R. *The Planting of New Virginia: Settlement and Landscape in the Shenandoah Valley.* Baltimore: Johns Hopkins University Press, 2004.

Kamoie, Laura Croghan. *Irons in the Fire: The Business History of the Tayloe Family and Virginia's Gentry, 1700–1860.* Charlottesville: University of Virginia Press, 2007.

Middleton, Arthur Pierce. *Tobacco Coast: A Maritime History of Chesapeake Bay in the Colonial Era.* Newport News: Mariners' Museum, 1953.

Rainbolt, John Corbin. *From Prescription to Persuasion: Manipulation of Eighteenth Century Virginia Economy.* Port Washington, N.Y.: Kennikat Press, 1974. Rainbolt's book treats economic diversification in the seventeenth century but was published posthumously with an incorrect subtitle.

Reps, John William. *Tidewater Towns: City Planning in Colonial Virginia and Maryland.* Williamsburg: Colonial Williamsburg Foundation, 1972.

Tarter, Brent, and *Dictionary of Virginia Biography.* "Edward Digges (1621–1675)." Virginia Humanities' online *Encyclopedia Virginia.*

Tarter, Brent, ed. *The Order Book and Related Papers of the Borough of Norfolk, Virginia, 1736–1798.* Introduction, 3–32. Richmond: Virginia State Library, 1979.

Tillson, Albert H., Jr. *Accommodating Revolution: Virginia's Northern Neck in an Era of Transformations, 1760–1810.* Charlottesville: University of Virginia Press, 2010. The book contains an excellent account of various craftsmen in that part of Virginia.

Chapter 26. John Wayles's Neighbors and His Families

Breen, T. H. *Tobacco Culture: The Mentality of the Great Tidewater Planters on the Eve of Revolution.* Princeton: Princeton University Press, 1985.

Evans, Emory G. "Planter Indebtedness and the Coming of the Revolution in Virginia." *William and Mary Quarterly*, 3d ser., 19 (1962): 511–33.

Evans, Emory G. "Private Indebtedness and the Revolution in Virginia, 1776 to 1796." *William and Mary Quarterly*, 3d ser., 28 (1971): 349–74.

Gordon-Reed, Annette. *The Hemingses of Monticello*. New York: W. W. Norton and Co., 2008.

Hemphill, John M., II, ed. "John Wayles Rates His Neighbours." *Virginia Magazine of History and Biography* 66 (1958): 302–6.

Chapter 27. The Candidates

Baine, Rodney M. *Robert Munford, America's First Comic Dramatist*. Athens: University of Georgia Press, 1967.

Canby, Courtlandt. "Robert Munford's *The Patriots*." *William and Mary Quarterly*, 3d ser., 6 (1949): 437–503. The article includes an informative introductory essay and the full text of the play.

Crawford, Meriah. "Robert Munford (d. 1783)." Virginia Humanities' online *Encyclopedia Virginia*.

Griffith, Lucille Blanche. *The Virginia House of Burgesses, 1750–1774*. Rev. ed. University: University of Alabama Press, 1970.

Hubble, Jay B., and Douglass Adair. "Robert Munford's *The Candidates*." *William and Mary Quarterly*, 3d ser., 5 (1948): 217–57. The article includes an informative introductory essay and the full text of the play.

Kolp, John Gilman. *Gentlemen and Freeholders: Electoral Politics in Colonial Virginia*. Baltimore: Johns Hopkins University Press, 1998. Kolp significantly corrects and replaces Charles S. Sydnor, *Gentlemen Freeholders: Political Practices in Washington's Virginia*. Chapel Hill: University of North Carolina Press for the Institute of Early American History and Culture, 1952; and Robert E. Brown and B. Katherine Brown, *Virginia, 1705–1786: Democracy or Aristocracy?* Lansing: Michigan State University Press, 1964.

McDonnell, Michael A. "A World Turned 'Topsy Turvy': Robert Munford, *The Patriots*, and the Crisis of the Revolution in Virginia." *William and Mary Quarterly*, 3d ser., 61 (2004): 235–70.

Tarter, Brent. *Constitutional History of Virginia*. Athens: University of Georgia Press Southern Legal Studies, 2023.

Tarter, Brent. *The Grandees of Government: The Origins and Persistence of Undemocratic Politics in Virginia*. Charlottesville: University of Virginia Press, 2013.

Chapter 28. George's Marked Face and Broken English

Chambers, Douglas B. *Murder at Montpelier: Igbo-Africans in Virginia*. Jackson: University Press of Mississippi, 2005. Chambers expertly traces several generations of descendants of natives of Africa as enslaved people at the plantation of President James Madison.

Costa, Tom. "The Geography of Slavery in Virginia." At www2.vcdh.virginia.edu, a free online database of digitized newspaper advertisements for runaway enslaved people in colonial Virginia.

Costa, Tom. "What Can We Learn from a Digital Database of Runaway Slave Advertisements?" *International Social Science Review* 76 (2001): 36–43.

Morgan, Philip D. *Slave Counterpoint: Black Culture in the Eighteenth-Century Chesapeake and Lowcountry.* Chapel Hill: University of North Carolina Press for the Institute of Early American History and Culture, 1998.

Rediker, Marcus. *Between the Devil and the Deep Blue Sea: Merchant Seamen, Pirates, and the Anglo-American Maritime World, 1700–1750.* Cambridge: Cambridge University Press, 1987.

Rediker, Marcus. *The Slave Ship: A Human History.* New York: Viking, 2007.

Stubbs, Tristan. *Masters of Violence: The Plantation Overseers of Eighteenth-Century Virginia, South Carolina, and Georgia.* Columbia: University of South Carolina Press, 2018.

Walsh, Lorena S. *From Calabar to Carter's Grove: The History of a Virginia Slave Community.* Charlottesville: University Press of Virginia, 1997.

Walsh, Lorena S. *Motives of Honor, Pleasure, and Profit: Plantation Management in the Colonial Chesapeake, 1607–1763.* Chapel Hill: University of North Carolina Press for the Omohundro Institute of Early American History and Culture, 2010.

Chapter 29. The Great Fresh of 1771 and Its Consequences

Coleman, Elizabeth D. "The Great Fresh of 1771: Rampaging Rivers Swept Men, Houses, and Tobacco Away in the Worst Natural Disaster in the History of Virginia." *Virginia Cavalcade* 1 (Autumn 1951): 20–22.

Murphy, Kathleen S. "Virginia's Great Fresh of 1771 and the Politics of Disaster Relief." *Virginia Magazine of History and Biography* 123 (2015): 292–328.

"Paper Money in Colonial Virginia." *William and Mary Quarterly,* 1st ser., 20 (1912): 227–62. The article reprints very two long letters that Treasurer Robert Carter Nicholas published in 1773 to explain the history of paper money in Virginia since the 1750s.

Scott, Kenneth. *Counterfeiting in Colonial America.* Philadelphia: University of Pennsylvania Press, 1957. 186–252.

Scott, Kenneth. "Counterfeiting in Colonial Virginia." *Virginia Magazine of History and Biography* 61 (1953): 3–33.

Tarter, Brent. "Benjamin Woodward and Other Atrocious Villains: Difficulties in Documentary Detective Work." *Georgia Journal of Southern Legal History* 2 (1993): 287–316.

Chapter 30. Patrick Lunan Exposed

Brydon, George MacLaren. *Virginia's Mother Church and the Political Conditions under Which it Grew.* 2 vols. Richmond: Virginia Historical Society, 1947–52.

Nelson, John K. *Blessed Company: Parishes, Parsons, and Parishioners in Anglican Virginia, 1690–1776.* Chapel Hill: University of North Carolina Press, 2001.

Seiler, William H. "Land Processioning in Colonial Virginia." *William and Mary Quarterly,* 3d ser., 6 (1949): 416–46.

Tarter, Brent. "Reflections on the Church of England in Colonial Virginia." *Virginia Magazine of History and Biography* 112 (2004): 338–71.

Chapter 31. Subversive Religious Doctrines

Buckley, Thomas E., SJ. *Establishing Religious Freedom: Jefferson's Statute in Virginia*. Charlottesville: University of Virginia Press, 2013. See especially chapter 1.

Isaac, Rhys. *The Transformation of Virginia, 1746–1790*. Chapel Hill: University of North Carolina Press for the Institute of Early American History and Culture, 1982.

Lindman, Janet Moore. *Bodies of Belief: Baptist Community in Early America*. Philadelphia: University of Pennsylvania Press, 2008.

Little, Lewis Peyton. *Imprisoned Preachers and Religious Liberty in Virginia*. Lynchburg: J. P. Bell, 1938.

Longmore, Paul K. "'All Matters and Things Relating to Religion and Morality': The Virginia Burgesses' Committee for Religion, 1769 to 1775." *Journal of Church and State* 38 (1996): 775–97.

Spangler, Jewel L. *Virginians Reborn: Anglican Monopoly, Evangelical Dissent, and the Rise of Baptists in the Late Eighteenth Century*. Charlottesville: University of Virginia Press, 2008.

Chapter 32. *Robin v. Hardaway*

Ablavsky, Gregory. "Making Indians 'White': The Judicial Abolition of Native Slavery in Revolutionary Virginia and Its Racial Legacy." *University of Pennsylvania Law Review* 159 (2011): 1457–1531. The article concerns this case but contains a few errors, including confusing attorney Thomson Mason with his brother George Mason.

Gallay, Alan, ed. *Indian Slavery in Colonial America*. Lincoln: University of Nebraska Press, 2009.

Gallay, Alan. *The Indian Slave Trade: The Rise of the English Empire in the American South, 1670–1717*. New Haven: Yale University Press, 2002.

Higginbotham, A. Leon, Jr., and F. Michael Higginbotham. "'Yearning to Breathe Free': Legal Barriers Against and Options in Favor of Liberty in Antebellum Virginia." *New York University Law Review* 68 (1993): 1213–71.

Kegley, Mary B. "From Indian Slavery to Freedom." *Journal of the Afro-American Historical and Genealogical Society* 22 (2003): 29–36. Kegley's article discusses two other cases of Indian enslavement that arose about this same time.

McCall, Kathy O. "The Revolutionary Political Thought of Thomson Mason." *Virginia Magazine of History and Biography* 1125 (2017): 98–137.

Nichols, Michael L. "'The squint of freedom': African-American Freedom Suits in Post-Revolutionary Virginia." *Slavery and Abolition* 20 (1999): 47–62. The article describes changes to Virginia laws respecting freedom suits after the American Revolution.

Sachs, Honor. "'Freedom by a Judgment': The Legal History of an Afro-Indian Family." *Law and History Review* 30 (2012): 173–203. The article contains detailed accounts of the cases that involved Judith Coleman's descendants.

Schwarz, Philip J. *Slave Laws in Virginia*. Athens: University of Georgia Press Studies in Southern Legal History, 1996.

Tarter, Brent, and *Dictionary of Virginia Biography*. "Richard Bland (1710–1776)." Virginia Humanities' online *Encyclopedia Virginia*.

Chapter 33. New Virginias in the West

Hofstra, Warren R., ed. *The Great Valley Road of Virginia: Shenandoah Landscapes from Prehistory to the Present.* Charlottesville: University of Virginia Press, 2010.

Hofstra, Warren R. *The Planting of New Virginia: Settlement and Landscape in the Shenandoah Valley.* Baltimore: Johns Hopkins University Press, 2004.

Hofstra, Warren R. *A Separate Place: The Formation of Clarke County, Virginia.* White Post, Va.: Clarke County Sesquicentennial Committee, 1986.

Hofstra, Warren R., ed. *Ulster to America: The Scots-Irish Migration Experience.* Knoxville: University of Tennessee Press, 2012.

McCleskey, Turk. *The Road to Black Ned's Forge: A Story of Race, Sex, and Trade on the Colonial American Frontier.* Charlottesville: University of Virginia Press, 2014.

Mitchell, Robert D., ed. *Appalachian Frontiers: Settlement, Society, and Development in the Preindustrial Era.* Lexington: University Press of Kentucky, 1991.

Mitchell, Robert D. *Commercialism and Frontier Perspectives on the Early Shenandoah Valley.* Charlottesville: University Press of Virginia, 1977.

Puglisi, Michael J., ed. *Diversity and Accommodation: Essays on the Cultural Composition of the Virginia Frontier.* Knoxville: University of Tennessee Press, 1997.

Tillson, Albert H., Jr. *Gentry and Common Folks: Political Culture on a Virginia Frontier, 1740–1789.* Lexington: University Press of Kentucky, 1991.

Wust, Klaus. *The Virginia Germans.* Charlottesville: University Press of Virginia, 1969. Wust supersedes the pioneering John Walter Wayland, *The German Element in the Shenandoah Valley of Virginia.* Charlottesville: J. W. Wayland, 1907.

INDEX

agriculture, 7, 8–9, 147–48, 186–88
alcohol, 98–102, 155–56
Appamattuck, 5–9, 13–15
Appomattox River, 152
Archer, Gabriel, 5–14

Bacon, Nathaniel, 56, 59, 69, 70
Bacon's Rebellion, 59–60, 62–64, 66–70
Baptists, 109–10, 170, 172–73
Barnes, Elizabeth, 83–84, 84–85
Berkeley, Frances Culpeper Stevens, 69, 70
Berkeley, Sir William, 59, 63, 64, 66, 147–48
Beverley, Robert, *History and Present State of Virginia* (1705), 98–100
Bibles, 25–26
Blair, James, 79–81
Bland, Richard, 162, 170, 178–79, 181–83
Book of Common Prayer, 25–26
Bray School, 107–8
Bucke, Richard, 25–27
Burton, Mary, 71–78
Burwell, Lucy, 80–81
Byrd, William, 111–16

Calendar Reform Act of 1752, 39
cannibalism, 18
Carter, Mary, 71–78
Carter, Paul, 71–78

Casor (or Casar), 39, 43–46
Catholics, 19, 173
Charles City County, 149–52
Chesterfield County, 147
Chickahominey, 61
Church of England (Anglican), 12–13, 19–20, 25–28, 79, 103–4, 112–13, 167–71; vestrymen, 156, 167–68, 170–71
coal, 147
Cockacoeske, 56–61
Conway, Timothy, 139–41
Cooper, Isles, 126–27, 129–29
Cooper, John, 129–30
Cooper, Susannah Sanders, 126–30
Cotton, Ann, 63
Cotton, John, 62–65
crimes, 22–24, 29–38, 71–78, 85–87, 123–25; capital punishment, 92–97, 135–37; corporal punishment, 33, 35–36, 137–38; counterfeiting, 164–65

Dale, Sir Thomas, 14, 22, 24
Dalton, Michael, *The Country Justice* (1618), 85, 87
Davies, Samuel, 109
debt, 149–52
De La Warr, Thomas West, Baron, 22–23
Dent, Archer, 141–42

{207}

Digges, Dudley, 148
Dinwiddie, Robert, 131, 139
Dunmore, John Murray, fourth Earl, 167

elections, 153–57
English law, 33, 48, 85–87, 89, 96, 136, 166, 173; common law, 24, 36, 41–42, 50–51, 55, 124, 126–27

First Nations, 1–4, 5–15; enslavement, 93–96, 111, 176–85. *See also names of individual tribes*
floods, 162–63
Fort Necessity, 139–43
Fraser, Jane, 142–43
Fraser, John, 142–43
French and Indian War (Seven Years' War), 139–43

Gates, Sir Thomas, 22–23
General Assembly, 25, 51, 64. *See also* House of Burgesses
General Court, 50–51, 55, 64, 76–77, 88–89, 92–93, 176–85
Germans, 188–89
Godwin et al. v. Lunan, 167–68, 170
Goldsmith, Samuel, 43–44
Gooch, Sir William, 128–29
Goochland County, 97, 123
Gordon, Lord Adam, 144
Great Awakening, 172
Great Meadows, 139–43
Great Wagon Road, 187
Grimstead (or Grimsted), John, 52
Grimstead (or Grimsted), William, 49, 50, 51–52
Grindon, Edward, 29–33

Hall, Thomas, 30, 31, 32–33
Hampton (enslaved man), 123

Hardaway, John, 178
Harrison, Sarah, 79–81
Hemings, Sally, 152
Henrico County, 68, 100
Henry, Patrick, 136, 154, 166
Higginson, Humphrey, 48–50
Hill, Luke, 84, 85, 89
Hite, Jost, 188
House of Burgesses, 51, 153–57, 173–74
hurricanes, 118–20

Indians. *See* First Nations
inns, 98–99
interpreters, 12, 57
ironworks, 14, 146
Isle of Wight County, 67–68

Jackson, Lowe, 135–36
James River, 5, 63–64, 162–63
Jamestown, 59, 62–65, 95, 155; Starving Time, 16–19
Jefferson, Martha Wayles Skelton, 152
Jefferson, Thomas, 136, 151–52, 154, 166; *Reports of Cases Determined in the General Court*, 167, 177
Jenings, Edmund, 94–95
Johnson, Anthony, 39–40, 42–45
Johnson, Mary, 40, 42–45
justices of the peace, 67–69, 156

Key, Elizabeth, 47–53
Key, Thomas, 47–49

Lee, Richard Henry, 154, 166
Littlefere, Richard, 30–31
local government, 66–70, 154–56, 168–70
Lunan, Patrick, 167–69, 170–71

Madison, James, 154
manufacturing, 144–48

Marshall, John, 153
Mason, George, 178
Mason, Thomson, 178, 179–81, 183–84
Mathew, Thomson, 56–58
Mattaponi, 59
Methodists, 109–10
Middlesex County, 95
midwives, 74
Mills, William, 29–35
money, 131–34, 163–65
Monroe, James, 153
Mottrom, John, 49
Muhlenberg, Frederick Augustus, 189
Muhlenberg, John Peter Gabriel, 189
Munford William, *The Candidates,* 153–57

Nansemond, 60
Nansemond County, 68–70, 167
Nauirans, 7, 12
Necatowance, 59
New Kent County, 126–30
Newport, Christopher, 7, 8
Nicholas, Robert Carter, 163
Nicholson, Sir Francis, 80–81
Norfolk, 116–22, 144–45
Nottoway, 14, 60

Opechancanough, 14, 56
ordinaries, 98–99

Pamunkey, 56–61
Parker, George, 43
Parker, Robert, 43–44
Parks, William, 135
Parse (or Pearce), John, 52–53
Paspehay, 14, 21
Percy, George, narratives, 4, 12, 14, 16–19, 20–21
petitions, 127–28, 139–43

plantation mansions, 111–14, 150–51
Pocahontas (Matoaka), 12
Portsmouth, 117–18
Powhatan (Wahunsonacock), 7, 8, 9–10, 14, 23
Powhatan, 5–14, 61
Powhatan Confederacy, 9–10, 59–61
Presbyterians, 109, 170, 172
Preston, William, 186, 187
Princess Anne County, 82–91
Pryse, Hughe (Hugh Price), 16, 18–19, 20
Puritans, 26

Quakers, 173

racism, 45, 54–55
Randolph, Peyton, 153
Rappahannock River, 162
religion, 18–21, 73, 74, 78, 84, 90, 112–13, 167–75; laws relating to, 23, 24; slavery, 103–10. *See also individual denominations*
Richmond, 163
Robin v. Hardaway, 176–85

Salvadore, 93–96
Scipio, 93–96
servants, indentured, 42–43
Shenandoah Valley, 188–89
Sherwood, Grace, 82–91
Sherwood, James, 83
shipbuilding, 118, 144–45
silk, 147–48
slavery, 92–97, 111–12, 158–61, 174; Christianity, 51, 54; education, 107–8; First Nations tribes, 59–60, 93–96, 111, 176–85; laws, 53–55, 176–85; life in, 103–10; origins, 40–43, 179–80, 181–82; religion, 51, 54, 103–10; runaways, 158–60; trans-Atlantic slave trade, 40, 41, 105, 150, 159–60
Smith, Captain John, 5. 7, 12, 17, 42

Sprowle, Andrew, 117–18
Statehouse, 64–65
Stith, William, 131

taverns, 98–99, 126–30
taxes, 67–69, 169, 188–89
Thompson, Stevens, 86, 94
Tios, Jane, 30, 31, 32, 33, 36
Tios, John, 30, 31, 32, 33
tobacco, 147, 150, 163, 169; as money, 32, 34, 67, 124, 132
Totopotomoy, 57–58
towns and cities, 116–22
Treaty of 1646, 59
Treaty of Middle Plantation (1677), 60–61
trial by touch, 73, 78
trial by water, 87–88
Tsenacomoco, 2, 6
Tuck, James, 72, 74, 75, 76

Upper Parish, Nansemond County, 167–68, 170–71

Virginia Gazette, 135–36
Virginia laws, 36, 48, 85–86, 123–25, 136; *Lawes Divine, Morall and Martiall,* 22–24; religious toleration, 172–75; slavery, 53–55, 93, 104
Virginia society, 101–2, 111–13, 149–51, 154–57, 187–90

warfare, 11–12, 58, 139–43
Washington, George, 139–43, 147, 153, 155
Wayles, John, 149–52
Webb, George, *Office and Authority of a Justice of Peace* (1736), 89–90, 125
West, Captain John, 57–58, 60
Weyanoke, 60
Williamsburg, 98, 135–37
wine, 98, 147–48
witchcraft, 82–91
women, 36–37, 52, 54; childbirth, 71–76; and property, 126–30; witchcraft, 79–81
Wright, Joan (Good Wife), 82–83

York County, 98

www.ingramcontent.com/pod-product-compliance
Lightning Source LLC
Chambersburg PA
CBHW031435160426
43195CB00010BB/745